Modernizing Patriarchy

Modernizing Patriarchy

The Politics of Women's Rights in Morocco

KATJA ŽVAN ELLIOTT

University of Texas Press ◆ *Austin*

First edition, 2015
First paperback edition, 2016

Requests for permission to reproduce material from this work should be sent to:
　Permissions
　University of Texas Press
　P.O. Box 7819
　Austin, TX 78713-7819
　http://utpress.utexas.edu/index.php/rp-form

All photographs courtesy of the author.

♾ The paper used in this book meets the minimum requirements of
ANSI/NISO Z39.48-1992 (R1997) (Permanence of Paper).

Library of Congress Cataloging-in-Publication Data
Žvan Elliot, Katja, 1978-
　Modernizing patriarchy : the politics of women's rights in Morocco /
Katja Žvan Elliott. — First edition.
　　pages cm
　ISBN 978-1-4773-0244-6 (cloth)
　ISBN 978-1-4773-0245-3 (library e-book)
　ISBN 978-1-4773-0246-0 (non-library e-book)
1. Women's rights—Morocco.　2. Feminism—Morocco.　3. Women—
Morocco—Social conditions—21st century.　I. Title.
　HQ1236.5.M8Z83 2015
　305.4096409′05—dc23

2014031033

doi:10.7560/302446

ISBN 978-1-4773-1220-9 (paperback)

To my babi, mom, and sister. For they are amazing women.

[H]ow can society achieve progress, while women, who represent half the nation, see their rights violated and suffer as a result of injustice, violence and marginalization, notwithstanding the dignity and justice granted them by our glorious religion?
—MINISTRY OF COMMUNICATION, 2003

Since acceding to the throne of his noble ancestors, His Majesty King Muhammad VI, our Chief Commander of the Faithful, may God protect him, has made the promotion of human rights a priority which lies at the very heart of the modernist democratic social project of which His Majesty is a leader. Doing justice to women, protecting children's rights and preserving men's dignity are a fundamental part of this project, which adheres to Islam's tolerant ends and objectives, notably justice, equality, solidarity, ijtihad [juridical reasoning] and receptiveness to the spirit of our modern era and the requirements of progress and development.
—PREAMBLE TO THE 2004 FAMILY CODE

His Majesty King Muhammad VI . . . has insisted . . . on making the Moroccan family—based upon shared responsibility, affection, equality, equity, amicable social relations and proper upbringing of children—a substantial major component of the democratization process, given that the family constitutes the essential nucleus of society.
—PREAMBLE TO THE 2004 FAMILY CODE

These provisions should not be regarded as flawless, nor should they be perceived from a fanatic angle. Instead, you should address them with realism and clear-sightedness, keeping in mind that this is an ijtihad effort which is suitable for Morocco at this point in time, in its endeavors to achieve the development objective it is pursuing a wise, gradual, and determined manner.
—MINISTRY OF COMMUNICATION, 2003

Contents

Acknowledgments

Writing acknowledgments is like saying good-bye to friends you are leaving behind. It is necessarily emotional and filled with fond, but also sad, memories. My father passed away only a few months before I could phone him to let him know that this manuscript, at the time still in the form of a PhD dissertation, is written. I wish we had more time to catch up on what was once almost lost. I wish we had more time to talk, listen to each other, and reconnect. *Yearning not death makes you cry. The dead find their rest in the earth* (Anti-Atlas *tazrrart*, quoted in Hoffman 2008). I hope you have found it. My grandmother and my mother are the two women in my life who taught me what it means to be a woman. Despite their enormous hardships in life, they always reemerged more beautiful and stronger than ever. They showed me how to survive, live, and love. It is to you, my dear babi and mami, that I dedicate this book. My sister is my role model. Her incredible achievements, dedication to her research, and integrity are sometimes frightening, but ever since we were little she has never once doubted my abilities and has always encouraged me to work hard(er). She also devoted much of her free time to comment on my drafts, for which I am immensely grateful. It is to you, my dear Matejka, that I also dedicate this book. I feel privileged to have the Elliotts in my life and that they have accepted me as their daughter. I am eternally grateful for their love and support, which has been more than generous. You, my dear Derek, to you I owe my sanity and serenity. Without your love, humor, and gentle reminders that there are things in life other than my work, without your carefully organized trips away from my desk, I would have had a much harder and much less enjoyable time writing this book. Also, watching you transform into a loving and tender father in a matter of seconds has been truly inspiring. And finally, when

I was sending out book proposals and turning my dissertation into this manuscript, I was eight months pregnant with our beautiful boy Phinneas and working in Morocco. I kept thinking then that although Phinn may not grow up in Morocco, wherever we will end up we will, unfortunately, encounter patriarchal mentalities, misogyny, and discrimination of any kind. The feminist struggle for a world free from any kind of prejudices and discrimination has not been won yet. But revisiting stories of hardships many women face in Morocco because of gender, their economic status, and demands placed on them by the patriarchal neoliberal state, as well as personal experiences of harassment because I am a woman made me even more determined in my resolution that Derek and I will raise a boy who will practice, believe in, and speak out in favor of equality, be it gender, ethnic, or economic. He is almost nine months now, and seeing him develop, imitate our trilingual talk by rotating his tongue and blowing raspberries, and light up when surrounded with people has been a constant reminder that as babies our mentalities continue to evolve (for the better) as well.

As for the persons outside my family who have helped me on my academic path, I have to first thank my supervisor at the University of Oxford, Michael Willis. It was he and his inspiring method of teaching North African Politics that landed me in Morocco and helped me frame my MPhil topic, which eventually turned into the dissertation on which this book is based. He has been an incredible mentor and of enormous support both in Oxford and Morocco. I am forever grateful for his immense patience with my questions, drafts, and knocking on his office door without an appointment. His genuine kindness and bonhomie will stay with me forever. Thank you! In Oxford, Middle East Center's librarian Mastan Ebtehaj and administrator Julia Cook, St. Antony's porters (Mick, John, Pat, Malcolm), and administrators (Gillian Crook, Kärin Leighton, and Rachael Connelly) helped me with my queries and laughed with me when I needed to; a thank you to Amy Joshi, though now in Delhi, who has opened up my eyes to feminism, discussed gender from a theoretical and practical point of view, and provided very insightful feedback on an earlier draft of this book; to Dorian Singh for our conversations, accommodation when I could not face another X5 ride back to Cambridge, and dirty martinis on my viva day; and to Lana Al-Shami and Nisrine Jaafar, for the enormous fun at our *dabkeh* practice and the conversations over these years. Thank you all for your generosity, love, and time!

I do not have enough space to thank all the people in Morocco individually who shared their thoughts and concerns with me, who devoted their time to answering my questions, but without you I would not have been able to write this book. A gargantuan thank you to you! A big thank you also to Amina Chibani, Hasna Ahmed, and Touria Benlafqih for their help with organizing interviews in Rabat and translations. Malika Enna-jeh and the Moroccan British Society offered their kind assistance with organizing interviews, while Malika and her husband also extended their generous hospitality, invited me to their home, fed me, and discussed politics and academia with me. I am grateful to Susan Schaefer Davis for sharing that long taxi ride from Ifrane to my field site, for providing much needed advice on how to survive in the field, for reading and commenting on my initial findings, and organizing interviews for me. I would like to keep the names of the families and my field-site friends hidden, but I will be forever indebted to the L., A., Gh., Gh., and L. families as well as to my girlfriends. This is a humble expression of gratitude to you who kept invit-ing me in despite my constant indiscretions. And you, *habibti* Habiba, you opened up your home and your heart; you shared your thoughts and your time with me; and you helped me with my questions, struggles, and frus-trations during my fieldwork. Here is a humble thank you and acknowl-edgment of a lasting friendship.

Note on Transliteration

I tried to keep transliteration of Moroccan Arabic words as close as possible to the way words are pronounced. I kept proper names in their colloquial form and as they would be written down by locals using the French transliteration style, for example, Ftouch, Aicha, and Oued al-Ouliya. However, because I also use official documents and newspaper articles, which are written in Standard Arabic, their transliteration differs from the colloquial form. It is for this reason that some words appear in two forms—*wa* and *ou*, *al-* and *l-*, *al-mar'a* and *l-mara*. Apart from that, for the transliteration of Standard Arabic I generally follow the system adopted from the *International Journal of Middle East Studies*, with certain modifications: I use *š* instead of *sh* or *ch* for greater clarification, and I avoid diacritics except for the hamza (') and the 'ayn ('). All Arabic words save for proper names and Standard English forms, such as the Qur'an, are italicized.

Abbreviations

ADFM	Association Démocratique des Femmes du Maroc (Democratic Association of Moroccan Women)
CEDAW	Convention on the Elimination of All Forms of Discrimination against Women
EU	European Union
HCP	High Commissioner for Planning
ILO	International Labour Organization
IMF	International Monetary Fund
JSO	Justice and Spirituality Organisation
LDDF	Ligue Démocratique pour les Droits des Femmes (Democratic League for Women's Rights)
MDGs	Millennium Development Goals
MENA	Middle East and North Africa
NGO	Non-governmental organization
OFI	Organisation de la Femme Istiqlalienne (Istiqlal Party Women's Organization)
PAIWID	Plan of Action for the Integration of Women in Development
PJD	Parti de la Justice et du Développement (Justice and Development Party)
PSC	Personal Status Code
PPS	Parti du Progrès et du Socialisme (Party of Progress and Socialism)
SAP	Structural Adjustment Program
UAF	L'Union de l'Action Féminine (The Union of Women's Action)
UDHR	Universal Declaration of Human Rights

UIDHR	Universal Islamic Declaration of Human Rights
UNDP	United Nations Development Program
UNFM	Union Nationale des Femmes Marocaines (National Union of Moroccan Women)
USAID	United States Agency for International Development
USFP	Union Socialiste des Forces Populaires (Socialist Union of Popular Forces)
WB	World Bank
WID	Women in Development

Modernizing Patriarchy

Introduction

Karima[1] was my primary contact in Oued al-Ouliya, a relatively small rural community in the southeastern part of Morocco, where I conducted my fieldwork. She was forty-two years old, single, and a literacy teacher with a degree in Islamic law. She was living in an extended family household with her mother, brother, widowed sister-in-law, and their families. Her personality was rather overbearing and she had "an old mind," prompting her nieces to conclude that "no wonder no one wants to marry her," but showed a much more submissive attitude toward her brothers, village elders, and married women. She was among the first in the family to wake up every morning to sweep the floors outside the house and eat breakfast before leaving for work at the local Association Oued for the Development of Women's Work (Association [Oued] pour le Développement du Travail Féminin). Her morning students were elementary school pupils whose parents could afford to pay for extra tutorials in reading, writing, calculation, and Islamic studies. After lunch, she and two other educated single adult girls were teaching three classes in the informal education program (*tarbiya ghair nidamiya*). Evenings, too, were taken up with private lessons she was giving to her neighbor's son. Karima was working full time, six days a week, and earning significant money for a *woman* in this community. Given the opportunity, however, married women mocked her status as a *girl*. (In Morocco, as elsewhere in the region, marriage and not age transforms a female's status from one of a girl to that of an adult woman.) Despite being educated and working outside the home, Karima's "advanced" age prompted many people to deny her status as physical adult and question her femininity. She was treated as *mskina* (poor thing) by her family and community rather than as the poster girl of development workers who promote the idea of education as a necessary if not the only way to women's empowerment and autonomy in the Global South.

The question of what defines a *woman* is not a new issue. Feminists, notably Simone de Beauvoir and Judith Butler, have discussed the topic at length, and their work has significantly influenced a diversity of approaches to the enhancement of women's rights within the international development community and national decision-making elites. The case of Karima is an example of how becoming a woman in Morocco is a political and legal question rather than a biological one. There are different categories of adult womanhood, and Karima belongs to that of the underdog. Being a female means that she is not entitled to own family property, and being unmarried inhibits her playing a part in the management of the household. Finally, being an unmarried girl implies that her personal autonomy and independence are severely restricted, regardless of her education, employment, and age.

What does it mean to be a *woman* and a *girl* in contemporary Morocco and who and what determine the characteristics of each? Each chapter of the book addresses these questions from a slightly different angle, bringing in new actors and their discourses of women's empowerment, such as that of the Islamists and the feminists, the neopatriarchal state (re-)creating a legal schizophrenia, and local society fighting these discourses in an attempt to survive in an invasive neoliberal state. Each chapter also introduces a new category of womanhood, be it women as a blanket term for all female citizens—be they married, divorced, or widowed women—or to denote educated single adult girls. As not all women are equal to each other, it is important to anatomize how the pervasive women's rights discourses affect the different categories of women that exist in a state. Such an analysis is necessary if we truly wish to gauge the impact of development policies tackling poverty and women's disenfranchisement.

"Zoom in on an unimaginable Morocco"[2]

Lying on the westernmost fringes of the Arab world, Morocco is a bit of an oddball in the region. Never part of the Ottoman Empire, ruled by the longest-standing Arab monarchy, the Alaouites, and never quite caught up in the Nasserist revolutionary fervor of the 1950s and 1960s, but rather developing its own multiparty parliamentary system, the country gives the impression that it is relatively modernized, moderate, and indeed progressive and liberal. Its elites, too, have for some time identified themselves more with the West than its neighbors to the east or the south. Today, the country is praised for its "model" legal reforms in the realm of women's rights, its liberalizing economic and political agenda, and of course for its professedly reformist king Muhammad VI.

Morocco, it is true, is historically, economically, politically, and culturally tied with the West, and the country's liberalizing reforms have been informed and often pushed and financed by the international development and financial institutions. The International Monetary Fund (IMF) and World Bank's (WB) Structural Adjustment Program (SAP) was introduced to Morocco in 1983. This coincided with the opening of United States Agency for International Development (USAID) office in Rabat that began with the Training for Development Project organized for educated Moroccans who were to work for the agency. In the mid-1980s, the NGO-ization of women's rights issues began with Morocco's banned Islamist organization Al-'Adl wa-l-Ihsan (Justice and Spirituality Organisation—JSO), establishing a women's section, and secular left-ist women creating Association Démocratique des Femmes du Maroc (Democratic Association of Moroccan Women—ADFM) and Union de l'Action Féminine (Union of Women's Action—UAF). (Members of all three groups assured me that *their* organization rather than the other two was the trailblazer.) By 2011 the number of women's groups in the country had escalated to such a degree that one Moroccan activist quite rightly concluded that establishing a women's rights association has become a form of (family) business enterprise for middle- to upper-class women. Such feminization of Morocco's civil society and its operation as a business has led to much competition for limited foreign and national funds and to competition for a leading position within the women's rights movement. Such a position, however, though a boon to obtaining funds, does not translate into the movement's wider recognition among the Moroccan general public and particularly by women, their supposed subjects. The issue of women's rights in Morocco today is as much a question of what kind of gender politics to adopt to genuinely ameliorate the position of women as it is a question of criticism of the universalist and Western feminist-inspired international development campaigns.

All indicators show that Morocco's human development indicators have improved, although the country still performs below the Arab average and below many of the countries within the category of medium human development. Morocco's 2005 report (Kingdom of Morocco 2005b) on the national progress of Millennium Development Goals (MDGs) shows that primary education enrollment increased to 87 percent in 2003–2004 compared with 60.2 percent a decade earlier, in 1993–1994. Its main beneficiaries were particularly girls from rural areas. Morocco's latest MDG report from 2009 (Kingdom of Morocco 2010) projects that the country is likely to meet the goal of universal primary education for girls and boys by 2015.

It is also true that a Moroccan woman under King Muhammad VI has more legal rights compared with the Moroccan woman under his father, Hassan II, in the 1990s. To paraphrase Moroccan sociologist and feminist Fatima Mernissi (1993), the king's project of modernizing the country has therefore ostensibly had as a consequence the emergence of women as citizens. In the government headed by Istiqlal's Abbas al-Fassi from 2007 to 2011, there were five female ministers and two secretaries of state, and 34 out of 325 members of parliament were female. While the number of female parliamentarians increased to 65 out of 395 members under the succeeding Islamist-led government, there was only one female minister in the original cabinet. When the coalition fell apart and the king appointed a new government in October 2013, an additional ministry was given to a woman. (It should be noted however, that the ministries "given" to women politicians can be considered as traditionally female sectors—Bassima Hakkaoui has been running the Ministry of Solidarity, Women, Family, and Social Development and Fatema Marouane has become the head of the Ministry of Handicrafts, Social, and Solidarity Economy.)

The 2004 Family Code (Mudawwanat al-Usra) reform gave women the right to choose to get married without their *wali* (legal tutor) upon reaching the age of majority, which is set at eighteen. This law also grants women the right to initiate divorce on the basis of irreconcilable differences and without paying compensation to her husband to release her (*khul'a* divorce).[3] Furthermore, a 2003 reform of the Labor Code recognized the principle of gender equality in employment and salaries. These are only a few examples of increased presence of women in Morocco's political life and reformed legal rights that have the potential to ameliorate the situation of women.

However, what does the enhancement of legal and civil rights mean in the context of persisting patriarchy within the state and family, as well as in the face of deteriorating economic conditions in more structurally marginalized regions of the country but also among the urban lower- and middle-class families? The IMF and WB's promotion of SAPs, of which Morocco was an early and eager student, as well as mismanaged economic liberalization have been recognized as among the main reasons for the deterioration of living standards not only in Morocco but across the globe. The Beijing Platform for Action, the main document produced at the 1995 UN Conference on Women, for example, recognizes SAPs as putting additional burdens on poor rural women and children. The document asserts that "[t]he number of women living in poverty has increased in most regions. There are many urban women living in poverty; however, the plight of women living in rural and remote areas deserves special attention given the stagnation of development in such areas" (UN, The Fourth World Conference on Women 1995). Morocco, similarly, wrote in its *Beijing +10* report that social expenditure for education decreased by 11 percent by the end of the 1990s, which had a negative impact on the enrollment of girls in school (Kingdom of Morocco 2005a). However, although the country recorded a 23 percent increase in educational spending in 2008, authors such as Silvia Colombo rightly conclude that "the low institutional quality of agencies in charge of channeling this investment . . . means that the poor quality of education in Morocco is unlikely to be tackled effectively" (2011, 6). Such an observation challenges the government's promise to achieve universal primary education by 2015. Inadequate utilization of funding is recognized as a result of Morocco's always having favored economic reforms over meaningful political and institutional reforms, which would address unaccountability, patron-client relations of which the monarchy benefits the most, corruption, and a dysfunctional electoral system (Colombo 2011; Joffe 2009).

Economic liberalization based on SAPs with concomitant austerity measures is seen as further harming women's integration in development and progress of their country. Valentine Moghadam in her book *Women, Work, and Economic Reform* (1998b) argues that in the Middle East and North African (MENA) region cutbacks in social spending (but also misallocated aid) impose additional burdens on women because in their role as housewives they are the ones responsible for the well-being and managing of the family budget. Similarly, Naila Kabeer (2003) reports that SAPs caused a "scissors effect" on women's time because women as the primary caretakers had to increase the amount of (unremunerated) hours to nurture and help those in need. Yet, at the same time many women had to take up poorly paid jobs in exploitative industries and/or the informal sector to compensate for either male unemployment or increased living expenses, if not both (Cairoli 2011).

What do such savings in social spending mean when linked with the state of human development? Illiteracy among rural females above the age of ten in 2004, when the last national census in Morocco was conducted, was still alarmingly high at 74.5 percent (HCP 2008). Women are also underrepresented in the Moroccan workforce, since in 2011 only 26.7 percent of the workforce was female; and women are more likely to experience longer-term unemployment (over one year) than men (HCP 2011). In 2010 only 17 percent of those employed had health insurance and while in urban areas the percentage was slightly better at 31.4 percent, in rural areas an abysmal 3.5 percent of those employed were insured (Agueniou 2010). Furthermore, 11.10 percent of all marriages concluded in 2010 were between an adult man and an underage girl and the rate was slightly higher at almost twelve percent in 2011 (Ministry of Justice 2011, 2012). The conclusion of the Moroccan government in its 2005 MDG report that "despite progress, Morocco is acutely aware of delays in social development and the fight against poverty" (Kingdom of Morocco 2005b), prompts one to ask, how well Moroccan *women* are integrated into the development of the state.

Or conversely, who are these *women* contained in the numerous statistics, reports, and development rhetoric arguing that Morocco is nonetheless making progress? Oyeronke Oyewumi is right in concluding that "[t]he woman at the heart of feminism is a wife" (2000, 1094). So, too, is this the case for the development community and for the Moroccan state. Much of the literature deals either with an unspecific category of *women* or with married women, giving the (false) impression that marital status does not play a significant role in women's position in society. Moreover, women's rights seem to be "hijacked" by rights of married women. At the heart of the reformed Moroccan Family Code, the leading and extolled legal document ostensibly improving the legal rights of *women* in Morocco, is a married woman (or a girl about to get married). The code's general silence on, if not marginalization of, the rights of single adult girls and, to a certain extent, also divorced and widowed women, subjects them to the whims of their families and local customs.

Islamist, secular, and state development agendas

I understand contemporary development (women's rights) discourse in Morocco to be directed by the international development agenda based on documents and guidelines such as, but not exclusively, the Beijing Platform for Action, the UN Convention on the Elimination of All Forms of Discrimination Against Women (CEDAW), and the MDGs. These three documents are among the main agenda-setting directives, informing much of the official government and (predominantly secular) NGO-led programs and campaigns for the amelioration of women's rights in the country. They furthermore supply material to two other, more specific approaches to women's issues in Morocco. The first one is the legalistic approach, promoted mostly by the Moroccan elite and secular feminist women's rights groups, such as the UAF, ADFM, and La Ligue Démocratique pour les Droits des Femmes (the Democratic League for Women's Rights—LDDF) that deem legal and constitutional reforms implementing gender equality as defined by CEDAW as a necessary prelude to changing people's mentalities and the advancement of society.

Its rival is the bottom-up approach to progress, advocated by the more moderate Moroccan Islamist movements, such as the JSO and to a lesser extent the parliamentary Parti de la Justice et du Développement (Justice and Development Party—PJD). Contrary to widespread belief I argue that these two latter organizations are not averse to societal progress in the realm of women's rights. Rather, their respective programs are ones of gradualism and seeking an "authentic" and specifically Moroccan Islamic solution to the problems and challenges arising from colonialism, modernity, and globalization. Legal reforms, which, for them, must be grounded in the contemporary rereading of religious texts, are a necessary consequence of society's readiness and ameliorated systemic conditions and not a precondition. And, as many other Islamist groups in the region have been arguing in the post–Arab Spring region, modernity and religiosity are not antithetical; instead, Muslim-majority states need to develop a pious modernity based on a "sound" reading of religious legal texts rather than by following the "foreign" and secular Western model. Though this is an important distinction that sets Islamist groups apart from the secular ones, one of the main distinctions between their social agendas is that the secularists focus their immediate attention on the promotion of strategic gender interests whereas the Islamists focus on practical ones. Nonetheless, the two groups share an end goal—women's empowerment. Chapter 2 will further explore this.

I call secular feminists as such because they promote secularization of the legal system, and most of them refer to themselves as feminists.[4] Zakia Salime (2011), on the other hand, terms feminists attached to the ADFM or UAF as liberal feminists.[5] I agree with her, but I nonetheless refer to secular feminism when describing them because their agenda is primarily secular in nature despite that some of them engage with the Islamic reference. As Salime contends, this was done with the purpose of furthering their universalist ideas of women's rights. I as well will demonstrate in

Chapter 2 that the utilization of religious language was a strategic choice rather than a genuine attempt at the Islamization of their evidently secular agenda. Their frame of reference is the international human rights law and they staunchly defend the universality of human rights, to which women's rights also belong. In their view, an Islamic framework of human rights, even when accommodated to address contemporary social, economic, and political developments, falls short of recognizing and institutionalizing gender equality because of such unresolved issues as polygyny, depriving women of equal inheritance shares, and the issue of veil, to name a few. Fatima Outaleb, the director of the UAF's Shelter for Women Victims of Violence in Rabat (the capital of Morocco) called the Annajda Centre, underlined this issue firmly in my interview with her in 2011: "We are secular and we will die secular. And we will do our best to remain secular."

However, although secular feminist activists seem to be proud of their label, mainstream society continues to associate secularism with atheism and thus considers it a Western notion, which has to be resisted and condemned as foreign and inauthentic.[6] The Islamists, on the other hand, advocate a need to devise a Moroccan Islamic epistemology in order to retain the country's ostensible cultural uniqueness and authenticity. Much of the Islamist discourse is still their attempt to liberate themselves from what they perceive as the neo-Orientalist and neo-imperial ideological onslaught.

The effect of state-led legal reforms

What is missing in this struggle for the hegemony of one ideological frame of reference over the other? The nonexistence of a constructive dialogue and the lack of tolerance between the secular feminists and Islamist activists harm those whom their campaigns are supposed to help—Moroccan women. Advocating for legal reforms and working with women and men on the ground in urban, rural, and remote areas have to be merged rather than promoted as two separate projects, as admittedly happens now. The conflict, however, is not easy to solve because it is mired in ideological debates about the appropriate human rights frame of reference. Should it be secular or religious? universal or culturally specific? Chapters 2 through 4 will examine in more detail these ideological binaries and their effect on society.

Furthermore, what is the purpose of legal reforms if not to both follow social reality and address social dynamism? Does waiting for society as a whole to metamorphose resemble waiting for Godot? These concerns bring me to the question to be dealt with in Chapters 3 through 5: How do laws and women's rights discourse affect social reality? It is well documented that the application of the Mudawwana has been slow, and this leads many to conclude that the law has had a rather uneven and minuscule effect on the changes in gender relations. Most of the literature contends that slow application is a result of continuing low literacy rates, women's ignorance in particular of the law itself, and corruptibility of judges (ADFM 2007; Ennaji 2008; Willman Bordat and Schaefer Davis 2011). I, however, contend that numerous campaigns organized by the state and various NGOs and the coverage of the topic in the media have resulted in raising public awareness of the reforms. Theater productions, for example, and government-sponsored soap operas dealing with such topics as the Mudawwana reforms, women's empowerment, and promotion of state-sanctioned modernization of female propriety in the public sphere have become a significant part of the regime's agenda to advance women's rights within a controlled and modernized patriarchal system (Jay 2013). The problem of (non)application thus necessarily lies somewhere else. Many women (but also the ʿadul, or religious notaries in charge of drafting marital and other contracts) themselves have adopted the attitude of "pick and choose" to the more exposed and therefore controversial provisions of the law, such as the legal age of marriage, women's right to choose to get married with or without the wali, and stipulating extra conditions into the marital contracts or concluding a prenuptial agreement. A discussion about the disconnect between modernity (represented by the law) and traditions (represented by people's attitudes) is salient, and it will feature prominently in Chapter 4.

Furthermore, material poverty, which forces many into either marrying off their daughters at an early age or maintaining a dysfunctional, if not abusive, marriage because women have nowhere else to go, is an important factor contributing to the lack of implementation or recognition of the law. Coupled with this is also the largely nonexistent infrastructure in more provincial and rural areas and police, medical, and other staff who are insufficiently trained to deal with women seeking help; however, it is also true that many men and women are not willing to help women because of their own personal biases (Terrab 2007; Willman Bordat and Schaefer Davis 2009).[7] Women thus have nowhere to go to and therefore submit to their "fate."

Finally, what is lacking in most debates about the Mudawwana is the recognition that the reformed law has failed to live up to its reputation.

The third and fourth chapters will demonstrate how the law is perpetuating patriarchal family relations rather than instituting gender equality.

Methodological considerations

This is an ethnographic study of women as the main subject of the contemporary Moroccan development and women's rights agenda. Borrowing the concept of the spiral of silence from Elisabeth Noelle-Neumann (1984; Gray 2008), the purpose of this book is also to break this spiral, because when the subaltern speaks she exposes the inherent malfunctions of the supposed (Moroccan) liberalizing project.

How is such a discrepancy between the image that Morocco has cultivated for the domestic and international public consumption and the reality on the ground possible? One problem is data collecting. Looking at the official census statistics for the community I studied, and especially data dealing with education and first-time marriages among girls, appeared to me as grossly exaggerated. I shall deal with the issue of the possibility of "politically correcting" data in Chapters 4 and 5; suffice it to say here that a cursory inquiry into how data were collected revealed that none of my interlocutors remembered being surveyed by a government official. In addition, by chance I came across a survey conducted by Morocco's statistical agency called Haut-Commissariat au Plan (High Commission for Planning—HCP) that dealt with the implementation of the Mudawwana five years after the reform. The results of the survey, however, were never published because, as I was told by a source at the agency who did not want to be named, they were "too sensitive politically."

The second important issue is the question of what numbers can actually reveal about the lived realities of people. I suggest that even sex-disaggregated data do not suffice in gauging the quality of women's and men's lives. Material poverty is, to a large extent, quantifiable and measured on the basis of various indicators, such as the somewhat outdated income per capita or the updated Multidimensional Poverty Index (MPI).[8] Yet even improved and expanded gender-related poverty indicators, such as the UNDP's Gender-related Development Index (GDI) and Gender Empowerment Index (GEM), though welcome for a general analysis, continue to portray the kind of picture that does not necessarily reflect people's perceptions of their own condition. Regardless, various leading international organizations recognize poverty first and foremost as material deprivation, and it is only recently that some authors and agencies have started to look at it from a multidimensional perspective. The WB's *World Development Report: Attacking Poverty*, for example, identifies poverty primarily in economic and material terms while also acknowledging the effect of "social norms, values, and customary practices" on the exclusion of women and other minority groups from actively participating in the national economy (2000, 3). This report furthermore specifies other areas of human development, such as low achievement in education, poor health, and substandard nutrition, all of which constitute human privation (World Bank 2000). The United Nations Development Program (UNDP) in its 2005 *En Route to Equality* report defined poverty as income, human, and time poverty.

Many academics as well agree that poverty cannot be reduced to pecuniary privation. Unquantifiable poverty, such as gender-based discrimination and lack of self-esteem, respect, and power, is gaining recognition. Hilary Silver and S. M. Miller (2003) write about the European Union's (EU) definition of social exclusion as distinct from income poverty and rightly argue that the notion of social exclusion offers a more holistic approach to and understanding of poverty. The EU "recasts exclusion as an inability to exercise 'the social rights of citizens' to a basic standard of living and as barriers to 'participation' in the major social and occupational opportunities of the society" (2003, 8). Naila Kabeer, too, argues that "[t]he well-being of human beings, and what matters to them, does not only depend on their purchasing power but on other less tangible aspects, such as dignity and self-respect" (2003, 80). It is such a definition of poverty as social deprivation or exclusion which is absent from most of the domestic and international institutional statistics and reports.

In other words, women's (and men's) lives reduced to numbers, while decontextualizing people's experiences can give a false impression of the nature of the country's progress. One often neglected reason thereof is that such indicators do not normally distinguish between different categories of women—according to marital status, age, and educational background. They thus reveal a generalized view of the state of women's rights in the country, while disregarding the fact that many *women*, despite lacking education and an independent income, may be satisfied with their societal status and life. In a number of societies, including the MENA region, the status of many women improves with both becoming a wife and giving birth to children rather than through generating income. Diane Singerman and Homa Hoodfar are right in concluding that Egyptian "working women may actually lose their power and status they had in the household because when they work their non-cash contributions to the household decline" (1996, xvii). Moreover, Fida Adely (2013) writes about the Jordanian gender paradox, echoing what seems to be an untapped market for research from other parts of the world about the misunderstood links between education and women's empowerment. Rather than education enabling women to find jobs outside the home, which is what development agencies so forcefully promote, education has become the means toward different ends. In the Jordanian case, as demonstrated by Adely, education has been linked with improving a girl's chances to get married. Marriage and not waged employment remains the primary ticket for the enhancement of a woman's societal status. However, whereas Adely's interlocutors in Jordan hoped to boost their credentials on the marriage market, in provincial Morocco sending daughters to bigger cities to complete their higher education resulted in many of them facing a different paradox. These educated single adult *girls* have not only been unable to climb the social ladder by finding good and respectable jobs but they have also been marginalized by their own communities due to their inability to get married. Contrary to Adely's findings, education of girls in Oued al-Ouliya, as well as in provincial Morocco more generally, has in many cases resulted in forfeiting the opportunity to (ever) get married and as a consequence failing to achieve full adulthood.

Again, the problem arguably lies in the way most leading international organizations, such as the WB and UN, define empowerment of women mostly in terms of increasing women's economic role and political agency—joining the workforce and having a greater say in the institutions of the state—rather than empowerment on a more personal level. In other words, it is empowerment for economic development of countries rather than empowerment of women per se which is being promoted (Chant 2007). Nicholas Kristof and Sheryl WuDunn in their development best seller, for example, make the link unequivocal by concluding that "the economic implications of gender discrimination are most serious. To deny women is to deprive a country of labor and talent, but—even worse—to undermine the drive to achievement of boys and men" (2009, 160).

Moreover, much of the development discourse has been preoccupied with the notion of feminization of poverty. This idea that poverty is somehow gendered has led to purposely invented slogans such as "female-headed households are the poorest of the poor," "to fight poverty, invest in girls," "educated mothers [*sic!*] get married later and have fewer children," and "women still constitute seventy percent of the world's poor" in order to attract generous donations for the women's rights project. In addition, such beliefs have, in the words of Srilatha Batliwala and Deepa Dhanraj, "become mythologized as they become development orthodoxy" (2007, 33). These notions have become so common*place* that many books, newspaper, and Internet articles referring to various aspects of female poverty and women's supposedly critical role for economic and human development, do not feel the need to reference their sources anymore. Yet, recognizing women as central to fighting national poverty has indirectly put the blame for poverty on women rather than on larger malfunctions and/or unabated patriarchy, supported and indeed promoted by regimes, as is the case in Morocco and elsewhere in the region.

Moreover, homogenization of women on the basis of, for example, household headship (male and female) does not say much about the range of diverse experiences of women and girls within these households, particularly when some women voluntarily "trade off" their personal autonomy for financial support and living in a male-headed household. Women may thus be poor materially but not in terms of power, psychological well-being, and/or personal security (Chant 1997, 2007; Davids and van Driel 2001). Trading the material security of living in a male-headed household for personal autonomy is thus an expression of self-determination applied to dealing with adverse situations; yet statistics do not display such female emancipation as such. On the other hand, focusing on the poverty of female-headed households also gives a (false) impression that women and children in male-headed households lead better lives. Again, disregarding the so-called secondary poverty or social exclusion of women and girls in such households (or any type of household for that matter) in poverty-alleviation programs and women's rights campaigns is dangerous and necessarily discriminatory against married women and single adult girls, whom both the literature and development community seem to neglect or mention only in terms of their assumed (future) roles as wives and mothers.

Further disaggregating data and paying attention to local gender attributes is thus pertinent to the discussion about poverty and women's empowerment and can reveal a much more nuanced picture than the one painted by numerous available statistics. Micro-level ethnographic research is therefore best suited to expose some of the misconceptions of the contemporary development discourse and to bring to light the intra-household inequalities and social deprivation of different categories of women. Particularly younger married and single women, though actively renegotiating their space and rights recognized by the state, carefully tread within the confines of locally delineated patriarchal rules of gendered propriety. Patriarchy thus is modernized, yet reaffirmed by the extent of the

trenchant development discourse, legal reforms, and specific socioeconomic conditions of particular communities. Nowhere is this clearer than
in the status of educated single adult girls, who will be the subject of the
analysis in Chapter 5.

Development activists and policy makers assume that women, if made
aware of their rights through education, will invariably be able to *choose* a
more autonomous and empowered life. There are two problems with such
a view. First, what does autonomy and empowerment mean for women?
Is there a universal definition that women the world over could relate
to? As suggested above, many women in this region become empowered
through marriage rather than by earning a wage and living an independent
life as (Western) development agencies make us believe. And second, this
book challenges such reductionist assumptions by looking at married and
particularly educated single adult girls from provincial areas and argues
that they are denied this right to choose. In the Moroccan case, this is a
consequence of the failure of the modernizing project presented in the
guise of the reformed Family Code, accompanied by the state's inability
and society's reluctance to enable educated girls to put their education to
work. As such, this book fits into a broader discussion on youth exclusion
in the contemporary MENA region as a result of the failure or ineptness of
governments to fulfill their part of the social (Nasserist) contract, the youth
bulge and unemployment, failed economic liberalization and neoliberal
reforms, the influence of mass media, and, finally, delayed marriage (Assaad and Ramadan 2008; Boudarbat 2005; Boudarbat and Ajbilou 2007;
Kouaouci 2004; Meijer 2000; Singerman 2007).[9] As Brahim Boudarbat
and Aziz Ajbilou writing on youth exclusion in Morocco rightly contend,
youth bulge should be looked at as a demographic gift because "by building the human capital of young workers and providing them with opportunities to use their skills, Morocco can increase income per capita, bolster
savings and improve social welfare" (2007, 5). Instead, young people in
the MENA region in general find themselves in a liminal space between
the familial ethos and the Internet era, between collectivity and individualism, between being physically adult but not adult in the eyes of society.
They are in the state of what Singerman (2007) terms "wait adulthood."
In her important and timely research on the economic imperatives of marriages in Egypt, she discusses young (male) adults who delay getting married well into adulthood in order to save sufficient amounts of money for
the wedding and accompanying costs. While waiting, these young (male)
adults continue to live with and depend financially and otherwise on their
parents. Such living situation and indeed delaying the foreordained can

create sexual and other frustrations due to the general conservative societal attitudes toward what initiates full adulthood, dating, and unwedded sexuality. Conflicts between the old and the new moral order abound and are played out in public, many of which were further exposed during the Arab Spring. The outrage provoked by the virginity tests in Cairo's Tahrir Square as by the Egyptian Alia al-Mahdy's nude photos, which she posted on her blog in November 2011, are only two such examples demonstrating the unresolved generational and ideological schism. And the 2013 Femen protests in Tunisia show that questions about women's freedom (or right) to choose and what constitutes justice will continue to be hotly debated in the post–Arab Spring region. There is a need among the youth to reinvent themselves to cope with the restricting realities of their modernizing societies, yet at the same time there is also the need to conform to the established patterns of propriety and social and family expectations to secure a future. This book is a contribution to this salient debate because it concentrates on the rural single adult girls in Morocco, a category much neglected in the literature, which for the most part deals with the urban educated (male) youth between the ages of fifteen and twenty-four. I have expanded this age bracket to include single adult girls beyond what academics define as youth because girls in their thirties, too, are part and parcel of the "waithood" phenomena experienced in the region. As will be demonstrated in Chapter 5, these girls experience waithood in a different way because they are marginalized from the labor market, realizing that education is not a strategy to climb the social ladder, as well as from the women's rights discourse simply because they are not (yet) *complete women*. Whereas Singerman (2007) concentrates predominately on the male waithood due to the high financial cost of getting married and Boudarbat and Ajbilou (2007) similarly conclude that in Morocco the extent of delaying marriage depends on monetary difficulties of both women and men, I question such assumptions based solely on a person's budgetary limitations. These authors neglect to address different societal and familial expectations placed on women on the one hand and men on the other, in addition to failing to recognize that the genders face contrasting repercussions when delaying marriage well into physical adulthood. Delaying marriage for girls may in fact translate into spinsterhood for life. A girl's (young) age and inexperience, rather than her education and employment, continue to define her as a suitable bride; whereas for a man, his mature age and experience of living away from his family while getting an education and/or earning money only confirms his masculinity or the ability to fulfill his masculine societal duties.

Case studies of consideration

The main analysis of this book focuses on two categories: married women and (educated) single adult girls in a provincial Moroccan community I call Oued al-Ouliya. The community lies in the Errachidia province, much of which is, according to poverty maps, among the more economically vulnerable and poverty-stricken regions in Morocco (World Bank 2004). An ethnographic analysis of the community will follow this introduction. I chose these two groups of women as being perhaps the most representative types and, what appears to be, on opposite poles of womanhood in this community in particular and in Morocco more generally. Although educated single girls represent a minority, they nonetheless form an important category not only because the majority of families in Oued al-Ouliya will have at least one such daughter but also because the development discourse places an enormous emphasis on the education of girls from poorer backgrounds. The singlehood of these girls could be one repercussion of higher education and as such warrants a closer look at their situation. Contrasting their experiences is thus necessary for understanding the impact of the development discourse on women's lives.

Poverty, understood as social deprivation, exclusion, or disenfranchisement, is manifesting itself in different ways in married women and single adult girls, regardless of the type of household they live in. Whereas being married is defined as fulfilling one's role in society, being single is failing in doing so. Daisy Hilse Dwyer in *Images and Self-Images: Male and Female in Morocco* (1978) contends that generally young girls were excluded from verbal denigration, whereas married, divorced, and widowed women were usually its target. I argue that being divorced or widowed, particularly with children, is not stigmatized to the extent that being an (educated) single adult girl is. Education, I suggest, has changed the perception of these girls since the 1970s, when Dwyer did her research. Postsecondary education makes them vulnerable to slander and gossip owing to their experiences of living away from the community while at the university. Looking at the so-called intra-household inequalities between women and men in general and different categories of women within households in particular sheds light on diverse experiences of social deprivation. Furthermore, adding education to women's status shows that although education is generally accepted as a positive and welcome contribution, there are negative consequences to being "too" educated. On the basis of analyzing education in Oued al-Ouliya in Chapter 5, I contend that in the case of educated single adult girls, higher education can be an impediment to fulfilling their feminine role. I demonstrate that the prevailing development and women's rights discourses and homogenization of women as one category obscures the experiences of many educated single adult girls. A combination of pursuing (post)secondary education, while deferring to a specific local social order, traps them in the space between traditions, symbolized in the community expectations of the ideal woman, and modernity, a quest for autonomy and individualized identity through employment and ownership of resources as promised by the development projects. In fact, these girls fail in fulfilling either their traditional feminine role or the modern one.

Despite their education, girls lack negotiating powers because opposing one's parents and brothers, whose role is to protect these girls regardless of their marital status, is like bringing a lifelong curse upon oneself and consequently losing protection and her identity. Although it is wrong to think of these girls as completely vulnerable—their power is seen in the way their behavior affects the honor of their male kin and family—it is precisely such gender-role ideology that forces families to control their daughters' movement and hence restricts their opportunities (Abu-Lughod 1999; Joseph 1994).

Why such inequality in women's statuses in society? The most apparent reason is found in the way society and the Family Code define a *woman*. I contend that a *woman* in the legal (and practical) context is a married woman regardless of her age. (It is for this reason, and following the local terminology, that throughout this book I use *girl* to denote an unmarried woman and *woman* as her married [or divorced and widowed] counterpart.) Single adult girls, albeit having reached the legal age of majority, continue to be treated as minors by the law and their families. In other words, legal majority does not entail or lead to personal autonomy. How has the "silent revolution," as the reform of the Family Code has been referred to in Morocco's 2005 MDG report (Kingdom of Morocco 2005b), ameliorated the position of these girls? Or has it?

Fieldwork

During the period of my final stage of fieldwork, which was conducted from October 2009 to June 2010 in Oued al-Ouliya, I lived with a local family of eight people belonging to three generations. This living arrangement gave me an invaluable opportunity to be an active participant observer of family life. Through the women in the household I met many other women and particularly single adult girls in the community for reasons which shall be illuminated in the following chapter. A few of these girls became my good friends, and therefore I cannot but disagree with Gesa E. Kirsch, who argues that "as feminist scholars . . . we need to understand that our interactions with participants are most often based on friendliness, not genuine friendship" (2005, 2170).

During this time I took four breaks: a three-week- and a four-week-long break to visit my family in Europe and to attend a conference in the United States, in addition to two shorter, five-day trips to attend a conference in Marrakech and to see my husband in Europe. I felt that these breaks from my life in the village and from the local family I lived with were necessary because lack of privacy and, at least at the beginning, my own frustration as a result of the inability to coherently communicate with people and to make sense of situations, proved to be quite challenging. My time away from the village was also an opportunity to reflect on my discontent, my dealings with people and situations, and on my research. "[B]eing an ethnographer," wrote Pat Caplan, "means studying the self as well as the other. In this time, the self becomes 'Othered,' an object of study, while at the same time, the other, because of familiarity . . . becomes part of the self" (1993, 180).

In Oued al-Ouliya I conducted thirty-three individual semistructured recorded interviews, two recorded discussions with both women and men, and a written survey among thirty-five girls attending informal education classes. I tried to choose the interviewed women and men on the basis of what I hoped was a somewhat representative sample of the community, paying attention particularly to their age, marital status, and educational background. In addition to my field research in this community, I interviewed women participants in the USAID literacy classes in four different provincial localities—El Hajeb, Douar Laouamra, Ben Slimmane, and Tamazirt—from October 2008 to December 2008. These interviews were an in-depth survey of the effect of literacy courses on women's lives outside of classrooms. Its analysis contributes to the understanding of how transformative education is for women living in conservative and lower-income households, communities, and regions.

Finally, during my various trips to Morocco from January 2007 to May 2011, I conducted interviews with secular (ADFM and UAF) and Islamist (JSO) women's rights activists in Rabat, Fez, and Casablanca. I concentrated on these three associations because they are among the most established and vocal groups dealing with women's rights in Morocco. I also tried to get interviews with the PJD female parliamentarians and particularly Minister of Solidarity, Women, Family, and Social Development Bassima Hakkaoui. However, getting to interview them turned out to be quite elusive. I had arranged a few interviews, including with Hakkaoui, but they were canceled at the last minute for various reasons, such as claiming I was late for the interview (when in fact I was waiting in the lounge of the PJD parliamentary cabinet, chatting with their party colleagues) or them assuming that they would not be a good person to talk to in terms of what they thought I was looking for. I try to compensate for this shortcoming by including newspaper articles and interviews, although I am aware that such secondary sources are insufficient for an in-depth analysis of the PJD's views and strategies. It is for that reason that I could not and did not include them in the same manner as the ADFM, UAF, and JSO to the discussion in Chapters 2 and 3.

I conducted most of the interviews with an assistant. The majority of my interviewees spoke Arabic and a few of them only Tašilhit. Although I felt I could have done the interviews with the Arabic-speaking persons by myself, I nonetheless felt more secure with an assistant because I wanted to avoid situations in which I and the meanings would be "lost in translation." I transcribed and translated most of the interviews into English together with Habiba, my closest field-site friend and assistant, in numerous weekend-long sessions. During these, we both got to know each other quite well, and our conversations, which accompanied our work routine, allowed me to get an additional insight into the community life through Habiba's comments on the interviews and interpretations of customs and sayings I was not familiar with. However, because we had run out of time, I translated the remaining interviews by myself upon my return to the United Kingdom and had the translations checked by Hasna and Amina, two English teachers from Rabat.

This book is a product of fifteen months of field research in Morocco and more than a hundred semistructured recorded interviews, in addition to numerous informal unrecorded conversations with people. The main arguments and ideas, however, are informed by my ethnographic work and life in Oued al-Ouliya, and it is this community to which I now turn my attention.

As part of their weekend activities, girls attending informal education classes at the old headquarters of the local association write down cookie recipes (November 2009).

CHAPTER 1

Ethnographic Reflections

I was on the night bus from Meknes to Errachidia and anything but confident about the research I was expected to do as part of my internship for the USAID-sponsored literacy project. I had never traveled at night in Morocco, and the thought of being dropped off at the bus station in Errachidia in the middle of the night and waiting for a morning bus to take me to Tamazirt, my final destination, was rather unsettling. The bus was filled with women traveling with their children, and so I pushed away the dark scenarios, which prevented me from feeling at ease. I drifted in and out of sleep and hoped that the bus would take longer than scheduled to arrive at Errachidia. My wish was not granted. Instead I was dropped off at the extremely uninviting concrete building that stood as Errachidia's main bus station. It was four in the morning and almost three hours to my next bus. I entered the station only to realize that the interior was dimly lit, cold, and frightening. Some shops and what seemed like a café were open. Men were sitting, chatting and smoking when I, with a great sense of relief, spotted a scarfed adult girl sitting with her back toward me in the corner of the makeshift café. I approached her and shyly asked if I could sit next to her. She smiled, invited me to sit down, and told me that there was nothing to worry about, despite the two men flanking us on either side and fixing their stare on me. Fatima, as she told me was her name, was waiting for dawn to come so she could take a taxi back to her nearby village. She had done this waiting many times because of her monthly travels to Casablanca to have birthmarks, which covered almost half of her face, removed. As we chatted about the Arabic language, Islam, and my research, the two men changed positions many times but not their object of interest. Three hours passed much more quickly than I had initially feared when stepping off the bus. Fatima took the grand taxi to her village, and I boarded the morning bus to the rural community of Tamazirt, one of the four communities where I would be interviewing female participants in the USAID-sponsored Passerelles (Pathways) literacy courses.

The morning bus ride was stunning: stone desert, dotted with occasional palm groves and adobe *ksour* (fortified mud-brick villages). Nothing but earth colors painted the scenery, which seemed welcoming and warm. After roughly an hour the bus arrived at Tamazirt. It was still quite early, but some boys were already up and playing in the dusty road. Men were hurrying to work, and I could not help but notice that women were absent from the morning village bustle. I would later learn that particularly in those villages where households no longer rely on subsistence agriculture, the day for most women starts around nine. I was picked up by Aissam, at that time still the director of the locally run Passerelles program, who introduced me to Karima, one of the teachers and my host for the duration of my short stay in Tamazirt. I spent a week in Taddert, one of the Tamazirt's villages, staying with Karima's family and doing interviews, but mostly visiting women, drinking syrupy-sweet green tea, and eating enormous quantities of food, which left me sleepless for most of my nights there. The community, with its enchanting environment and proverbially hospitable people, instantaneously captivated me.

Almost a year later I returned to the village to start my yearlong fieldwork. This time I took a daytime bus ride from Marrakech. Crossing the High Atlas Mountains at Tizi n'Tichka pass, the road drops to Ouarzazate, where the scenic tourist Road of One Thousand Kasbahs begins. The road is dotted with palm groves and the remains of as well as the still-inhabited tawny *ksour* villages with ubiquitous satellite dishes; roses and other flowers or plants, depending on the season; and women washing their clothes and rugs in shallow streams, which during the summer dry to merely a trickle of water. What is displayed through the bus window is an enchanting view of earth-colored structures and life adapted to the semiarid desert climate, which is one of the main reasons for this region to attract many (Western) tourists.

Tamazirt

Nestled in an oasis on the southeastern side of High Atlas Mountains lie a series of mostly Berber-speaking villages belonging to the rural commune (*baladiya*) of Tamazirt (Homeland in the local Berber dialect Tašilhit). This provincial locale is divided into two administrative communities (singular: *jami'a*)—Oued al-Soufla (Lower Wadi) and Oued al-Ouliya (Upper Wadi), which is the site where I conducted my fieldwork. Approximately twenty thousand people live in Oued al-Ouliya's twenty-three villages of various sizes and distances from the main road.[1] These villages are called both *ighrman* (singular: *ighram*) in Tašilhit, or *ksour* (singular: *ksar*) in Arabic. In the past, all the original villages were fortified and as Walter B. Harris (1888) and Vicomte Charles de Foucald (1895) reported in their nineteenth-century travelogues, the oasis of the river Oued was extensive and hosted a number of *ksour* on both sides of the then flowing river.[2] Its main economic hub, *ksar* Al-Souq (the Market) was, according to Harris:

> the largest village we had yet come across in the Sahara, enclosed in high *tabia* walls, and boasting a number of well-built houses, and even a few shops. . . . In fact, [Al-Souq] may be more fitly described as a town than a *ksar*, for within its walls it is divided up into streets, many of them of the same tunnel-like formation as one is so used to see in Fez, for instance, the houses meeting overhead. (194–195)

De Foucald reported two market days on Sunday and Thursday, a practice which, according to locals, had been discontinued after independence but revived in the last few decades. Today, many of these fortifications are in ruins as villages expanded beyond the old sun-dried adobe walls. Reasons for the expansion include the end of tribal conflicts in the postcolonial time, building of a new *baladiya* of Tamazirt for the purposes of administering the oasis, and taking on a life of its own with a weekly market, which plausibly caused the termination of Al-Souq's biweekly market (Naciri 1986). The road, which now connects Tamazirt with the two major cities in the southeast of Morocco—Errachidia to the north and Ouarzazate to the south—not only enhanced the movement of people and goods into and from the community but also brought with it new ideas and values, which have weakened traditional structures. Further reasons for weakening of traditional structures include floods having ruined the original dwellings and forcing its inhabitants to build new villages; droughts;[3] the influx of remittances; and a general improvement of living standards, which allowed for rural gentrification. A devastating flood in 1979, which left much of Al-Souq in ruins and killed one person, as I was told, resulted in establishing new *ksour*, such as my field-site home Taddert (Home) and Qtaa al-Oued (Across the Wadi). Such developments culminated in various *ksour* forming a continuous stretch of houses without clearly defined boundaries or uninhabited land between them. To a large extent, original fortified villages remain only as a decayed reminder of the past, although a few of them, including Al-Souq, have been restored with the aim of attracting tourists and providing or improving housing for locals.

Most people are building houses with more expensive and "modern" materials, such as locally made cinder blocks. They have largely replaced mud bricks, which are also made on the spot from clay, water, and straw and left to dry in the abundant desert sun. Despite the inferior insulation properties of cinder blocks, locals prefer them to mud bricks as a building material. The efficient retention of heat and cold is an important detail when wide daily and seasonal temperature fluctuations are taken into account. Winter nighttime temperatures can drop to minus five degrees Celsius from a comfortable daytime high of twenty degrees; and summer days can be as hot as 44 degrees, dropping to the cooler mid- to high twenties during the night. To me, these new cinder-block houses in winter felt like refrigerators, especially because women aired their houses throughout the day and all year-round; whereas in spring and summer these houses feel like saunas, prompting people to sleep outside on the roofs or terraces of their homes. Despite these effects, "modern" materials are preferred because of their durability and, hence, aesthetic appeal; they are less prone to decay.

Many of the community's villages, including the ones surveyed for my research, lie on the main road. There are many tourist attractions situated close by, but life in the community remains largely unaffected by mass tourism. Economically and politically, Tamazirt remains of peripheral importance. The region of Meknes-Tafilalet, which is where Tamazirt is situated, is among the poorest in the country. Morocco's High Commission for Planning (HCP) reported in its 2007 poverty report that this region was the fourth poorest among sixteen regions in the country. Its poverty rate, defined as the proportion of those living with less than 3,834 dirhams (approximately 460 dollars) per person per annum in urban areas and 3,569 dirhams (approximately 430 dollars) in rural areas, was 12.2 percent (HCP). In addition, 21.4 percent of the population was recognized as vulnerable, meaning that although they were above the threshold of relative poverty they were vulnerable to falling below this line due to the vagaries of the socioeconomic situation of the environment in which they were living. Moreover, the poverty rate in Tamazirt at 13 percent with additional 24.7 percent vulnerable to poverty is slightly higher than in the region as a whole. Poverty is a countrywide problem in Morocco, but as David Crawford (2002) rightly argues, the most poverty-stricken areas can be found among rural, mountainous regions that are mostly populated by a Berber-speaking population.

Political decrees reach the community, but the voices of locals are, as those of many others in Morocco, not heard in Rabat's corridors of power and consequently not included in the decision-making process. Yet life here in Tamazirt is very much affected by the decisions of the country's political elites. Crawford is right in stating that Berbers are often ignored by academics and policy makers alike, or at best dealt with only in historical and apolitical studies. And although this is not a study of how one Berber-speaking community copes with changes brought by modernity and globalization, but rather a study of how peripheral communities more generally deal with such effects, it nonetheless offers an important insight into the workings of marginalization of Berbers in Morocco and therefore attempts to also contribute to rectifying the issue of the "invisibility of Morocco's Imazighen" (Berbers) (Crawford 2002).

The family and me

The father and the head of my field-site family died approximately twenty years before my arrival. His wife, Khalti Ftouch,[4] became a widow, but with adult children and working sons, some of whom by that time had already brought home their young brides, she was secure in her position as family matriarch. At the time of my fieldwork, she was most probably in her seventies. Despite her mature age, wrinkly face, and somewhat gaunt body, which she hid underneath multiple layers of clothing, she was remarkably agile. She devoted much of her time to prayer, visiting women, and worrying about the whereabouts of her unmarried daughter, Karima. Khalti Ftouch had divorced two husbands before she finally married her late husband, with whom she had three daughters and four sons. She was a Chrifa, tracing her descent to the prophet Muhammad, and thus enjoyed quite a lot of respect in the community, some of which was also attributable to her advanced age and motherhood. She was very critical of the younger generation of women, and one day she told me the following:

> In the past women didn't have rights. They made carpets without being paid. Now women have rights, they stay in the house, throw their husbands out [of the house] and they are in control. . . . She tells him "give me my house! I don't want your family!"

This is a strong critique of younger women, and I suspect her attitude has something to do with her daughter-in-law Hind, who might have been the reason for Khalti Ftouch's son Hicham to look for a job away from her and his home. Hind was treated differently from Amira—Khalti Ftouch's youngest daughter-in-law. Women in the house constantly complained about Hind's alleged laziness, carless cleaning, bad cooking, and, finally, her badly behaved son. My host family's female neighbors often told me that Hind was indolent and not a good daughter-in-law. But my impression of Hind was quite different. She was bubbly and loved to talk, and one often saw her carrying a wide smile on her face. Although she was admittedly slower in completing her chores than the other women in the house, at the end of the morning when she finished her tasks, her cooking tasted very similar to either Amira's or Mama's, the widowed and eldest daughter-in-law of Khalti Ftouch. My conclusion of women's criticisms of Hind is that she had deviated too much from the image of the ideal woman in this family and in the community in that she was vivacious, extroverted, and quite possibly acted as the decisive factor in influencing her husband to move away from the rest of his family and the community.

Karima was Khalti Ftouch's youngest daughter. She was forty-two years old at the time of my fieldwork and still unmarried: a girl and not yet a woman. Only Karima and one of her brothers had a university degree, whereas her two older sisters were illiterate. This pattern is quite common to many families in this community, whereas particularly in the not-so-distant past older daughters were still raised to get married at a young age and the youngest daughter was perhaps sent to school but definitely kept around for much longer, helping her mother and other womenfolk in the family. Naturally, marrying off all daughters and getting married in general is the ultimate goal in a girl's and her parents' lives. Karima's age was considered to be very advanced by most people in this community, in which girls in their early twenties complained about already missing the marriage train. Married women lamented Karima's situation by never forgetting to stick the epithet "poor thing" (*mskina*) to her name and looking extremely saddened, if not distressed, by the thought of her never experiencing *complete* womanhood. Despite being a teacher in the local women's association, teaching both illiterate women and girls who had dropped out of school and devoting much of her free time to various other educational activities, such as tutoring other women's children and leading aerobics classes, that she was single determined her lower status compared to that of married women. Many married women doubted that she could perform the duties of a woman—cleaning, cooking, and looking after children—and they discredited her efforts of working outside the home simply because that was not the purpose and role of a woman in this society. Karima thus, as most other single adult girls, was determined to get married despite her "old" age. She was aware that without marriage she would not be treated like an adult or "become a woman," and she would ultimately fail in fulfilling her societal role. In other words, she would not be treated as an equal by the other married women.

Amira was married to Khalti Ftouch's youngest son Zakariya, who was also the only adult man living in the household and thus acted as the head of the family. Amira was a beautiful twenty-four-year-old woman, who married Zakariya when she was nineteen. Upon obtaining a high school degree, she enrolled in a university course. However, just before the academic year started, Zakariya came to her house to ask for her hand. (This, in fact, was a strategic move on his part because, as will be seen in Chapter 5, university-educated girls are subject to an array of negative stereotypes reflecting on their reputation. Marrying Amira before she began to attend university was a strategy to prevent her from getting a university education and, by indication, compromising her reputation.) He came from a respected family and worked as a public school teacher, which made him too good of a match to turn down, particularly given the fact that many girls who chose a degree instead of a suitor ended up being single and without a full-time and well-paying job, like Karima and Amira's two older sisters. Despite Amira's being the youngest one of the women and coming to the household as the last one, she wielded quite a lot of power. This power is attributable to her status as the wife of the head of the household, the mother of a son, and her personal idiosyncrasies. She was very hardworking, a good cook, and often quiet and withdrawn. Hardly ever did I catch her smiling, and never once did I see her visit a female friend. She only left the house to visit her mother and sisters or other family relatives. Other women in the household treated her with the utmost respect, commending her on her cooking abilities and other household skills and loudly praising the behavior of her three-year-old son. Amira rarely returned the compliment, and she admitted to me once that when Khalti Ftouch passes away, Karima gets married, and Mama returns to her father's house when her two boys get married, she and Zakariya would be able to live in a single-unit household. Many girls in the community described Amira as conceited because, given the opportunity, she emphasized her status as a married woman in order to show her superiority compared to the other single girls and particularly those, who, at the time, had chosen university over marriage. Amira sneered at these girls, asserting that it was better for them to take any man who would propose as they were not in the position of bargaining anymore. In other words, their marriage train departed when they chose to go to the university.

Khalti Ftouch's oldest son died suddenly of a heart failure, leaving his bride, Mama, with two young boys. Contrary to what was customary, the family asked Mama to stay with them at least until the boys grow up, create their own families, and move out. The older of the two boys, Muhammad, who was twenty-one years old at the time of my fieldwork, twice during my stay with the family attempted to quit his vocational training to become a mechanic. His paternal and maternal uncles, who because of his father's death acted as Muhammad's legal representatives, forced him to return to school. In February 2010, however, Muhammad finally ran away from home to Casablanca, as we found out a few nerve-racking days later. Soon thereafter, when he realized that he would not be able to find a job on Casablanca's oversupplied job market of untrained manpower, he moved to Taroudant with his uncle Hicham and his wife, Hind, much to the relief of the women in the family, who had been agonizing about his future prospects. His mother was anxious about him to the point of asking me whether my single sister would be willing to marry him and take him to Europe, where he, Mama was confident, would be able to find work. Khalti Ftouch once told me that a boy of scrawny build and without any skills, like Muhammad, would never succeed in finding a job in Morocco. The fact that my sister was thirteen years his senior, among other substantial differences, did not matter because such a marriage would be one of convenience—not only for Muhammad but also for my sister, whom Mama regarded as "that poor girl" because of her status as single and adult.

Mama, a deeply religious middle-aged woman, spent every free moment reading the Qur'an or watching religious programs broadcast on numerous Gulf TV channels. She often initiated conversations about Europe and unjust global relations. I, who epitomized her conception of a stereotypical "Frenchwoman"[5] and in fact was the only European she had ever had contact with, was able to come to Morocco whenever I desired and traveled to Europe much more frequently than local immigrants do to visit their families. Despite my conscious attempts to deemphasize what to her appeared to be on the one hand my "privileged" background[6] yet on the other merely a typical European life, I ultimately failed to demonstrate to her (but also to the rest of the family and the community) that life in Europe and for Europeans is not as unambiguous as the stories and the "wealth" manifested in cars, renovated and extended houses, and flashy gadgets of returning immigrants seem to portray. I often felt I was being "Othered" and my personality oversimplified. Many locals thought of me merely in terms of such attributes as a Frenchwoman, a city girl, a daughter of a doctor and a nurse, and a non-Muslim.

But I, without a doubt, was different and privileged as a result of being a European, and the dissimilarities became increasingly prominent and complicated as months went by and my departure date was approaching. At the time of my fieldwork I was thirty-one years old and married for a bit over a year. The fact that I returned without my husband and still a student was rather peculiar, oftentimes criticized, but nonetheless shrugged off as being one of those odd European idiosyncrasies. My neighbor and friend Nour's brother, twenty-four-year-old Abdallah, during my interview with him continually emphasized the much more advantageous position of women under Islam compared to that of women in the West. At one point he concluded that in comparison with Morocco, women in Europe had fewer rights. "Honestly, I think that maybe [men] don't care about [women]," he speculated about European gender relations, and continued that women in Morocco have the right to freedom:

> You can't find any woman now who'd live as if she was imprisoned. The husband doesn't tell her "you can't go out." *Ya'ni* ["that is" but used more as a filler without specific meaning], thank God, there is freedom. Women go out but within limits. After the sun goes down or before darkness it's in her interest, it's better for her to stay inside so that no one harms her. There are many problems on the street. It's better [for her], do you understand?!

Knowing one's limits and staying at home in order not to cross boundaries entails protection and, more important, being protected is a woman's right. My travels to foreign places unprotected signaled to them exactly the opposite of what this means in Europe—that my family perhaps cared too little or not as much as their families would. But it also raised the question of whether I was *mastura* (a girl of good reputation and morals)?

Women judged the relationship with my husband and the "freedom" I enjoyed and thought I was silly. Many people I met in Morocco, and certainly women and girls from my field site, asked similar questions in the same progression: "Where are you from?" to "Are you married?" followed by "Do you have children?" and finally "Why don't you have children?" Particularly toward the end of my fieldwork women concluded that I should return home immediately and get pregnant. Most people I encountered and developed a friendship with believed I was spending an excessive amount of time away from my husband and postponing having children to, for them, an illogically distant future, while leaving my poor husband at home alone. They did not perceive me as a conventional woman, and they often reprimanded me for what they considered my frivolous attempt to pursue a career when it was obvious to them that I could not possibly escape my feminine destiny now that I was married. My single girlfriends could not understand why I, as a married woman, denied myself the pleasure of being a *complete woman* and enjoy the fruits of everything this status engenders when that was all they indeed longed for. Time and again, women and girls in assertive yet pleading voices urged me to finish, if not terminate, my research without further delay and get pregnant.

Being "too free" and individualistic is hence neither desired nor encouraged. In fact, such a behavior conveys to people that the girl is a bad girl and not *mastura*. I, by all means, behaved as such. In addition to my autonomous individualism, I spent much time engaged in activities such as the following: visiting my friends; walking alone (or taking a taxi) to Tamazirt; sitting an hour a day on average in the cybercafe, talking to my family and friends at home; drinking coffee or an occasional orange juice with an American male Peace Corps volunteer at a village café; putting lip gloss on my chapped lips absentmindedly in public and without realizing that this was *haram* (forbidden), as I was attracting male attention by doing that; wearing the kind of clothes inside the house that showed too much of my contour; and being in many ways extremely individualistic in following my own daily routine. Much of this was done when I realized that the women in my field-site family followed their own daily routine and without showing much incentive to include me in any way beyond inviting me to accompany them when visiting friends or family or to join them in their weekly visit to the *hammam* (public bathhouse). Most of the time, however, they left me to my own devices and sometimes not uttering a word unless I started a conversation. Once I made friends with neighboring girls, I was indeed happy to escape the rather somber atmosphere of my field-site family. I created my own rules of what I thought was an appropriate and tolerated behavior for a *faransawiyya* (Frenchwoman) with the aim of not losing too much of my own identity in, at times, the extremely challenging environment. The first few months of my fieldwork were eye-opening for me. Before my arrival I had been determined to be as malleable as possible, but I soon came to the realization that unless I asserted myself I would not be able to finish my research. This exposed many of my own idiosyncrasies and defects and inevitably led to the deterioration of my relationship with the women within the household. Unknowingly at the time, this also unearthed my preconceptions about the community and led to what I hope is a greater understanding of gender relations, hierarchies, and the inner workings of patriarchy.

Toward the end of my fieldwork I painfully learned that my field-site family was aware of every step I made and boundary I crossed. After all, the family honor could be compromised by my ostensibly immoral behavior. I never intended to keep anything hidden from them and always told them where and why I was going out and when I would be returning. I limited my sleepovers at my girlfriends' homes to once a week, turning down persistent and numerous other invitations, which, had I accepted them, would turn me into a nomad sleeping at a different house every night. Perhaps more than my frequent outings, though that was also a topic of their conversations, something I learned later when I was able to understand the language better, their criticism was directed at my having coffee and spending money at the cybercafe. Girls and infrequently also married women certainly used the Internet in cybercafes, but they did so occasionally, money permitting, and did not order drinks while Skyping or surfing the Internet. Sitting in cafés, drinking coffee, and socializing with friends outside the house is admittedly something that only men do; women meet their female friends and family members at home. Furthermore, when spring came and with it high daily temperatures, I started wearing a long black *jabador* (a loose-fitting long garment) inside the house in order to keep cooler. I had not realized that I might be dressing inappropriately. After two days, however, Karima, visibly embarrassed, asked me to put on woolen tights underneath the *jabador*, ostensibly "because of [Zakariya]." I was showing too much of my lower leg and disrespecting the boundaries of proper female sartorial modesty upheld by women within the household in the name of men, but also in their own name.

I was the exact opposite of Tamazirt's ideal woman, but my behavior was condoned because of their hospitality, the fact that I was only interrupting their way of living for a short and hence bearable moment in time, and because I seemed to only confirm their perception of a Frenchwoman. I was a foreigner and therefore allowed to cross the boundaries their girls and women could not if they did not want to risk family and community expulsion. My field-site family was merely monitoring my behavior in order to ensure that *their* reputation would not be affected too seriously by my "amoral" conduct. This is one of the keys to understanding the position of women within the family in this community (and arguably in Morocco in general). A woman is an integral part of the family and the one who is entrusted with the daunting task of preserving her family's honor. Thus, even though the traditional idea of the ideal woman as being an obedient and quiet wife and daughter-in-law differs from the contemporary ideal of a woman who is more assertive yet still deferential to her husband and his family, the woman cannot be conceived of as being outside her family. To secure her position as a member of the family, she has to comply with the locally constructed rules of feminine propriety. What is being debated today as a result of the penetration of modern media, the development discourse on women's rights and greater mobility is the renegotiation of the position and status of women and girls within the family.

True, I was married, but apart from that nothing about me, my behavior, career, or life choices defined me as a *woman*, let alone an ideal woman, in their sense. On one occasion, a few friends of mine, girls of my age, confirmed this observation, saying that despite my wedding ring I was just like them, a *bint*, or a single girl. This perception of me determined the attitudes of my host family, as well as women and girls I associated with, toward me. Even after my husband visited me, their behavior toward me did not change. In hindsight, this was also a consequence of my talking about my relationship with my husband too candidly—I often said that I missed him and particularly women at the aerobics class I attended often laughed at me when I told them that a three-week-vacation with my husband was too short, whereas they concluded that a few days with him was more than enough. When I questioned their own relationships with their husbands based on what they were telling me, they reticently assured me that their marital relationships were good and that they were well taken care of. Gender roles are clearly defined and divided and so are gender relationships. Spouses do not spend much time together and do not appear to have many common interests. In fact, women who lived in separate households from their in-laws told me that they preferred their husbands to be away because they felt much freer and could visit their girlfriends without compunction. Furthermore, talking about feelings is strange for particularly older women, and although younger girls talk and certainly think about such topics as love much more openly, they only do so among the right audience, which is among girlfriends.

The recognition that I was more a *girl* than a *woman* only fully developed when I returned home in June 2010 and had time to thoroughly reflect on my experience. It was also then that I became aware of the depth of the social deprivation imposed on (educated) single adult girls compared to married women.[7] My education, life experiences, intractability, autonomy, feminism, and subsequent outspokenness, which were often taken as annoying, certainly did not enhance my reputation in a positive way within the community. Quite the contrary, these characteristics shed a bad light on the family I was staying with and hence led to their increasing criticism of me in public. In other words, my "empowerment" was not a ticket to an approved trespassing of boundaries. If anything, my social attributes created many problems for me and potentially for my field-site family.

New houses built with modern materials belong to families with one or more male members living and working abroad (November 2009).

CHAPTER 2

Politicization of Gender

In October 2006, Moroccan weekly liberal newspaper *TelQuel*, being one of the rare news publications in the country intent on pushing the boundaries of appropriate and uncensored "free" speech, ran a cover story entitled "Blad Schizo," or the "Schizo[phrenic] Country."[1] Its authors Réda Allali and Hassan Hamdani described Morocco as a country "[c]aught between modernity and tradition, pretense and true lies, feigned morality and poorly adopted religion. Moroccans seek their identity. And they are pretty lost on the road to the point of becoming schizophrenic" (2006, 42). They define schizophrenia as "a destruction of personality, a painful illness marked by profound anxieties, delusions, and a disconnect from reality. At the basis of the malaise is of course the question of identity" (44). It is such a state of mind that is recognized as the key illness of the contemporary Moroccan society. Morocco is a country considered by the outside world to be modernizing and one of the leaders among the MENA Muslim-majority countries in the enhancement of women's rights, while at home it is a country where "change is a priori considered as negative," where the past and its traditions are glorified and sacred (45). The authors are no less harsh in their observation that Morocco is "a culture of appearance" (46). Moroccans, at least on the surface, are in denial about the existence of the parallel world of "immoral" behavior, such as drinking alcohol, eating during the month of Ramadan, and having sex outside wedlock. Instead, people explain such social or cultural "deviances" through the supernatural forces of *jnun* (spirits) and the subsequent usage of "therapies," to use Vincent Crapanzano's (1981) nomenclature.[2] Allali and Hamdani urge their fellow citizens to accept the inevitable social and moral evolution, but they are also aware that breaking taboos and transforming mentalities "is anything but easy" (2006,

46–47). If, as another *TelQuel* journalist writes, "[m]odernity is a project of social emancipation," and if this project "has the advantage of encouraging a constant questioning of self, social norms, and values" (Berkou 2010, 39–40), then Morocco as a country and Moroccans as individuals still have much work to overcome the stifling duality in order to free themselves of the "schizo" mentality.

I started to study and visit Morocco in 2006, and since the beginning I have been intrigued by what appeared to me to be a society teeming with curious dichotomies. Both Rabat and Casablanca, Morocco's political and economic hubs, respectively, have older parts of town that look rather decrepit, where women and men sell their homegrown produce or homemade goods and where numerous cafés are almost exclusively frequented by men. I would often attempt to ignore this reality and sit on the café patio only to be overcome by an unsettling sense of breaking the unwritten rules. Both cities have large *bidonvilles* (shantytowns) at the outskirts, visible from the train, but they both also have swanky new, clean, and spacious city centers, well stocked with shops selling Western clothes, accessories, brands, high-end jewelry, and, naturally, overpriced patisseries, where women and men sit side by side.

In addition to the apparent architectonics, easily discernible even to the most superficial tourist exploring both rural and urban Morocco, there are other indicators of an increasingly liberalizing and hence deeply torn society. Browsing through daily newspapers and weekly magazines, such as the more secular *TelQuel* and *Le Journal*, or any Moroccan women's magazine, reveals that the country is indeed engulfed in the battle of values (if not the battle of the sexes and the generations) caused by modernization and the increasing influence of *foreign* ideas.[3] By *foreign* I do not necessarily refer to the routinely evoked Western imports only but also to "innovations" coming via satellite dishes from numerous religious Gulf TV channels—such as Al-Fajr, Iqraa TV, and Al-Resalah—which were watched daily by my field-site family as well as by other families I visited on a regular basis. So much has the pervasiveness and popularity of foreign TV channels, shows, and imported soap operas "transformed and disturbed" the world of Moroccans, that one Moroccan journalist labeled such modernity as "telemodernity" (Berkou 2010, 39–40). As a consequence, the country seems to be split between those who are "Westoxicated" and those who are "Eastoxicated"—between those who emphasize the universality of human values and those who call upon a more culturally specific, if not an "authentic" approach to rights and freedoms. It is this question of what *kind* of modernity—one situated within the global or the alleged local world—that permeates Moroccan and regional discussions on the enhancement of women's rights and, more generally, a national identity. In this chapter I will not retell the story of Morocco's nearly two decades of struggle for the reform of the Personal Status Code (PSC), as this has been done numerous times (Brand 1998; Buskens 2003; Freeman 2004; Ghazzala 2001; Maddy-Weitzman 2005; Sadiqi 2008), the most recent and eloquent of these accounts being Salime's (2011) in *Between Feminism and Islam: Human Rights and Sharia Law in Morocco*. Instead, the focus will be on the analysis of the intentions, ideological motivations, and divisions of some of the most fervent activists involved in the process—the secular feminists and the Islamists—as well as on the (lack of) interaction between the two movements. The discussion of these binaries, which mirror yet intensify the schizophrenic character of Moroccan society, will inform the textual analysis of the official discourse on women's rights and of people's attitudes toward such topics as gender equality dealt with in the following chapters.

Authenticity or hybridity?

Oued al-Ouliya's and Morocco's in general social and moral order continue to be rooted in a system of classic patriarchy, as defined by both Deniz Kandiyoti (1988) and Suad Joseph (1993, 1994). Using Joseph's definition, I understand patriarchy to mean the "dominance of males over females, elders over juniors," where "the positions of power are gendered (masculinized) and aged (seniors) but not sexed" because older women often use their seniority and status to advance their position (1993, 459–460). In the Moroccan patriarchal system positions of power are also dependent on marital status, as the following chapters will demonstrate. Women have developed a set of strategies, which Kandiyoti (1988) terms patriarchal bargains, to enhance their status within the hierarchical system and their families without losing the protection, security, and sense of belonging it affords.[4] Patriarchal bargains are not static; they are "susceptible to historical transformations that open up new areas of struggle and renegotiation of the relations between genders" (Kandiyoti 1988, 275). Kandiyoti's argument that the current transition period, which is seeing the erosion of classic patriarchy, is resisted by the generation of women caught in between "because they see the old normative order slipping from them without any empowering alternatives" (282–283). Although Kandiyoti wrote the article over twenty years ago, such resistance to the new moral order can still be observed in communities such as Oued al-Ouliya.

Despite popular beliefs in the West, Moghadam, as well as others, rightly observes that patriarchy "should not be conflated with Islam but rather should be understood in social-structural and developmental terms" (2003a, 123). Nonetheless, it is exactly such patriarchy, which people themselves embed in Islam, that gives gendered and discriminatory traditions and customs their potency, as well as a sense of immutability and authority. Emphasizing the significance of customs and traditions and situating them within *a* "genuine" version of Islam would be superfluous if it were not for the intrusion of something foreign and, ipso facto, in direct conflict with the "authentic." Yet, such conjuring up of a culture free from influences and borrowings from the "Other" appears rather absurd, not least because cultures do not come into being or exist in vacuum. (We should not forget that Islam, too, at the time of the Prophet was heavily influenced by Judaism and Christianity.) In Hobsbawmian sense (2009), inventing contemporary "authentic" *Islamic* customs and traditions to establish the link with the purported unadulterated era of the Prophet in this process of purifying the culture is crucial for the continuation of patriarchy. Homi Bhabha, one of the key postcolonial authors on cultural hybridity, rightly contends that

> the enunciation of cultural difference problematizes the division of past and present, tradition and modernity, at the level of cultural representation and its authoritative address. It is the problem of how, in signifying the present, something comes to be repeated, relocated, and translated in the name of tradition, in the guise of a pastness that is not necessarily a faithful sign of historical memory *but a strategy of representing authority* in terms of the artifice of the archaic. (2006, 156; italics added)

Bhabha concludes that "the hierarchical claims to the inherent originality or 'purity' of cultures are untenable, even before we resort to empirical historical instances that demonstrate their hybridity" (156–157). Public moralizing by the Islamists—as the performative act of the claim, if not the demand for the purification of culture—is one such effect of the penetration of modern and imported values particularly from the West. It is these values that are presented as attacks against the "true" Muslim identity of people and the country, against the Moroccanness of the country's identity.[5]

However, the discussion on corruption of values through "heresies" is anything but a postcolonial issue. Throughout the centuries, Muslim religious scholars have been fighting against the intrusion of *bidaʿ*, or heretical innovations, into the "original" Islamic principles and practices. What is new in this debate is that perhaps more than ever before the simultaneous existence of multiple ideological frames of reference is personally affecting ordinary people. This creates confusion among people and leads to more pronounced divisions within society, a topic which shall be explored in the following two chapters. Arguably, these divisions are visible more today than in the past simply because they have the ability to cut across geographical, educational, and class divisions as a result of modern technology, education, greater mobility, and urbanization. Borrowing Zygmunt Bauman's (2007) concept of liquid modernity and somewhat adjusting it illuminates the situation. Contemporary Morocco as an "open society'" is at a stage where outside influences markedly shape national discourses and as a result notably affect social patterns. Old structures become liquid because they are continuously remolded, but there is no time for them to make a visible impact or difference, leading to the fragmentation of lives. It remains to be seen *which* "foreign" referent will triumph and *how* it will affect Moroccans in the long run, but it is evident that such debates have divided society and left many people confused and others shocked because liquid modernity entails quick adaptation to new realities.

In recent years there have been many such shocks against the entrenched moral order, but one that perhaps inaugurated a new era was the 1993 Tabit affair. This affair uncovered an enormous collection of pornographic videotapes, showing Tabit, a high-ranking policeman, engaging in mostly nonconsensual sex with more than five hundred women. Tabitgate, as the scandal came to be known, exposed not only the extent of corruption at the highest levels of Moroccan officialdom but it also, and perhaps most importantly, revealed the hidden reality of violence against women.[6] *TelQuel* regards the affair as "the greatest moral scandal in the Kingdom" (El Azizi 2007) and Jamila Bargach reports that the scandal was perceived in Morocco as "a sign of loss of values, moral decadence, and abrogation of tradition" (2002, 40).

The debate, which ensued and was carried out by both the Islamists and secular feminists, also appeared at the time when the UAF fought to obtain one million signatures for its campaign to change the PSC. If anything, Tabitgate opened the floodgates for the discussion on violence against women and led to the opening of the first shelters for female victims (or survivors) of violence. (Shelters continue to be prohibited by law because Penal Code recognizes harboring a woman who escapes from her husband as a criminal act. But, as I was told by a Rabat judge and Moroccan activists, there exists an unwritten understanding between courts and shelters of no prosecutions.)

As Tabitgate presented an opportunity for the women's movement to start the debate on violence against women, the reform of the PSC, officially inaugurated at the beginning of the 1990s, represents the point of departure for the discussion as to *how* to ameliorate the position of women in society.

Genealogies of Moroccan women's rights ideologies

Hisham Sharabi in his *Neopatriarchy: A Theory of Distorted Change in Arab Society* (1988) forewarned of the power of the women's movements. He called them "potentially the most revolutionary" of all groups confronting state power in this age of economic and political liberalization and "the detonator which will explode neopatriarchal society from within" (154). In fact, many have argued (or questioned the idea) that *real* modernity and democracy go hand in hand with women's liberation (Abu-Lughod 1998; Joseph 1996; Keddie 2007; Mernissi 1993; Moghadam 2003a; Moghissi 1999). Although Sharabi wrote the book well before the Arab Spring's toppling of some of the regime leaders, it is true that the question of women and hence national identity is, and certainly will form, an important part of future debates in postrevolutionary countries. An essential element of these debates is how to define liberation of women.

In Morocco, there are generally two trends within the women's movements whose frames of reference have led to, at least on the surface, conflicting definitions of womanhood and women's liberation. The main protagonists in this clash are Westernized (francophone) and secular feminists, and their nemesis, the Islamist women. Both are more or less obligated to engage with the pervasive (Western) international development discourse on women's rights and poverty as well as with the conservative agendas popularized through various religious TV channels and recorded sermons sold at mosques and in the *mudun* (old parts of towns, distinct from the normally French-built *ville nouvelle*, or new city). As such, their agendas are necessarily shaped by such discourses either by applying it to the Moroccan context or reacting against it.

Contemporary Morocco has been embroiled in discussions about the construction of an "ideal" modern Moroccan woman since the time of the country's resistance against the French in the first half of the twentieth century. Although women were actively present in the national struggle of the 1940s and 1950s against the country's colonizers, their possible advances were lost in the immediate independence era, much like in neighboring Algeria (Lazreg 1994). In fact, as Liat Kozma (2003) argues, the nationalist historiography was written through a male perspective, denying these women their deserved place in Moroccan history (Abouzeid 1989). It was only in the 1980s, with the emergence of feminist magazines and a more proactive engagement of female academics and authors in the debates about women's status, such as Fatima Mernissi and Leila Abouzeid, that nationalist women's contributions were incorporated into the official historiography to represent them not only as national heroines but also as feminists. (It should be noted that the more prominent voices heard were not of just *any* women but generally belonged to the urbane Rabati and Fessi families, if not its elites.) Oral historian Alison Baker in her book *Voices of Resistance: Oral Histories of Moroccan Women* (1998) presents the stories of some of the women who actively participated in the independence movement. She concludes that although admission of women to the masculine public space was not further promoted in the postindependent nation building, "what *was* permanent was the transformation in these women's consciousness, in their concept of themselves as women" (280; emphasis in original). This paradigm shift in women's perceptions of their own societal roles was what, for Baker, ignited women to slowly "reclaim" the public space and eventually led to women's political activism by some of the Marxist-Leninist women in the 1970s. In addition to this, the ideologically charged international climate of the Cold War era, decolonization, the expansion of education to include girls at least in the urban areas, and since the 1980s economic and political liberalization created an opportune climate for greater women's political engagement and activism.

Latifa Jbabdi was one of the educated radical leftists who clashed with the authorities in the 1970s and was, like many of her female and male colleagues, imprisoned for her activism and ideological beliefs. At that time, these Marxist-Leninist women were members of such leftist parties as the forerunners of the parliamentary Union Socialiste des Forces Populaires (Socialist Union of Popular Forces—USFP) and the Parti du Progrès et du Socialisme (Party of Progress and Socialism—PPS).[7] Their activism was consumed by the notion of class struggle and hopes to bring about a socialist system in which, at least for the time being their female members were told, there was no space for a specific women's rights agenda (Baker 1998; Brand 1998).[8] The enhancement of women's rights was largely absent from political agendas of not only these socialist parties but across the political spectrum because of its potential to unleash divisive and disruptive sentiments among the public (Naciri 1998). (Their fears were substantiated a few decades later during the One Million Signatures Campaign and after the announcement of the government Plan of Action for the Integration of Women in Development [PAIWID] at the end of the 1990s, an issue that shall be addressed in continuation.) Marginalization of women's issues led these women to gradually distance themselves from political parties, although, as Rabea Naciri, the former president of the ADFM reports, the break has not been complete. In fact, Naciri writes, "women's associations remain divided between their desire not to cut the umbilical cord from their leftist roots and their desire to affirm their own political identity and their independence from these same groups" (1998, 95–96). Or, as Azzedine Layachi (1998/99, 61–62) argues, these organizations are not accountable to their party of origin yet continue to espouse the party line. Much of the work of the secular women's organizations, which today involves lobbying for legal reforms, depends on the access to political elites, and hence maintaining such connections is in their pragmatic interest. But the government as well utilizes many women's associations to carry out some of its educational and other poverty-alleviation projects, such as literacy, reproductive health, or micro-finance projects and, since the reform of the Family Code in 2004, also various awareness programs intended for the general public as for those charged with implementing the laws—court officials, lawyers, police officers, and medical staff.

One of the first acts of women's disengagement from strict politics, while promoting women's issues in the public arena, was the emergence of Morocco's first women's magazine in 1983 called *8 Mars* by Latifa Jbabdi and her female colleagues. (It is not insignificant that the first issue of the magazine coincided with Morocco embarking on SAPs.) *8 Mars* was written in Arabic and was financially and editorially independent. Its stated goal was women's consciousness building and sensitization of public opinion to women's social and legal issues. The magazine ceased publication in 1995. Another women's magazine, *Kalima*, was published for the first time in 1986. The idea behind it was Noureddine Ayouch's, who in 1995 established Morocco's leading micro-finance foundation called Zakoura. Fatima Mernissi was among *Kalima*'s writing staff. The magazine inquired into provocative and, at the time still considered taboo topics, such as (male) prostitution, domestic violence, and single mothers, in addition to elucidating for the general public complex legal and political issues.[9] However, both *8 Mars* and *Kalima* were attacked by the Islamists, the religious establishment, and the government, which eventually led to their closure. Journalists of both magazines were accused of all evils— working for the Polisario, undermining Morocco's image, and destroying the sanctity of the divine word, among other verbal attacks (Mrabet 2009; Skalli 2006). In short, the divisive issue, which attracted public scrutiny, was the question of national identity and its adaptation to the constantly evolving (inter)national environment.

Islamist women's voices, too, became more assertive in the 1980s. There were two main avenues: female members and supporters of Al-Islah wa-l-Tajdid (Reform and Renewal), led by Abdelillah Benkirane (later to be secretary-general of the Islamist PJD and appointed prime minister in 2011), published articles in their magazine called *Al-Forkane*. At first these women dealt with the changing nature of Moroccan womanhood as a result of women's improved access to particularly (post)secondary education, but they later focused their discussion on gender hierarchies within the Islamist movements. At the beginning of the 1990s, they openly voiced concern with and reacted against the secular feminist One Million Signatures Campaign to reform the PSC. The UAF, as the main protagonist of the campaign, mobilized the public to sign their overtly secular petition, in which they called for equal divorce rights with those of men, abolition of polygamy, instituting equality in marital rights and obligations, the right of women who have reached the legal age to be legally competent, among other demands. The initial draft of the petition was even more subversive. During our interview, Leila Abouzeid, who participated in the royal Union Nationale des Femmes Marocaines (National Union of Moroccan Women—UNFM) and was approached by Jbabdi to sign the petition, recounted the following:

> Latifa Jbabdi wanted to change laws that are explicit in the Qur'an like polygamy, to abolish polygamy and inheritance, to make daughters share [inheritance equally] with boys. And this couldn't be accepted by the Muslims, even by Muslim women. She came to me, she wanted me to sign [the petition], but I refused . . . because I said: "You have to remove these two things [polygamy and inheritance] because people who are engaged in Islam, who are Muslims, would never sign this because this is explicit in the Qur'an!"

In effect, the petition was a demand for secularization of the family legislation and consequently of society. As such, it did not only challenge the supremacy of Islamic legal principles in the family legislation but also undermined Hassan II's religious role as Commander of the Faithful and therefore his right to decide upon matters pertaining to the religious realm as well as the legal aspect of gender relations. The UAF obtained the signatures but caused a major uproar among certain segments of society, such as the religious establishment, or the official 'ulema', the nascent women's movements, secular as well as the Islamist, including the so-called independent 'ulema'.[10] In fact, Salime (2011) argues, it was young female activists within Al-Islah wa-l-Tajdid, rather than its male members, who were the main agents in fueling the controversy surrounding the feminist campaign. Men on the other hand were vehicles for formulating their contention in the form of an official legal religious opinion (*fatwa*) because women by their very nature of being female did not have the authority to do so. In addition, some of the independent 'ulema' called upon the Islamist women to form an organized answer to secular feminists.

The JSO presented the second avenue for the Islamist women's activism. During my interview with Nadia Yassine, perhaps the most well-known and controversial female Moroccan Islamist and the daughter of the founding father and spiritual guide (*muršid*) of the JSO, shaykh Abdessalam Yassine, it was she who began to politicize the question of women's participation within the organization. Her feminine outspokenness was not received well by the (male) members despite having the support of her father, to whom, Nadia Yassine asserted, it was clear "that women have to represent half of [the JSO's] actions and our movement." Nadia Yassine explained the background of the problem:

> But men who began to work with him [Abdessalam Yassine] had great and deep baggage. At the beginning, it was impossible to have the same thinking. . . . They brought two influences: of the Muslim Brotherhood . . . and the Wahhabis. . . . The Muslim Brotherhood is very typical of Egypt and it's [therefore] very difficult [for the organization] to have a universal influence. It's not like Wahhabism. Wahhabism was very dangerous. Why? Because [everything] is white and black. *Haram, haram, haram* [forbidden]. Another really important thing with Wahhabism is petrodollars, which finance dissemination [of these ideas]. . . . But those men who came to the *Jama'a* [JSO] to work were not Wahhabis. You have to understand that Wahhabism is not a doctrine, it's a virus. . . . There is no such thing as being a Wahhabi. It's like a virus, you know, seropositive. . . . You don't know that you are a Wahhabi, but you are

because there is the influence of TV. . . . There is great confusion. There
are some Ikhwan Muslimin, some *rijal tabligh*.[11] . . . There are many influences, but . . . the biggest influence is Wahhabism. There is much talk
on the TV, and [the TV is popular], there is no immunity, no antibodies
against this. When my father wanted to build this movement, the men
[who joined, brought this influence]. . . . The challenge was to educate, to
bring them away from this mind-set, to unite them in many activities and
projects. At the beginning thus it was a great struggle for the women's
section. So I fought very hard to build this section, there were some
people in the *majlis al-iršad* [council of guidance] who were not in accord
with the *muršid* and the others. At the beginning we worked with some
clandestinity.

The dispute, she continued to explain, went so far that one of the
members of the supreme decision-making body—*majlis al-iršad*—left
and wrote a doctoral thesis about the issue, in which he argued that the
woman's place "is in the kitchen and in bed." Although she felt that to a
certain extent the arguments of men were legitimate due to the political
repression experienced by the JSO particularly in the 1980s and 1990s,
she admitted that such attitudes were still part of that dominant patriarchal discourse.[12] "They were afraid for women. . . . [They wanted] to protect them, you know. This classical discourse, that women are like a little
egg [that needs to be protected]. It's horrible. . . . We don't want to be
diamonds and hidden away." As a consequence of such persistent pressure
from some of the male membership on the one hand, and adamance of the
women on the other, Nadia Yassine, too, left the organization in protest.[13]

Although all the JSO women I interviewed were pleased with the
progress of the organization as regards changing gender relations and
mentalities of men and women, the issue of women's political activism,
however, is far from resolved. JSO women have grown: "they are better
informed now, they know their rights, and they are ready to fight for
them," Yassine asserted.[14] As such, the women's section, which was established in 1998, began with training fifty female scholars (*'alimat*) to propose a revivalist and feminine rereading of the Qur'an and the prophetic
traditions. (During our interview, Merieme Yafout, the former president
of the JSO's women's section, likened the project to Amina Wadud's
[1999] book *Qur'an and Woman: Rereading the Sacred Text from a Woman's
Perspective* but added that JSO women nonetheless need to come up with
a *Moroccan* women's rereading of the sacred texts rather than a *Western*
Muslim one. Here, too, JSO's purported objection to *any* Western influ-

ence, even if coming from a Muslim woman, is more than evident.) The purpose of this training was to expose and fight against corrupt interpretations, which imposed masculine hegemony and marginalized women through such restrictions as the veil, unequal sharing of inheritance, or women's legal inability to share marital property. Their work in this regard is indeed revolutionary. Souad Dkkali, one of the female members of the JSO, explained their work to me:

> We want fifty women who have a higher education, doctoral degrees, so that when they discuss things with the *fuqaha'* [experts in Islamic jurisprudence], their words will have weight because they are officially learned women. We want fifty learned women, whose opinions will have an effect on the opinions of men in society. When a learned woman says something, it's not like a regular woman saying it, such as me, even if I am a professor of scientific translation. Through our education inside the movement, we have developed a new and interesting view about the issue of women. No one will pay attention to what we proclaim unless we hold a respectful degree. We want specialization; we want women who are specialists and will be able to change the situation. . . . [We want] different specializations to change the conventional opinion.

Through such work, female members of the JSO are actively challenging the patriarchal mentality within and outside the organization, but also modernizing—dare I say Westernizing—the traditional image of what constitutes an ideal woman, to which some male members strongly object. Nadia Yassine voiced her concern with the situation in 2011 and told me that she was leaving the organization again in protest to show support for the women's section and their "controversial" project:

> For the last two or three years my father has been ill and he completely disengaged from the work of the movement. So he doesn't have any influence on the work of the movement. The resistance has been renewed but this has nothing to do with the past. These are new issues.

In fact, women in the JSO appear to be too liberal for the male members because, Nadia Yassine continued.

> we're not feminist but we have [a different] view of the links within the family that we think deeply and surely are the real teachings and revelations of the Prophet. . . . What bothers them [male members or the Orga-

nization] even more now is that with the ʿalimat they are not able to tell them: "You don't have the knowledge, what you said is not correct."

The struggle of the women's section may be different from the one in the 1980s and 1990s, but it is a direct consequence and perhaps even a logical continuation of Nadia Yassine's and other women's struggle to establish their voices as equal parts in the otherwise still male-dominated Islamist organization. She, too, is admittedly contributing to the fight against the marginalization of women in Moroccan society despite getting the inspiration and theoretical rationale from different ideological sources than the secular feminists, such as Jbabdi or Naciri.

Politicization of women's rights

If the Islamist women were becoming more assertive within their movements, the birth of secular feminist women's magazines gave Moroccan feminists the impetus to establish the first (semi)autonomous women's organizations. These women's rights activists believed that the time was finally ripe to engage Moroccan society in the debates about what constitutes a contemporary ideal Moroccan woman and, inevitably, to push for legal reforms. From the 1980s onward, therefore, the country saw a proliferation of women's associations.[15] These organizations were much more politicized because they were challenging the established masculine public space, while at the same time intensifying the schizophrenic character of the Moroccan national identity. Their campaigns advocating for reforms in the realm of family, nationality, and other legislation were more controversial and divisive than, for example, the work of the more or less charitable Organisation de la Femme Istiqlalienne (Istiqlal Party Women's Organization—OFI) or the royal UNFM.[16]

If these early attempts to promote women's issues in the public arena were initiated by the urban educated secular leftists like Jbabdi or Mernissi, it became clear toward the end of the 1980s that they would need to change their tactic and "overtly secularist" (Hackensberger 2006) and universalist tone in order to appeal to a broader audience. Morocco, after all, was still a generally conservative society, and to discuss the advancement of women's rights, which belonged to the remnants of Islamic law, outside the religious framework was considered to be an act of apostasy (Brand 1998; Buskens 2003). In fact, Salime rightly argues that both the secular feminists and the Islamist women shaped each other's agendas. The UAF's "movement moment" (Salime 2011, xix)[17]—as she calls important turning points such as the One Million Signatures Campaign, the PAIWID, and the women's marches of 2000—led to the feminization of Islamist women's discourse and activism, already set in motion through the above-mentioned campaigns. The feminist campaign, therefore, gave Islamist women an external push to discuss the status of women in society on the eve of the twenty-first century. Salime (2011, 31) perceives feminization of the Islamist agenda as threefold: it exposed Islamist women to the universalist discourse of women's rights; it led them to challenge the feminist claim to speak on behalf of all Moroccan women; and their greater assertiveness resulted in challenging the male dominance of leadership positions within their own movements.

The next "movement moment," or the "show of force," by the Islamists manifested in the Casablanca March in 2000 as a reaction to the government's PAIWID led to, what Salime calls, "Islamization of the feminist agendas," which she uses to "refer to the articulation of feminist agendas and Islamist politics by the feminist movement" (70). PAIWID was a project initiated by the Alternance (rotation) government, which was led by the USFP from 1998 to 2002. It represented USFP's main government project because the party had to abandon the idea of promoting its leftist economic agenda, which would necessarily have been in opposition to the neoliberal SAPs that the regime had been implementing for over a decade. The nomination of Saïd Saadi, a member of the PPS, to the position of secretary of state in charge of drafting the plan was, according to him, a "godsend because I was convinced that the status of women is an important cause for Morocco" (Hachimi Alaoui 2002). For the feminist organizations and particularly the ADFM, which was invited to participate in the drafting of the Plan, the appointment of Saadi was a stroke of luck as well because they shared their views on the question of women's position within society. (ADFM was also still indirectly associated with the PPS.)

The essential guide for the social politics of the Alternance government and the issue of women's rights within it was the 1995 negotiated Beijing Platform for Action. As such, the PAIWID followed a liberal, universalist, and secular Women in Development agenda,[18] as its name already suggests. It comprised 215 measures aimed at ameliorating the position of Moroccan women within society. The Plan's main areas of priority were expanding education; improving women's health, including family planning; integration of women in economic development; and strengthening women's legal and political status (Buskens 2003; Freeman 2004; Maddy-Weitzman 2005; Salime 2011). This last area was directly linked with reforming discriminatory legal codes, such as the Penal Code, to criminalize violence against women, Nationality Law to grant Moroccan nationality to children born to Moroccan mothers married to foreign husbands, and the PSC. The draft of the Plan, however, caused much controversy among the conservatives—the Islamists as well as some members of the leftist parties—which prevented it from being adopted. In an interview for *Le Journal* in 2003, Saadi commenting on the failure of PAIWID asserted that the problem was not only the PJD, who, being reactionary,

> could not have had a different position. This is a social project, which advocates a modern and tolerant Islam, adapted to the conditions of the 21st century. [The PJD] has a different vision and a different reading of Islam. For them, Islamic law means to cut off the hands of thieves and they encourage polygamy as a solution to being single. (S. 2003, 18)

More than the Islamists being the sole problem, Saadi continued, "it's the whole culture. Our society is still misogynist" (19). In a different interview, but seven years later, Saadi illuminated his damning portrayal of Moroccan society, concluding that "[m]ale thinking in Morocco is still inhibited. Masculinity concentrates on virility, hegemony, physical power, and guardianship, whereas the true masculinity is gallantry, chivalry, interest in the other, extending one's help to the other. The solution to all problems regarding the application of gender equality, which many give value to, is to curtail such masculinity" (Halaq 2010, 29). Abraham Serfaty, Moroccan dissident and political activist, in a similar manner described Moroccan society as "deeply chauvinist" and added, "What we lack is the courage of a Bourguiba" (Beaugé 2002, 4).

In the subsequent Moroccan analysis of the failure of PAIWID, many journalists on the other hand blamed the Alternance government for undermining the project by being split on the issue of the appropriate ideological framework—the first draft was based entirely on the universalist human rights and international development agendas—but also by underfunding Saadi's department, which according to Saadi himself, was done deliberately by his minister in charge (S. 2003). (The split was not only between the socially conservative Istiqlal and the leftist USFP but also within this seemingly socially progressive party.) *Le Journal*'s journalist concluded that "[t]ouching the foundations of society without having the legitimacy, without representing 'the will of the people,' was enough to condemn the action of the government" (B. 2002, 12). The article, furthermore, addressed the issue of the WB's contribution of twenty thousand dollars to Saadi's department, a fact that served as one of the essential rallying points for the Islamist March in Casablanca in 2000. Nadia Yassine asserted in my interview with her in 2011 that the motivation of the JSO to join this march was not their opposition to the reform of the Mudawwana, which is what many journalists and the opponents of the JSO like to emphasize. Rather, she continued, they were against the "cultural intervention" into Moroccan affairs, which the JSO saw in the WB's financial contribution toward the funding of the PAIWID's agenda dealing with women's reproductive health. For Nadia Yassine, the WB's intervention was a clear indication of "international eugenics."[19] Nonetheless, the journalist of Le Journal's article added that the sum of twenty thousand dollars would not have been necessary had Saadi received sufficient financial and human resources from his government to not only complete the project but also be able to run a campaign to raise support for it. "Should we not doubt," the article quite rightly concludes, "the sincerity of the government's will, when the project that determines the fate of every country and its democratization is born with too little resources? The real issue is: wasn't the project doomed from the start?" (B. 2002, 13).

PAIWID, as already mentioned, was not implemented, but there was no need to. Beijing's Platform for Action and the MDGs have been adopted as the principal foundation of many government-led poverty alleviation programs, such as the National Initiative for Human Development, known under its French acronym INDH, diverse adult literacy and women's empowerment projects, which are funded by UNIFEM, WB, the EU, and the like.[20]

Although Salime (2011) places Islamization of the feminist agenda as a reaction to the negative outcome of PAIWID in the form of the Islamist Casablanca March of 2000, it is my understanding that the UAF was among the protagonists in moderating its feminist agenda already in their 1992 campaign. These feminists exploited the Islamic referent strategically, which is manifested in their switching from the French language to Arabic in order to garner support for their universalist and WID frameworks of women's rights, rather than truly Islamizing their agenda. In other words, using Islamic law and somewhat peppering their usage of Arabic with Islamic references to promote an otherwise secular women's rights agenda, was more a means to an end than a genuine end. Jbabdi's evolution is a case in point. In 2006 she revealed in an interview that she progressed from being a radical leftist to being a strong advocate of democracy. Jbabdi furthermore conveyed: "I am a feminist Muslim, but not a feminist Islamist. I am a citizen of Morocco and belong to a Muslim society. But, above all, I adhere to the universal values of human rights" (Hackensberger 2006). That utilizing Muslimness as a cultural dimension of her identity was more opportunistic than a real feeling became evident to me during my second interview with Outaleb in April 2011, amid the Moroccan Spring and the civil society eagerly working on drafting their motions for the reform of the constitution. I asked Outaleb about Jbabdi's apparent reconciliation between being a leftist and a Muslim feminist when Outaleb, quite appalled that I would suggest something like that, replied: "Who said that?! Never, she has never said that! Latifa has never said that she was a Muslim feminist." I continued: "I think I read it in one of the online . . . —" when she interrupted me, still visibly shaken by the thought, and said: "What you read is one thing because I know that not all journalists are objective. . . . She has never said 'I'm a Muslim feminist' because this was our divergence with the PJD-ists at the CSW. . . . I think you're [alluding] to . . . a journalist who wrote about Latifa and Nadia Yassine?"

"I think it was in a German . . . ," I tried to explain, but she was adamant: "Yeah, yeah, that. I know [it]. It's not true."[21]

What this anecdote reveals is that Jbabdi's declaration in fact lacks both depth and meaning. The thought of being associated with the religious movement is dismissed by all means. The disagreement with the PJD that Outaleb was referring to occurred at the 54th Session of the UN Commission of the Status of Women (CSW) in March 2010. (This Session is also called Beijing+15 because it was celebrating and evaluating fifteen years of Beijing's Platform for Action.) Before discussing this particular issue in more detail, it is important to first emphasize that the UAF's conflict with the PJD, and in fact with the Islamists in general, goes beyond this particular UN meeting. Moreover, this conflict is not confined to the UAF but is endorsed and promoted by other secular feminist associations, most notably the ADFM. The following anecdote exposes the issue.

I met Amina, the daughter of Nadia Yassine, in 2008. She was anything but the stereotypical image of an oppressed veiled woman one often hears about in populist Western media. At our first meeting she was wearing a blue loose and long skirt with a pullover and a *hijab* as it was a rather cold March Fessi evening. Her English was perfect and she spoke with a clear and not at all demure voice. When she drove me back to my host family, we spoke about our future plans and she told me about her master's program in education and her plans to apply for a PhD. The next time I saw her was in 2011 in Rabat, where she lived with her husband and two boys. She was a PhD student and told me that she spent a semester at the University of Cambridge earlier that academic year. Her character was as ebullient as I remembered it to be and she made it easy to forget that she, after all, was a member of the Yassine family. During this final research trip to Morocco she helped me meet with many of the female members of the JSO, her mother, and Fathallah Arsalane, JSO's spokesperson, but she also helped me conduct an interview with two members of the ADFM. I knew that this could potentially cause problems, if not for conflicting with the Weberian rules of objectivity (Salime 2011, xxvi), then for being accused of having a hidden agenda. Despite these concerns, I went ahead and invited her to help me conduct the interview. The interview went well, and neither Amina nor I felt the need to reveal Amina's family background as she was with me in the role of an assistant. When we left the ADFM headquarters in the leafy Quartier des Orangers, one of Rabat's more prosperous areas close to the old city walls, I mentioned to Amina that I got a somewhat negative feeling from one of the interviewees. She was not unfriendly and by all means was extremely talkative; yet at the same time she appeared slightly too formal for what I certainly was used to when interviewing or talking to other Moroccans and women's rights activists. I thought that perhaps I was asking them rather provocative questions, but Amina reassured me that it was probably because of her wearing a *hijab*. At the time I thought this was a rather sweeping explanation, until Outaleb a few days later and not aware of this episode confirmed Amina's suspicion by relating the following to me:

> Some of our leaders just say "No!" [to opening a debate with the religious people]; [they are] stigmatizing [the girls]: "That one is [wearing] a veil so I'm not going to talk to her." No! I have to talk to her, I [will] judge her according to her speech and also according to her actions. I'm not judging her according to her appearance, I don't mind if she has a veil or if she has a skirt. Stigmatization has really done a lot of harm to our society and it's time that our secular leaders change. (Cf. Salime 2011, 94–96; Guessous 2011)

Amina, standing beside her car and contemplating the situation at the ADFM, concluded: "We're women, too, and we want education, justice, and respect. No woman wants to be oppressed!"

What the issue of the veil signifies is exactly one aspect of the problem that Outaleb was referring to when she talked about the UAF's "divergence with the PJD." More specifically, it is this issue that epitomizes the conflict over the Moroccan identity, its schizophrenic character, as discussed at the opening of this chapter. Secular feminists perceive matters such as polygamy, Islamic inheritance laws, and the veil to be in direct opposition to universal women's rights. For them, there is no reconciliation between such discriminatory laws and justice for women—one cannot support polygamy and disproportionate inheritance shares and at the same time cannot, by any means, also champion women's rights. "The problem with these people [the Islamists]" Outaleb explained,

> is the double discourse. That's the problem. They have a discourse they are preaching and [having] in Morocco and within the institutions, elected institutions like the Parliament and the Chamber of Councillors, and they have another discourse of freedom and nondiscrimination outside [of Morocco] to bring in money, to get money. So either you believe in gender equality and women's rights fully, no division, fully, no concessions, nothing, or you just believe in your things, polygamy, and all that stuff. So that is the problem, and I think this happened also in the early nineties when we were signing the petition. They were against us, they even had that *fatwa*, you know, but [then] when the king said yes [to reform the PSC] and he announced it in his speech, they applauded. But still, [they have a hidden agenda].[22]

I then told Outaleb that I interviewed some of the women from the JSO, including Nadia Yassine and Yafout, and related to her the organization's women's project of rereading the Qur'an from a woman's perspective. She was very intrigued to hear about it and challenged me with questions about their conclusions on polygamy, inheritance, and "the *niqab*, and women and the *niqab*? [Are] they against it?" she finally asked in disbelief. "They're looking at the sources to see whether it is really necessary [to wear a *hijab*] or not, and I had a feeling that they are going toward [the idea] that it is not really necessary," I reported.[23] But she was not convinced. "Why are they [using a different language] when they are recruiting ordinary people?" I continued, somehow trying to persuade her to believe me and believe the good intentions of the JSO women:

> They made it [seem] that if they were [speaking] for equality [in public] that there was going to be a backlash against them and they're trying to be a bit more pragmatic because if they try to propose things that are too revolutionary in this society, which is still quite conservative, you know, their message may not get through. And they are trying to work step by step.

Outaleb, however, was still unimpressed. "Who said that? Nadia?"

"Yes, I interviewed Nadia and I interviewed the president of the women's section of Al-'Adl wa-l-Ihsan. And they seemed very . . ." Here, Outaleb finally heard enough and interrupted me by saying: "That's why! They succeeded in impressing you!" A bit shocked that she would think I could be that impressionable, I tried to make a case for my position, but she would have none of it.

> That's what they're looking for. We never trust them. . . . We don't trust them because you come here for a certain period of time and they have a certain message they want to transmit to you just to gain your sympathy, more supporters. It's a tactic. It's very tactical. But when they go, for example, to mosques, when they preach in mosques, when they preach in caves [sic!], in *suqs*, and I don't know where [else] . . . [W]e are Moroccans, we don't come from Europe, we live here and we go to special events, marriage, or *sbu'* [naming ceremony on the seventh day after the birth of a child], mourning and you hear that lady who is [referencing] a *hadith* [prophetic tradition] — it's terrible, it's really terrible.

I tried to provide possible explanations and pushed the "gradual approach" strategy once more. But Outaleb was adamant.

> No! Either you believe in something and you defend it or you don't. . . . The difference between them and us is that we say that religion and politics are two separate things, [whereas] they are mixing them. They are just looking for . . . political gains, using religion, and that is why they [use] that language. That is why they will never impress me. That is why we are stuck, we lock ourselves. Because the danger is that you Europeans, Americans, donors, you believe in that speech, you give them that space and you give them that opportunity. . . . You see what happened in Egypt now with the constitution. Seventy percent were for the constitution, amended constitution and let's say fifty percent of those seventy percent, let's say they're fundamentalists, they are Ikhwan Muslimin. . . . I think that voting has just shown us the reality, has just proven to us that within our societies we are the minority.

"Secularists?" I asked.

> Secularists. We are a minority. And please try . . . the West has to be very prudent, very careful when spreading that message. How can we [per-

suade] you that they have a double [discourse], they can [use the kind of] language and [give] speeches which call for discrimination, employment—men should have work first, that women should obey their husbands, that [girls] can be married at nine.

"Oh, you're talking about Al-Maghraoui," I interrupted her because only a few days prior to our interview, the Salafist shaykh Muhammad bin Abdelrahman Al-Maghraoui returned from his exile in Saudi Arabia. When asked at the airport in Marrakech upon his arrival whether he retracted his *fatwa*, in which he wrote that a nine-year-old girl has the same sexual capacity as a woman of twenty and above, effectively sanctioning a marriage with a child, he said: "I do not have the right to define the marital age. Only God himself has the right [to do so]" (Al-Basri 2011, 1). Outaleb started laughing for the first time during the quite intense interview: "Al-Maghraoui *Hmar* [jackass]!"[24] and then immediately changed her tone to a somber one: "Because of him I had [to] campaign throughout all of Morocco and I'm still working on early marriages." I wondered whether he even had a large following in the country. But for Outaleb, shaykh Al-Maghraoui was not a problem.

Not Al-Maghraoui. No, no, no! Not Al-Maghraoui at all. You know what happened? When he said that [girls as young as nine can be married off], many women [who] have nine-year-old girls just rejected him. But then the fundamentalists, Nadia Yassine and her followers, they were for him, they defended him because [this is what] the Prophet [had] said. Anyway, I'm angry.

Shaykh Al-Maghraoui and other Salafists may not be taken seriously by many people; the JSO and the PJD on the other hand, have a significant following, and hence secularists like Outaleb cannot dismiss their activities lightheartedly. For these feminist activists, the JSO and PJD Islamists are the truly powerful and dangerous "fundamentalists" in Morocco.

Secularization or re-Islamization of the law and society?

What these anecdotes and the snippets from the interviews reveal is that both the feminists and the Islamists believe that they alone possess the right medicine to cure the schizophrenic national identity. The feminists are convinced that harmonizing Islamic principles with universalist ideals of women's rights is, in the end, absurd. More than that, through utilizing Islamic legal sources, the UAF believes to have shown in the past that "correct" rereading of such sources brings an analogous result to that of universalist principles contained in the Universal Declaration of Human Rights (UDHR) or CEDAW. The ADFM, too, has remained more or less resolute in advocating a universalist reading of women's rights as *the only* reading leading to women's justice. In its *Memorandum Presented to the Advisory Committee for the Revision of the Constitution: For a Constitution That Guarantees Effective Equality of Women and Men as an Indicator of Democracy*, issued in April 2011, the complete absence of any reference to Islamic sources is striking. In fact, when defining the underpinning reference of the new constitution, the ADFM calls for

> [e]xplicit acknowledgment of the primacy of international human rights instruments and conventions over domestic laws and the harmonization of the latter with those conventions in a way that ensures respect for universal human rights and fundamental freedoms as recognized universally, without any discrimination based on **sex**, color, race or belief." (ADFM 2011; emphasis in original)

Moreover, Naciri in her chapter on the women's movement in Morocco writes that Islamism is an ideology that "is clearly opposed to their strategic interests as women" (1998, 100). Women who use religion to further their goals thus may look for short-term solutions as a "strategy of resistance for educated women from modest social backgrounds who have, nonetheless, higher aspirations" (101). For Naciri, the veil allows these educated, although not yet fully emancipated, women to penetrate the male public space, but eventually they will need to address the issue of universal women's rights and accept a secular law. In short, for feminist organizations such as the ADFM and UAF, Islamist women have internalized a false consciousness or are, at best, unaware of their best interests. Interestingly, in her discussion of the two approaches to women's emancipation in contemporary women's movements, Naciri only considers the feminist approach advocating "the universalist philosophy of the rights of the individual of either sex" as a "progressive approach" (101–102). The other, which is utilizing *ijtihad* for interpreting Islamic legal sources, is merely presented in her analysis as *an* approach. She concludes that the women's movements adhere to one or both of these approaches, "depending on opportunities and the interlocutors" without this being in conflict of interest (102). In other words, the utilization of religious sources and language is a strategic tool for the feminist women's rights activists, helping them promote a secular family law in a conservative society when need be. For Naciri and her other fellow secularists, only such a law can bring about women's full and genuine emancipation.

For the Islamist women on the other hand, the universalist framework can be promoted, albeit within certain immutable limitations. This is much in line with what Muhammad VI said in his speech at the opening of the fall session of Parliament, in which he inaugurated the reformed Family Code, on 10 October 2003:

> As regards the issue of the family law and the status of women, I raised this fundamental problem, shortly after acceding to the supreme position of the Commander of the Faithful, by asking the following question in my address of 20 August 1999: how can a society achieve progress, while women, who represent half the nation, see their rights violated and suffer as a result of injustice, violence and marginalization, notwithstanding the dignity and justice granted them by our glorious religion? . . . In my capacity as Commander of the Faithful, I cannot make licit what God has forbidden, nor forbid what He has made lawful. (Ministry of Communication 2003)

I will discuss the Mudawwana in the following chapter, suffice it to say here that tampering particularly with polygamy and inheritance is out of bounds both for the king and the Islamists, at least for the time being.

Weakened secular feminists

Interestingly, however, the moderating language of the UAF used in public since their 1992 petition, sowed a seed of dissension between them and the ADFM. This dissension was also due to the limited international funds both organizations were applying for and the unresolved question of which women's organization (and which female leader) is at the helm of the feminist struggle for women's rights. ADFM remained a more or less staunch advocate of secularizing family and other legislation, despite in 1999 participating in the National Network for Support of the PAIWID, which issued a communiqué in the PPS's newspaper, the party that ADFM is affiliated with. In it they used the principle of *ijtihad* to legitimize the Plan (Salime 2011). This group in 2001 created a coalition called Printemps d'Egalité (Springtime of Equality) with the aim to form a unified feminist opinion to approach the Advisory Committee, which Muhammad VI established to put forward the recommendations for the reform of the PSC. But the unity was not long lasting because members of the coalition differed in their opinion of the king's committee. The UAF and a few other organizations endorsed the committee and established the National Coordinating Committee for Women's NGOs, whereas the ADFM and the LDDF opposed it. Outaleb in 2011 explained to me the depth and the consequences of the continuing lack of coordination and cooperation within the feminist organizations:

> I'm disappointed. I am one of those who is disappointed by everything that is happening here. The time it took, all the time it [has taken] us to move some things. And we're old, all of us are more than fifty [years old], and are we sure that we have secured our children's future? I'm not sure of that. Believe me. I'm not really sure of that.

I was quite struck with Fatima's lack of optimism, particularly when compared with her attitude in 2008, when I first interviewed her. At that time, she seemed optimistic about the developments and, if anything, she was realistic in saying that to change society they needed time:

> Politics is slowing our work. Every time we're optimistic and we know we can achieve something, very quickly a political event like Palestine or Iraq comes and this hinders our work. I just imagine our work as a . . . you know, a fish which has a lot of hands and is trying to struggle with each [of these hands].[25] So this is what we're facing. Roots, traditions, culture, and mentalities. Material obstacles. It's hard, but it doesn't matter. We will die with it. We know we will die achieving something [and] we paved the way for our daughters. We don't want to be pessimistic about it, though sometimes it happens.

Perhaps I caught Fatima in one of these pessimistic moments in 2011, but her teary eyes revealed that although the feminist momentum is not lost it is "confused, totally confused." Such doubt when put in the context of the Moroccan Spring of 2011 was perhaps quite telling of the prospects to bring about meaningful change. Outaleb explained the confusion in 2011:

> Women, many women like me are totally confused. And also, we shouldn't deny that women's NGOs are part of that confusion. This is my

point of view and [just so] you know, most of them are now working in palaces, in five-star hotels, advocating for I don't know whom, and getting money from the West. And the leadership crisis, all of them want to be leaders. There's a big gap between those women's NGOs, those leaders, and the population on the ground. For example, ADFM, just because they are ADFM, and sometimes even UAF, why not, "Oh, yes we're going to do some training for some NGOs, we're going to bring people from Tunisia, from Algeria, from I don't know where, and we're going to have a conference on [some] recommendations that are never implemented." And on the ground you feel nothing, we just left the population [to] themselves.

Secular feminists are caught in a leadership and funding struggle, which ultimately weakens them as well as their cause, but it also gives their "opponents" a reason to perceive them as hypocritical.

Nadia Yassine offers her opinion of the problems the feminist movement is facing in Morocco. For her, most important, there is no feminist movement in the country. The women claiming to be feminist are in her opinion first and foremost partisan women (*nisa' muhazabat*).

In the past it was fashionable to have feminists in the parties. But there are [very few] feminist figures, like Fatima Mernissi. Very few women. . . . But these women don't have a social base because they were Westernized. They were influenced by Simone de Beauvoir, here they were influenced by the French feminism. . . . These are very small Westernized elites. But this isn't the problem, the problem is that they don't care about social justice; all they care about is how to prosper and about consumerism. . . . You know, it's the elite around the palace, but there was no intellectual level to have a link with this feminism. And the other reason is illiteracy. People don't have access to those ideas, and they consider everything that comes from the West to be against religion (*kafir*). It isn't religious, but against religion. So there is confusion and such feminism couldn't thrive in Morocco. No way! Practically ever since we created the women's section . . . we tried to build a relationship with them [the feminists]. We prepared this feminine elite, who could really bridge the gap between the feminists and their ideas, and the people. [We did this] to understand them and to build something with those feminist activists, especially since the majority of these Westernized feminists have converted [*sic!*] to some more or less religious discourse. . . . We tried to build something, but they rejected us because they were partisan before they were feminist and [members of] political parties that were part of the *makhzen*.

Nadia Yassine frequently mentioned her role as a mediator, not only within the JSO but, as this example shows, also between the Islamists and the other women's organizations. One important aspect of such building of bridges is that the feminist women's movements and the JSO work on two different levels and using two different ideological approaches to achieving similar ends—that of ameliorating the lives of women. For the time being, however, conflicts within their own associations as well as feuds cutting across ideological divides further polarize the public opinion about the enhancement of women's rights and the essence of national identity, as well as weaken their cause(s) vis-à-vis the regime and the governing elites more generally.

Women's interests and priorities

Organizations such as the UAF and ADFM are following a more or less legalistic approach to the question of women's issues. Although they work with ordinary people, particularly through their women's shelters, listening centers for female victims of domestic violence,[26] and literacy classes, they see their primary role as lobbyists to change discriminatory state laws. JSO however, perhaps also due to the nature of the relationship between the organization and the regime, is engaged primarily in a bottom-up project to *resocialize* the masses through purging local traditions of what they perceive as centuries-long accumulation of corrupt practices. These two approaches correspond to Maxine Molyneux's (1985) two conceptions of gender interests—strategic and practical. The former are represented by the feminist organizations and can be discerned in their advocacy to change the legal reality of the Moroccan state. Examples of their campaigns include lobbying to change discriminatory family, nationality, labor, and penal codes, increase women's quotas, and institutionalize gender equality in all spheres of public and private domains. The preoccupation of secular feminists with strategic gender interests is also a consequence of the fact that, as Bohdana Dimitrovova (2009) rightly concludes, Moroccan civil society is elitist and as such has a weak social impact. This furthermore corresponds to Outaleb's disenchantment with the feminist activists discussed above. Since the 1980s, Morocco has witnessed a change in the approach to the promotion of women's rights to one of a business. More than that, as Abu-Lughod astutely observed, in the region as a whole Muslim women's rights have become an industry of its own, "[creating] careers, [channeling] funds, [inspiring] commitments" and have as a consequence "an extraordinary social life" (2010, 1, 33). Without denying the significance of fighting for the amelioration of strategic gender interests, campaigns, such as lobbying for women's quotas and encouraging women to stand for office, are simply urban middle-class concerns. The prime focus of liberal feminists the world over is on the utilization of education and the importance for women as individuals to pursue their potential. There is the assumed *right* to participate in the free market economy and the assumed *ability* of women to choose their own trajectory if only they would be educated. An example of such an agenda can be seen in the survey of the International Foundation for Electoral Systems (IFES) on the status of women in Morocco conducted in 2009–2010.[27] IFES concludes that "a very low rate of formal schooling among women limits their ability to pursue careers, contribute economically to families, or to be *self-sufficient if they so desire*" (IFES Educational Attainment 2010). The following three chapters will demonstrate that such attitudes and conclusions fail to take into account the overarching institutionalized patriarchy and inauspicious macroeconomics and instead perpetuate the idea that the solution is in women themselves. Or, perhaps, that it is women who are ultimately to blame for their own predicament.

Furthermore, lobbying for women's quotas has produced an effect opposite the one expected by the feminists. Batliwala and Dhanraj (2007) writing on India assert that the policies toward increasing the numbers of women in politics have been more than successfully co-opted particularly by the socially and religiously conservative political parties. However, while this should not be regarded as the conservative women having false consciousness because they are indeed active agents, it does show, authors argue, that "fundamentalist movements have created a genuine *political space and role* for women. Regrettably, this is something that none of the so-called 'progressive' forces have done on the same scale" (29; emphasis in original).

Moreover, merely having more women in politics does not necessarily lead to gender mainstreaming to the feminist liking. The March 2012 case in Morocco of the suicide of the sixteen-year-old Amina Filali, who had been raped and then forced to get married to her rapist, is a case in point. Following the event, women's rights activists organized a demonstration for the repeal of article 475 of the Penal Code, which, rather strangely, stipulates that the person "who, *without violence*, threatens or frauds, abducts or diverts, or attempts to kidnap or divert a minor under eighteen years of age" shall be punished (emphasis added). However, when the victim "marries her *kidnapper*, he cannot be prosecuted" (emphasis added). Hakkaoui commented after the demonstrations that "[a]rticle 475 of the Penal Code is unlikely to be repealed overnight and under pressure from the international public opinion. Sometimes the marriage of a raped victim to her rapist does not cause real damage" (Belabd 2012). The following chapter will further elaborate on the conservative agenda of the Islamists such as Hakkaoui toward gender equality and CEDAW, which contradicts the secular feminist politics.

As the following chapters will show, the conservative Islamist agenda reflects the opinions of the general public, which not only opposes the feminist beliefs but also perceives the heightened women's rights discourse as largely irrelevant in the face of worsening economic and other societal problems. The mission to ameliorate women's and men's practical interests, addressing people's immediate needs, such as their material poverty and its immediate manifestations, has been taken up by the Islamists, and particularly the JSO. The regime's control over JSO's activities forces the organization to operate through local sympathizers, who apply for official permits to set up associations and cooperatives in many provincial and urban localities across Morocco. The work they do is versatile, but poverty-alleviation is the overarching issue. "In general," said Dkkali, JSO's activist,

> women here in Morocco suffer from a number of problems and among
> them the biggest one for Moroccan women is poverty. Poverty seems
> to stand in the way of women knowing and learning many things. What
> we try to do is, within the limits of our very restrained resources, we try
> to alleviate poverty as much as possible. We have a famous trilogy to
> describe the situation of women in Morocco; the first element of that
> trilogy is poverty. The second and third element[s] are injustice and igno-
> rance. Under the broad heading of injustice we find societal injustice—
> the position of women in our society is not what it should be; women
> are belittled, marginalized, and looked down on by men. We try our best
> to fix that through educating women and giving them back confidence in
> themselves so that they feel that they are a worthy societal constituent.
> We try to help women shed their shackles—societal shackles, shackles of
> traditions, shackles of religion. The third element of this trilogy is illit-
> eracy. A great number of women suffer not only from actual illiteracy

but also from a number of other types of ignorance. Political ignorance among others, even ignorance of basic medical skills: you find mothers in charge of a whole family who don't know anything about first aid or basic medical notions because no one cared to teach her. What we do is we start by teaching these elemental notions, we teach women the alphabet, but also hygiene. We actually invite doctors to our meetings to teach such things. We teach women how to manage their household and we invite experts to do that. If there are any legal issues we try and invite lawyers and legal experts to raise awareness about the subject, though in these matters we need to be very consistent and provide regular follow-ups. The means we have only allow us to focus on raising awareness, and we hope that once we have better resources we will be able to engage in more practical aspects.

In addition to such life-learning projects, JSO also helps women set up income-generating cooperatives. Although for Molyneux these practical gender interests do not challenge systemic forms of oppression or patriarchy, JSO's activities and political agenda nonetheless do have an ideological and hence strategic component to them. I interviewed JSO's spokesperson Arsalane at his home in the outskirts of Rabat. When I asked him what his organization's view of women's rights was, he explained that they perceived liberation as necessary for both women and men.

Jurisprudence . . . has to be liberated from jurisprudence which justifies oppression and oppressive judges. We think that if a man is humiliated and oppressed, we have to liberate him. But women are oppressed twice: by judges and by men who are ignorant about their true religion. Customs and traditions oppress women and deny them rights in the name of religion and Islam.

What society requires for its own liberation, continued Arsalane, is democracy. Morocco today is a stratified society, and this is not only a gender problem but also a problem, he continued,

between a man and a man and another man. There's no democracy, no justice, there's oppression in everything—between a woman and a woman, between a man and a man, the judge and the judged. But in this atmosphere where there is no democracy, justice or freedom, I think that oppression affects everybody, but mostly the weak and here, the woman is weaker than the man. . . . If we want to give women rights, we have to educate society, [give them] basic education, and then bring justice and rights.

JSO in their emphasis on education as the main tool of societal transformation does not differ much from secular women's organizations, despite their primary preoccupation with legal reforms. Where they diverge, however, is in their intentions. Whereas the feminists see the purpose of their campaigns in engendering a just and equal society based on universal values of human rights, the main intention of JSO's grassroots activities and their ultimate goal is that of spirituality—to purge religion of corrupt and oppressive customs and to bring people (back) on the *true* path to God. In order to achieve that, I was told by two female JSO activists who wished to remain anonymous, people's livelihoods and their personal dignity have to be secured first. Only then will people be able to turn the attention to their spiritual well-being.

What both movements have in common is that they assume that they, rather than the "Other," have the key to what they deem to be common women's interests. Molyneux (1985) argues that the notion of women's interests creates a false consciousness among women's rights activists that *all* women have the same interests. In Morocco, the feminists and the Islamists are promoting a sense of societal unity or an image of Morocco as a homogenous society. The feminists see it in the way of promoting the "right" kind of education for women in particular, to equip them with the knowledge of the (universal) human rights that should by definition, they believe, lead them to accept empowerment and refuse the patriarchal bargain that maintains their oppression. These feminists are convinced that veiled women, as Amina's case demonstrated, have a false consciousness and need to be reeducated. Only as such will Amina and other veiled women be able to truly enjoy justice and dignity.

The Islamists, on the other hand, already perceive Morocco as a Muslim society and hence a unity of believers, but one which needs to be strengthened through purging the centuries-long accumulation of corrupt customs to finally bring about genuine Islamic justice to both women and men. Both movements are fighting for the triumph of their own view of a modern Moroccan society—an imagined community of mythic unity— but in doing so they leave little space for diversity and indeed tolerance. Production of knowledge, information, and alternative opinions to one's own are severely restricted not only by the state but, more importantly, by its agents. As Molyneux quite rightly argues, "a theory of interests that has an application to the debate about women's capacity to struggle for and benefit from social changes must begin by recognizing difference rather than by assuming homogeneity" (1985, 232). In Morocco, however, it is secular feminist voices that are sidelined and excluded by the general public because it is these feminists who do not (or refuse to) speak the language of Islam.

Conclusion

This chapter has demonstrated the conflictual nature of Morocco's civil society struggle for women's rights, which is a consequence of the evolution of Moroccan national identity, of what it means to be Moroccan in the globalized world. As these debates about the nature of women's liberation, how to approach a multitude of women's interests, and the definition of the ideal Moroccan woman in the twenty-first century continue to be fought in the public space and circulated by newspapers, TV shows, mosques, and informal groups, they have inevitably contributed to the schizophrenic character and behavior of ordinary Moroccans and state responses.

Moreover, the struggle for the reform of the PSC as the struggle for a redefined and modernized national identity is significant because it has contributed to the opening up of the political space to alternative voices. It is tempting, however, to assume that this evolution has resulted in the feminization of Moroccan politics, as Sadiqi and Ennaji assert (2006).[28] The political liberalization process underway in the country since the mid-1980s gradually allowed marginalized groups, such as women and the Islamists, to enter the public arena. However, neither genuine Islamization nor feminization of politics have occurred, but it is true that both -isms have influenced politics and politicians, as well as secular feminists and Islamist women to the extent that ignoring women's issues or following overtly secular agendas negatively affect their political and social agendas and work. It is my understanding that Moroccan politics has never been secular and that there has never been a genuine disengagement from the religious modus operandi as regards personal status, civil freedoms, national identity, sections of the Penal Code, or issues of (public) morality more generally. If anything, the 1980s and particularly the 1990s saw politicization of women's questions within a continued conservative political climate. It is the question of how this politicization has materialized in concrete legal reforms that I now turn to.

A typical street in Taddert (October 2009).

CHAPTER 3

The State, the Public, and Women's Rights[1]

A discussion of Morocco's women's rights would be deficient without an analysis of its Family Code because, as Moghadam rightly stated, family legislation showcases the state's social agenda, in addition to being "a key ingredient of the state's gender policy" (2011, 114–115; Brand 1998; Charrad 2001; Esposito 2001; Mir-Hosseini 1997; Tucker 2008; Hallaq 2008; Welchman 2000, 2004).

On 10 October 2003 King Muhammad VI announced the much anticipated reforms to the old PSC, which regulated marital (rather than gender) relationships, child custody, and inheritance. The king placed the Family Code firmly within the development discourse, with a clear aim and commitment to further reforms heeding societal evolution. As such, the king asserted that the new Mudawwana is not "flawless" but "an *ijtihad* effort, which is suitable for Morocco at this point in time" (Ministry of Communication 2003). He furthermore made the reform an essential and indispensable ingredient of his democratization project, which requires ameliorated living conditions of all Moroccans and a culture of responsible and committed citizens (Ministry of Communication). According to the king's speeches, the long-term project is one of liberating and empowering his people because only such citizens will be able to actively contribute to the building of a democratic society and fully enjoy their freedoms.

The notion of gradualism is perhaps the most salient guiding principle when analyzing the Family Code, or the reforms may be otherwise dismissed as falling short of the feminist expectations and the international praise much the same as the 1993 reforms. Morocco's activist communities ascribe to conflicting ideas as to what it means to liberate women, and which category of women at that, based on the ideological utilization of what appear to be not necessarily compatible legal frameworks—those of the Islamic legal sources and international human rights conventions, specifically CEDAW, UDHR, and Convention on the Rights of the Child (UNCRC). The contemporaneous existence of multiple frames of reference resulted in the law to reflect this somewhat schizophrenic backdrop discussed in the previous chapter. If anything, the current Mudawwana demonstrates the pragmatism of the king to placate the conservatives while at the same time recognizing the legitimacy of feminist demands.

In this chapter, I do not intend to approach the law and its stipulations in a systematic manner. Instead, I will analyze the "unwritten," the implicit character of the Mudawwana's stated goals because it is these, rather than the stipulations, that undermine the overall result of the reform and taint the positive image of the reformed law.

Justice and the Mudawwana

The Preamble to the 2004 Family Code declares that the aim of the law is threefold: "doing justice to women, protecting children's rights, and preserving men's dignity." That the authors of the Mudawwana included preservation of men's dignity among the stated goals is understandable given the backlash against the reform and the fact that many people still refer to the Family Code as the "Women's Code," demonstrating people's supposition of the law's asymmetrical preoccupation with women's situation. However, such progressive language in the preamble may and, in the case of the reformed Family Code, does obscure reconsolidation of gender inequality and indeed patriarchy.

The new Mudawwana is certainly presented to the international (donor) community as one giving the impression of a progressive law. When I visited the Ministry of Solidarity, Women, Family, and Social Development in Rabat—the main government body in charge of promoting women's rights—the official immediately handed me a number of brochures and booklets on various national women's rights projects. One of them was "La Moudawana, autrement" ("The Mudawwana, Differently"), which is an attractively colorful booklet of the "most important provisions of the new Family Code" replete with witty caricatures comparing and contrasting the old and new "moral order" (Seftaoui 2006). It is written for international aid workers, educators, and civil society activists in French and Arabic. The "problem" with the booklet is that it includes principally those articles which present Morocco and the reform in a positive, progressive, and democratic light. It includes for example article 25, granting women of legal majority the right to choose to get married without her *wali* or to delegate this power to her father or any other relative. The booklet also contains various articles enhancing women's right to seek divorce, in addition to article 51, which spells out mutual obligations and rights between spouses. It is this article which is often invoked to showcase Morocco's apparent determination to institute legal gender equality.

However, the booklet omits those articles that in fact reaffirm patriarchal relations and perpetuate gender inequality. For example, article 194 obliges the husband to financially provide for his wife and children, and article 236 designates the father as the primary legal representative of his children regardless of whether or not he has custody over the children (Zvan Elliott 2009). Although many Moroccan women and men interpret article 194 as benefitting women, it nonetheless confirms gendered division of space into the female domestic and male public spheres. In other words, because men are legally obliged to provide for their families, whereas women are not, it was such reasoning that some of my interviewees put forward when making a case for discrimination against female candidates on the labor market. The obligation of men as family breadwinners also raises family expectations, if not demands, that their daughters(-in-law) stay at home after they get married. The law therefore reaffirms local customs and attitudes toward women's work outside the home and as such has serious repercussions for the extrication of women's financial and legal dependence from their husbands and male family members. By obscuring discriminatory provisions, the law is veneered with a thin layer of progress.

Enhancing justice for women through revising those clauses that allowed men arbitrary behavior in the past, such as marrying off daughters without their consent or knowledge[2] and taking a second wife without informing the first (or without informing the second wife of the existence of the first wife),[3] can be read as overhauling those aspects of the established moral order that diverged from the principles of Islam—justice, equality, and amicable social relations.[4] In addition, the law responded to the changing social circumstances, such as women working outside the home. It is for these reasons that the new Mudawwana grants a married couple the right to stipulate further conditions into the marriage contract (articles 47 and 48) and to sign a prenuptial agreement in which the couple settles on comanagement of marital property (article 49). (In the absence of such an agreement, however, marital property is separate.)

What judges, the ʿadul, and people themselves make of these reforms will be discussed in the following chapter.

However, one of the less-researched questions is how does the law interact with people, or rather, how do people interact with the Family Code's stated goals of doing justice to women and preserving men's dignity? This is important because the very wording of the code's goals can be read as an attempt to satisfy opposition to the reform, coming from those circles that perceive the enhancement of women's rights as a zero-sum game.

Moreover, examining the stated goals of the reformed law reveals a multitude of veiled connotations. Dignity has a compound meaning of honor and respect, of which particularly the former has been a constant research topic among the academics working on the MENA region (Abu-Lughod 1999; Latreille 2008; Meeker 1976a, 1976b; Peristiany 1974; Welchman 2007). Honor, echoing Abu-Lughod (1999), represents the moral basis of hierarchy. And, in the words of Martin Latreille, "under the guise of honor and its correlates [such as shame and modesty, which are attributes of women] we find norms dictating behavior and interaction" (2008, 601). This is a potent conclusion, which also applies to the spirit, if not the letter, of the Mudawwana, since honor as an aspect of dignity specifically belongs to men. (While women's behavior significantly impacts the quality of such honor.) Therefore, the law by declaring that it is preserving men's dignity maintains the role of men as heads of the family because it is *their* honor, and consequently that of their family, which is affected by doing justice to women. As the law and its reformers do not operate in a vacuum, it is important to contextualize the meanings and explain the rationale behind the goals, which is arguably best done through ethnography. What does the law mean when it proclaims that it is bringing justice to women and preserving men's dignity? And why was there the need to formulate these goals in such a way where "doing justice to women" is juxtaposed to the possibility of compromising men's dignity?

Explaining the contradiction through ethnography

In an unusually heated interview with the faith healer (*fqi*) in Oued al-Ouliya, he explained the idea of honor as a protective force for women. I asked him whether he had heard about the notion of gender equality, to which he replied:

Thank god there is equality even here in the Qur'an! The Qur'an is the core of Islamic law. It glorifies women. I know what you want to say. There is a statement in the Qur'an that the foreigners are fixed on and this statement in the Qur'an says, "Beat them." You [Westerners] can't stand this. . . . You want to eliminate this. You say it's not right, this is inequality. The woman has honor (šaraf) in Islam. Islamic law came to give her rights, which protect women. . . . It is honor which protects women and [which protects them] against violence. . . . What is the cause for violence outside the house? It is adornment. That smile and image bring violence to her. Seduction. Do you understand? It's outside the house, not inside. If she goes out, if she shows her beauty she may be hurt. So, this is honor in Islam. And you want to get rid of this issue?! You or somebody else will get hurt because of your image. Do you get it? Seduction. He doesn't have conscience (damir) and he's [li]able to assault [a woman].[5]

While the reformed code claims it is "doing justice to women" by allowing them to tread outside the protective boundaries of gendered propriety, such behavior may indeed have serious repercussions for the woman. In my field site as in many other similar areas across Morocco, neither women nor men are regarded as autonomous individuals, which is in opposition to the principle of individuality contained in the universal human rights concept, something that Morocco purportedly adheres to as will be addressed in continuation. Lawrence Rosen eloquently described the nature of Moroccan society as one that has an individual rather than a collective at its center. However, centrality of the individual does not also entail her autonomy. Significance is attached to this individual only when she is placed within the collective (family, tribe, or village), when her origin (asel) — in terms of her family and place — is established. When inquiring about an individual, as for example to determine whether she is an appropriate match, her asel and not her profession or age, as is normally the case in the West, is of prime interest and importance. "Such an inquiry," writes Rosen,

give[s] the inquirer a key piece of information, for it suggests who this other is connected to and the ways in which [s]he is used to forming such ties given the customs and practices of the region from which [s]he comes. . . . In Arab culture the individual is a unit into which the features of background, context, and association are poured and through which the characteristic ways of forming ties to others are played out. Tribe, family, village and quarter form an outer structure that provides the material that will cohere in the person. (1998, 12, 15)

Marriage arrangements are a relevant example of what Rosen meant. The most important prerequisite for parents to start marriage arrangements in Oued al-Ouliya is to determine the tribal affiliation of the candidate's family. Such affiliation is associated with skin color, although I sometimes would not be able to differentiate a person with "lighter" skin tone from a person with "darker" skin color. The issue was further confusing because I could not tell whether it was the tribe or the skin color that was important and whether one is predicated upon the other. I came to the conclusion that tribal affiliation defines skin color, albeit every so often even the "right" tribal affiliation would not help the person. This was the case when her skin tone was too dark because the local beauty ideal dictates skin to be as white as possible, in contrast to the West's obsession with having suntanned skin. Belonging to either a generally "lighter-skinned" tribe, such as Cherfa, Egguramen, and Aït Merghad or to "darker-skinned" people, called pejoratively Heratin, significantly defines a person to this day.[6] (My friends explained to me that the Heratin do not have a tribal affiliation and are, at least among the "black" people, further distinguished according to the shade of their dark skin color—Ismkhan are perceived as darker than the Heratin.)[7] Despite both "lighter-skinned" and "darker-skinned" families living in the same *ksar* and socializing with each other—the elected president of the community, Hamid, is Heratin—intermarriages are nonetheless rare and considered inferior. Families make an exception only, I was told, when a Heratin or Ismkhan man is wealthy. But even then "white" women can shun the "white" bride for marrying someone without, essentially, a tribal affiliation. The Heratin cannot (or perhaps were denied the ability to) trace their origin back like the Berber tribes can and are therefore without the *asel*, or genealogy. Tribal profiling and speaking of someone's darker skin or "African physical characteristics," as I often heard, as something bad or ugly (*khayb*) is associated with many stereotypes and misconceptions, significantly affecting the nature of matchmaking. Girls belonging to one or the other "white" tribe told me that, for example, the Heratin were less educated, that they refused to send their children to school, and that they married their daughters off without a thorough background check on the man. In other words, for "white" families the fact that the would-be bride or groom belongs to the Heratin is a valid reason to refuse the proposal outright.

Once someone's tribal affiliation or skin tone is approved, a more in-depth inquiry into the reputation of the family commences. Women in particular are mobilized to help with the research if the family is from a different village or town. With the extensive web of family relations extending into neighboring or more remote villages and towns, it seems that there will always be someone who has "firsthand" information about the family under scrutiny. Good reputation of the family hinges upon the evaluation of many factors. As shown below in Soukaina's case, the fact that the mother of the groom-to-be failed as a mother to the children from her first marriage was the rationale given by Soukaina's mother to refuse the marriage, rather than Soukaina being underage. Moreover, hardworking, pious, wealthy, with modest female family members, and scandal-free family history are some of the positive idiosyncrasies associated with a good reputation of the family. The bride's family will also look at the employment background of the groom and will be quite reluctant to give their consent if the groom is not a public servant or if he does not have a permanent job. Habiba's mother once explained to me that a man who is not a public servant only has to have one headache for his wife and children to go hungry. The preoccupation with employment in the public service is to an extent understandable, as jobs in the private or the informal sectors for the most part do not come with social benefits, but there is also a discernible sense of prestige still attached to public servants. That one of the members or even the candidate himself is working abroad also contributes to the favorable evaluation of the proposal because it implies that the daughter will be taken care of and shall perhaps even move to Europe. (This possibility increases the reputation of the girl's family.) In the hierarchy of reputations, that of the family firmly stands above the individual.

The person, therefore, is indebted to this collective because "one's *asel* is one's social identity" (Rosen 1998, 12), which crucially determines the behavior of other people toward this individual and consequently her future. Borrowing Joseph's concept, it is connectivity that binds family members to each other and requires "continuous interaction between significant others for a sense of completion" (1994, 55). Individuals need to be connected to their family members for "security, identity, integrity, dignity, and self-worth" (55).

To better understand the concept of an individual in Moroccan society, it is necessary to examine the interaction between the law, custom, and religion as well as the popular understanding of such interplay. Rosen, again, in his numerous studies of the impact of custom on law with an emphasis on Morocco concluded that "custom and law are not discreet categories but are, in many instances, conceptually merged" not only in people's minds but also as regards judges' interpretation of the substantive law (1995, 206). The issue of *wali* is a good example of this, as it has been one of the more contentious reforms presented by the new Mudawwana. As mentioned, the law gives the engaged girl of legal age a choice to conclude her marriage contract by herself or entrust her legal guardian to do so on her behalf. "One of the most important things that women have gained from the new law is that *guardianship is her right*," concluded the Ministry of Justice's *Practical Guide*, because "like the man she exercises it according to her choice and her interests without being subjected to any supervision or consent" (quoted in Welchman 2012, 71). In a similar manner, one of my interviewees from Oued al-Ouliya, Aissam, a thirty-eight-year-old teacher with a degree in Islamic law, welcomed this article, saying:

> It's good because at least it doesn't make the woman feel insignificant. That means that a woman getting married should have the authority over taking decisions and of taking the responsibility for her decision. This means that we affirmed that a woman is mature and knows what's good for her and her future.

However, such opinions do not reflect the actual situation. Official statistics of the Ministry of Justice presented in the table below show that less than a quarter of all brides of legal age concluded their marriage contracts by themselves.

These statistics, however, do not disaggregate data to show how many of these brides did not have a legal guardian, either because they were orphans or their father was deceased or absent, or how many were getting married for the first time. (I often heard that when a divorced or widowed woman remarried she was less likely to be reprimanded for choosing the spouse and signing the contract without seeking the consent of the family and/or her *wali*.)

My interviews with women and men in Oued al-Ouliya support such low national percentage and manifest two prevailing attitudes toward women choosing to get married without their legal guardians. There was either overwhelming discontent with this reform or, particularly in the case of my female interviewees, welcoming the reform in principle but not in practice, particularly in cases in which the girl does not have a *wali* or works outside the home,[8] while for those with a *wali* such a choice

Table 3.1. Number and percentage of marriages by selected year in which the bride of legal age signed the marital contract outside the presence of her *wali*

Statistical year	Number of brides	Percentage of such marriages
2006	60,095	22.01
2007	62,162	20.88
2009	64,125	20.40
2010	65,299	20.84
2011	66,620	20.47

Source: Ministry of Justice 2008b, 2009, 2010, 2011.

was unimaginable. Yasmin, a divorced woman in her forties, for example explained:

> Women can't [get married without their *wali*] and unemployed women should always have [one]. And if she signs the contract by herself people will talk about her as if she is a bad girl. This means that she always needs someone who'll guide her because she's not employed. . . . But there aren't any girls who have parents and would sign the contract by themselves and not allow their father to be present. It is impossible. But those who don't have a *wali* or someone to depend on can sign the contract by themselves.

There are a variety of reasons for such varied responses, which the interviewees put forward, but they can be summed up as having to do with religion and customs (oftentimes used interchangeably). Such views corroborate Rosen's claim of the interconnectedness between the two categories. Youssef, a teacher in Taddert's primary school, reflected on the issue in the following way: "Well, she has the right, but despite this it's necessary for her *wali* to be with her. These are our customs and it's not the law (*qanun*) because there are customs and there's the law." I then asked him about his opinion of the woman's right to choose and he weighed the options further:

> It has negative and positive sides. A positive side is . . . when a girl gets to a certain level of maturity and she's convinced that marriage is good

for her, why wouldn't we give her the right to get married by herself?!
Because it's her future and not someone else's. Whereas the negative
side is that, for example, if we let go of this issue, well, there will be disorder (*siba*). We'd find that when a girl meets someone she'd marry him
without getting to know him [which is not good] because the family
still wants to know the man who is marrying the girl. Here, people still
want to know this person. They should know him! That means that they
have a certain knowledge, even if it's simple, about the husband, a special
knowledge—who is he, where he comes from, what is his job, what he
does, etc. [His] economic, financial, and family situation.

Marriage arrangements therefore, remain firmly in the hands of the
family. Boutayyeb, the director of Taddert's primary school, who was at
first very reluctant to be interviewed and was later slightly defensive about
his culture (which is ostensibly being eroded by *my* culture and globalization), had strong views of the Mudawwana and the issue of *wali*:

If we want to go into the [issue of] just treatment of women, whether
a woman is treated justly or not, we should go back to the religious
'*ulema*'. They explain the ruling on guardianship. . . . It touches our
honor, honestly. You won't understand me well because you didn't grow
up here. You have your own culture and we have our own culture.

When I asked him about whether women know about this right, he
said confidently: "Yes and they refuse it. The majority of women refuse
this. They think that this doesn't come from religion, from the Islamic
law." What is more, stated my field-site neighbor Abdallah, "Islam says
that if she gets married without the permission of her parents, [the mar-
riage] is invalid. In Islam, there has to be a *wali*—her father, the one responsible for her." In fact, Boutayyeb explained, this right is discredited
in people's opinion (as it is in his) because "the majority of people think
that [the Mudawwana] came from abroad and that its origin is not from
here. . . . It hasn't originated in our culture, from our way of thinking,
and from our own volition." It is for this reason, that "this [right] makes
me feel disgusted, honestly. Maybe you won't understand this, but I do,"
he concluded.

For people in Oued al-Ouliya, religion and its texts are what lends cre-
dence to customs, whereas substantive law does not have that stamp of
authenticity and is thus rejected for it may bring disorder on many levels.

One of the likely repercussions for women of denying the legal guardian his customary right to marry off his daughter is that such violation of the established order absolves her family from its moral obligation to protect her in times of tribulation. A twenty-one-year-old Ghizlane, who at the time of the interview was finishing high school and recently became engaged, insisted that it is indeed illegitimate to get married without a legal guardian. She explained why:

> No, she doesn't have the right because if there's a problem, which could arise tomorrow, she wouldn't be the only one who would carry the burden, but these people as well, this *wali*, will also carry it. He was present on that day [of the signing of marital contract], which means that he'll also carry the burden. . . . [This law] is illegitimate (*ghair mašruᶜ*).

Zoulikha was a middle-aged married woman, who perhaps spoke from her experience because, at the time of my fieldwork, her husband was in a mental institution in France for assaulting someone. She therefore lived with her parents because her husband was unable to support her, and she was not able to join him abroad.

> It's possible [to get married without the *wali*]. But here are customs. It is customary that the father and the mother of the girl and the man have to be present when she wants to sign the contract. It's a custom. In this region, if they're not present, such marriage will be considered as *naqisan* [inferior, defective]. In legal terms it's considered as a marriage, but if parents are not present, it's *naqisan*. You know why? Because of our traditions and our Islam. There is an *aya* [Qur'anic verse] that states this, but I don't remember it. Consultation is good because you can have problems with your husband or with your in-laws, [and] who will help you [if this happens]? This means that you'll have to go to your parents, and if you didn't respect them before they'll tell you: "Since you did everything by yourself, finish it up by yourself!"

My conversation with the *fqi* further reveals such perception of incompatibility of this right with the customary order and/or Islamic law. When I asked him whether women were aware of their right to get married without their *wali*, he replied that only if they were over the age of *nisab*, which, according to him denotes a girl who "is over the age of twenty-five or [who] is an orphan or doesn't have a father. Otherwise she must consult her father." But I wanted to hear his opinion of this freedom rather than what local customs dictate. "Because," he explained, "if God brings divorce where will she go? If she didn't consult her father and she comes back he won't want her back. Do you understand? You as well perhaps have the same thing; if your father and mother don't accept . . ." I interrupted him here and told him in a slightly curt manner that "it's not their business (*maši šughluhum*)." There was an incredulous gasp coming from all three people sitting in the room with me—*fqi*, his wife, Aicha, and Karima. He and Karima repeated in unison: "It's not their business?!"

"No," I continued, "because in the case of divorce, she won't have to go back to her father or mother. She has an apartment. The marriage is between a wife and her husband and not between her and his families." The *fqi*, however, still disbelieving what he was hearing, reiterated the question: "But if God brings divorce, where is she going to go?"

"To her own apartment," I repeated somewhat matter-of-factly. He pursued the issue further, asking, "What if she doesn't have an apartment?" I tried to explain that most women in the West have a source of income and could thus rent an apartment if need be, but he interrupted me before I was able to relate this to him as if finally getting to the bottom of the issue on his own. "So, the government gives you apartments, houses. But not here! If she doesn't obey her parents, she is out. To consult her parents is a right. The *wali* should be present at the first marriage." *Fqi*'s incredulity was not unforeseen, since in Oued al-Ouliya not many couples, let alone single or divorced women, rented their own apartments or houses separate from the husbands' families. More than this being a consequence of financial constraints, it is the essence of a patriarchal system with built-in demands for women to bargain in order to improve their position within family and, accordingly, society. Yet the presence of the *wali* is not only a strategy for the girl to secure for herself continuous physical protection of her kin, but it also demonstrates to the community that she is modest. Khalti Ftouch, the matriarch in my host family, for example, explained this in the following way:

> If she doesn't have a *wali*, she's not a good girl. . . . Girls today get married by themselves even if they have fathers. They don't care about them. . . . [But] it's not good if you don't put your hand in your father's hand.

In Oued al-Ouliya the presence of the *wali* is in fact required by the *ʿadul* and hence automatic, regardless of what the law stipulates. The local 'adul told me that he insists on the presence of the *wali* "because that is a custom. If the father or someone else is not present, it is something shameful." When I asked him why it was shameful to get married without the *wali*, he explained:

> It is shameful, yes. At the beginning, if a man is interested in getting married, he goes to see her father directly to ask for her hand. He does not go to the girl. According to customs, if he goes to the girl without going to the father, it's a bit stupid. Thus, you have to go to the father. It is in the interest of the girl, he defends her. He looks at what is good for her. Do you understand? This is guardianship, the meaning of guardianship. The problem is that many people do not understand its role; even the father or parents don't understand what is guardianship. Guardianship means protection for the woman, to protect her, so that not just anyone can come and marry her; for example, an alcoholic or a homeless man. Do you understand? But even fathers don't understand guardianship. Anyone can come and they give him the girl. But in reality in Islamic law, the guardian acts in the interest of the girl, to protect her. The father chooses the right person for his daughter to live a good life with him, [a life] which continues.

What all these snippets of interviews demonstrate is that protection for the girl equals shelter, a physical and an emotional shelter. It signals having a roof above the head, as well as having a social identity, the *asel* that Rosen spoke about. It also means being able to interact with people because the girl is recognized by the community as a law-abiding individual. In essence, having protection implies being able to exist as an accepted member of the community. On the other hand, however, overriding the right of *wali* to marry her off puts the girl in a precarious position: she may well miss the opportunity to (ever) get married, and she risks losing the right to protection because she has brought shame to her family.

But shame as an attribute of women's modesty is also something that women are proud of because, as Rachel Newcomb concludes, "it represents a civilizing force" (2009, 148; Abu-Lughod 1999). The girl demonstrates her maturity, her *'aql*, which Abu-Lughod aptly translated as "social sense and self-control of honorable persons" (1999, 108) and hence secures her good reputation by honoring the customary right of her *wali* to oversee the marriage process. Enjoyment of such customary rights as protection is in fact conditioned by the satisfactory performance of one's duties, which is what *fqi* meant when he said that consulting parents was a right. In other words, the girl can claim her right to protection when she successfully fulfills her customary obligation to treat marriage as a family affair. It is important to note, however, that even despite their fulfilling their customary duties, many women face difficulties in such cases, for example, as that of marital discord. The result is that women stay in abusive marriages because their families refuse to take them back. It is, in Bassam Tibi's words, "the collectivity, not the individual, and duties, not rights, [which] rank highest" (1994, 296). It is such conditioning of rights which reinforces the argument that the current Family Code, despite the reform, continues to be embedded within the customary (Islamic)[9] Weltanschauung rather than a more universal, if not a secular, one. Moreover, this example further demonstrates a discrepancy between the two conceptions of human rights.

A conception of human rights in Morocco's legislation

It is important to see the reform of the PSC in light of the heightened international pressure to define women's rights as human rights, which is a debate that Morocco has not been able to escape. Therefore, the debate about the conflict between the Islamic and the universal concepts of human rights in Morocco's official discourse is germane because of the country's constitution proclaiming to adhere to the universal concept of human rights, as well as because of the repercussions that this reform has had for women in general and single adult girls in particular.

On the one hand, the king was clear in his speeches that the reformed Mudawwana is informed by and based on a modern rereading of religious legal texts. On the other, the Preamble to the country's 1996 constitution declares that the Kingdom of Morocco "fully adheres to the principles, rights, and obligations arising from the charters of [international] organizations" and that it "reaffirms its determination to abide by the universally recognized human rights."[10] In a similar manner, the newly promulgated reformed constitution of 2011 declares the following:

> Aware of the need to strengthen its role on the global stage, the Kingdom of Morocco, as an active member within the international organizations, is committed to adhere to the principles, rights, and obligations set forth in their respective charters and conventions; [and] it reaffirms its commitment to human rights as they are universally recognized.[11]

However, article 19 of the 2011 constitution complicates the issue of the utilized legal frameworks. While it initially states that women and men enjoy equal civil, political, economic, social, cultural, and environmental rights in accordance with the international conventions ratified by Morocco, these rights are nonetheless subject to "*des constantes* [in Arabic, *thawabit*] of the Kingdom and its laws." The choice of words in both Arabic and French is interesting because of the ambiguity in meaning and could refer to any established or, indeed, immutable law or customs, pillars of society. In other words, what is meant by *des constantes/thawabit* is that the state will guarantee gender equality *except* when it contradicts those laws and customs emanating from Islamic/Maliki law. Such a constitutional provision is in accordance with its 2005 Beijing +10 report, in which the Moroccan government wrote that the reformed Family Code respects "the sacred values of Islam and universal values of the rights of individuals" (Kingdom of Morocco 2005, 3).

Furthermore, Morocco ratified (or adheres to) a range of international human rights conventions and declarations, such as the UDHR, Beijing's Platform for Action, and CEDAW, in addition to committing itself to reaching the goals of the MDGs. Such declarations and activities strongly manifest Morocco's adherence to universally recognized human rights standards, at least in principle, while at the same time reveal inconsistencies in the country's working definition of an individual and her rights and obligations, if not, as will be shown, discrimination against certain categories of womanhood.

Moreover, the contradictions in the utilized legal frameworks are manifested in the conception of a *woman*. The Moroccan Family Code is clear in designating the family, rather than the individual, to be the core of society when declaring that the family is "a substantial major component of the democratization process, given that the family constitutes the essential nucleus of society." This, however, contradicts what Tibi (1994) postulates as a prerequisite for developing a modern society, namely the process of individuation and the concept of human rights as entitlements of an individual. Leila Rhiwi, the former director of a feminist ADFM-led initiative called Spring of Equality and currently Maghreb women's rights coordinator for UNIFEM, stated that "[t]he new Family Code acknowledges the identity of a woman and hence her citizenship and freedom to be a human being" (2004, 16). I argue instead that the current Mudawwana does not represent a historical breakthrough in Moroccan women's rights politics exactly because of the failure to define women's rights as rights of autonomous individuals. Or, keeping in mind the gradual approach of the king as concerns the issue, this process of individuation and recognition of rights as entitlements rather than a consequence of fulfilled duties is the challenge for the future reformers of the Family Code. For the time being, however, Morocco fails to comply with the international order, to which it has committed itself at least on paper.

Gender equality and the state

The case of gender equality as defined by CEDAW and how the state deals with it further calls into question Morocco's professed adherence to the international human rights standards and further sheds light on the discrepancy between Morocco's stated adherence to such standards and the country's *constantes* (*thawabit*) as expressed in article 19 of the current constitution. Moreover, many conservative Western and Moroccan women's rights activists oppose the notion of gender equality, which surrounds the heightened international and domestic discourse on women's rights, poverty-alleviation projects, and legal reforms. Analysis of Morocco's government responses to international conventions and action plans dealing with women's rights, such as CEDAW and the MDGs, responses of both feminist and Islamist activists, as well as people's perceptions and attitudes toward gender equality, manifest misinterpretation and misappropriation of the notion of gender equality by different groups and for diverse purposes.

CEDAW recognizes discrimination against women to be intrinsically linked with lack of gender equality. It defines gender equality in a holistic manner, applicable to both the public and the domestic spheres, in addition to situating it within the international (universal) regime of human rights. "In fact," argue Alda Facio and Martha I. Morgan, "without equality, human rights have no meaning" and CEDAW makes this association unequivocal (2009, 3).[12] CEDAW, therefore, establishes an international standard for gender equality and as such forms the basis of numerous other international legal standards and poverty-alleviation campaigns, such as the Beijing Platform for Action and the MDGs.

Morocco ratified CEDAW in June 1993 shortly after the first reform of the PSC. However, it entered several reservations to clauses granting women equal rights with men as regards the nationality of their children (to article 9 [2]) and to article 16, which spells out key principles of gender equality within family and marital relationships. It is this article that is recognized by the drafters themselves to be one of CEDAW's two core provisions. (The other being article 2, to which Morocco entered a declaration. I shall address the issue in a later chapter.) Morocco entered these reservations because gender equality as defined by the convention in the domestic realm, but not in the public domain, was considered to be incompatible with the Islamic law, "which guarantees to each of the spouses rights and responsibilities within a framework of equilibrium and complementarity in order to preserve the sacred bond of matrimony" (UN Division for the Advancement of Women). It is thus separate individual rights and obligations rather than equal rights that govern gendered (marital) roles in Morocco. These reservations not only nullified the object and purpose of CEDAW but also confirmed that Islamic law took precedence over the international law in cases of the conflictual nature of some of its articles with the domestic legislation[13] (in addition to asserting that the Islamic law—*des constantes/thawabit*—and universal human rights law use incompatible definitions of gender relations). The remark of the Euromed report, *Women's Human Rights and Gender Equality: Morocco*, saying that Morocco enters reservations "essentially for conventions dealing with women's rights" (2010, 39) is not insignificant in this respect and only reaffirms the supremacy of religiously based laws in family legislation in particular. In other words, the ostensible incompatibility of Islamic law with the international human rights standards was not invoked with other CEDAW articles dealing with gender equality in the public space, such as articles 3 (equality in political, cultural, economic, and social fields), 8 (the right to represent her government internationally), 10 (equality in education), or 13 (the right to family benefits, bank loans, etc.). Moreover, Morocco also did not object to other international legal human rights instruments protecting particularly rights and freedoms in the public domain, as for example the UN International Covenants on Civil and Political Rights as well as on Economic, Social, and Cultural Rights, or such International Labor Organization (ILO) conventions as the Equal Remuneration Convention or Night Work (Women) Convention.

On 8 April 2011 the king's promise made in several of his speeches, in which he expressed the imminent withdrawal of reservations and declarations to CEDAW, was finally partially fulfilled.[14] Although Morocco withdrew its reservations to articles 9 (2) and 16, it kept its declarations to articles 2 and 15 (4). Article 2 is important because it spells out state obligations. It requires signatory states to institute gender equality in their legal orders, including their national constitutions, and urges countries to foster a culture of equality—(Committee on the Elimination of Discrimination Against Women 2008a; Committee on the Elimination of

Discrimination Against Women 2008b) as such it is recognized as defining the object and purpose of the convention; whereas, article 15 (4) specifically regulates the individual's right to freedom of movement and the freedom to choose her residence and domicile. But, the difference between reservations and declarations is not always clear-cut. Hence, the Human Rights Committee in its General Comment No. 24 specified that in determining the effect of declaration,

> [r]egard will be had to the *intention* of the State, rather than the form of the instrument. If a statement, irrespective of its name or title, purports to exclude or modify the legal effect of a treaty in its application to the State, it constitutes a reservation. Conversely, if a so-called reservation merely offers a State's understanding of a provision but does not exclude or modify that provision in its application to that State, it is, in reality, not a reservation. (Office of the High Commissioner for Human Rights 1994; emphasis added)[15]

Therefore, following this general guideline, it is important to identify Morocco's intention as regards the application of particularly article 2 and the institution of gender equality in the national legislation. In its declaration to this article, Morocco maintains that it shall comply with the international legal rules set by CEDAW unless

> [t]hey . . . conflict with the provisions of the Islamic Shariah. It should be noted that certain of the provisions contained in the *Moroccan Code of Personal Status* according women rights that differ from the rights conferred on men may not be infringed upon or abrogated because they derive primarily from the Islamic Shariah, which strives, among its other objectives, to strike a balance between the spouses in order to preserve the coherence of family life. (UN Division for the Advancement of Women)

This declaration, therefore, clearly excludes and modifies the legal effect of CEDAW in its application to Morocco, demonstrating that it can indeed be treated as a de facto reservation.

Keeping the reservation to article 2 in its original form is peculiar for two reasons. First, it limits the effect of Morocco's removal of reservation to particularly article 16 (defining gender equality) because it declares that as long as gender equality, as defined throughout the text of the convention, does not contradict the now abrogated PSC, the country shall be bound to the international order. And second, even after the removal of some of the reservations, Morocco kept the declaration in which it continues to refer to the old PSC, despite the Code's being not part of the country's legal order anymore. Retaining the abrogated PSC in place is further reiterated in its declaration to article 15 (4), concerning freedom of movement and residence, in which it refers to two articles abrogated or replaced by the new Family Code, saying that

> [t]he Government of the Kingdom of Morocco declares that it can only be bound by the provisions of this paragraph, in particular those relating to the right of women to choose their residence and domicile, to the extent that they are not incompatible with *articles 34 and 36 of the Moroccan Code of Personal Status*. (United Nations Treaty Collection 2012; emphasis added)

Article 34 of the PSC regulated the rights and obligations of the married couple, which was replaced by article 51 in the new Mudawwana—the celebrated article, introducing comanagement of household affairs; and article 36 stipulating the wife's obligations toward her husband, or simply, this article set down the rights of the husband. The article was revoked by the new Family Code as it goes against the letter (and spirit) of its article 51.

The peculiar case of Morocco's withdrawal of reservations to CEDAW is complicated by the fact that the pre–Arab Spring government headed by Istiqlal's Abbas al-Fassi did it without consulting the parliament.[16] The PJD member of parliament, Bassima Hakkaoui, is seen protesting during a parliamentary session in early 2011 at such unilateral governmental initiative in a video posted on YouTube. She asked whether in the time since the reservations were published in the *Bulletin Officiel* in 2001 and 2011 "the pillars (*thawabit*) have changed, or has the Islamic law changed, or has society and its identity changed? What exactly has changed to prompt this?"[17] Hakkaoui also protested against what she, as will be shown, considers to be mechanical gender equality contained in CEDAW's article 16. Speaking in the name of Moroccan society, she is seen asking the parliament whether such equality meant that women would be responsible to pay *nafaqa* (maintenance paid to the wife) and the deferred bridewealth upon divorce to their husbands because "this is the kind of equality that the article 16 is talking about," she concluded.

That the government submitted its withdrawal of the reservations at the UN during the Arab Spring and amid predictions of a PJD victory in the forthcoming elections leads me to conclude that the withdrawal was due to international and domestic pressures, as well as a strategy to protect the image of Morocco as a progressive Muslim-majority country in the region engulfed in revolutions and advances by the Islamists. Moreover, does this episode also demonstrate the incompetence or at least unfamiliarity of those in charge with withdrawing the reservations with the country's legal order?

Gender equality and the Mudawwana

How does the reformed Mudawwana address the issue of gender equality? This is an important question particularly considering that the law is frequently presented by the more secular members of the country's political elite as establishing gender equality. The Preamble, for example, declares that the Moroccan family is "based upon shared responsibility, affection, equality [*musawah*], equity, amicable social relations and proper upbringing of children." Both the Preamble and article 400 recognize Islamic values to be about "justice, equality [*musawah*], and amicable social relations." The Preamble, furthermore, mentions "[e]quality [*musawah*] between women and men with respect to the minimum age for marriage, which is now fixed at eighteen years for both" and article 41 stipulates that polygamy shall not be authorized "[i]f the man does not have sufficient resources to support the two families and guarantee all maintenance rights, accommodation and equality [*musawah*] in all aspects of life." The word *equality*, or *musawah*, is therefore used fairly liberally throughout the text but never in the form where it could be interpreted specifically as *gender* equality in the CEDAW sense. Instead, the reformers introduced the concept of *mutuality* of rights and obligations (*al-huquq wa-l-wajibat al-mutabadila*), which in fact renders both the wife and husband *equally* responsible for the success of their marriage, household management, and upbringing of children but does not confer on the partners' equal rights and obligations. Nonetheless, it is this notion of mutuality contained in articles 4 and 51 that is often invoked to emphasize the putative gender equality agenda of the reformed law and Morocco in general.[18]

A more thorough reading of the Family Code reveals its many inconsistencies. To be specific, rather than the understanding of mutual rights and obligations being that of equality, a wife's and a husband's roles remain based on individually defined rights and obligations within the system of complementarity. In fact, it is a husband's obligations toward his wife and children that are much more clearly spelled out than those of a wife. (It may also be this fact that prompted people to label the Mudawwana as the Women's Code.) Article 199 stipulates that husbands are legally responsible for the financial maintenance of their wives and children whereas mothers are only required to provide for the children if their father is "wholly or partly unable to pay maintenance to his children, and the mother is affluent, the latter shall become responsible for their maintenance in proportion to the amount the father is unable to pay."[19] Furthermore, it is fathers whom the law nominates to act as legal representatives of their children even if, in case of divorce, they lose custody over them. This somewhat uneven division of responsibilities, however, does not ipso facto liberate women or make the law necessarily more just to them. Quite the contrary: on the basis of replacing articles 1 and 36 contained in the PSC and introducing the concept of mutuality the law gives the family a more democratic and just appearance while it maintains the patriarchal character of the family by the very fact of explicitly spelling out only a husband's various obligations toward his family. By implication, therefore, the law designates him as the family breadwinner and its legal representative. While wives are, at least in theory, taken care of, such entitlement to financial security and protection comes with a series of duties, which is a topic that will be explored in more detail in the following chapter. Suffice it to say here that although the reformers repealed obedience as a wife's legal obligation and a husband's right, many men (and families) continue to condition enjoyment of a wife's rights on successful fulfillment of her obligations.[20] (This is what Moghadam (1998b) refers to as a patriarchal gender contract.) Not insignificant in this respect is the IFES survey, which reports that 71 percent of women and 85 percent of men believe "that a good wife should obey her husband even if she disagrees" (2010b, 13–14).

Accordingly, the reformed Mudawwana reproduces the patriarchal idea that women need protection, which denies them individuality, autonomy, and agency. The Family Code continues to operate as a protective and corrective document rather than a nondiscriminatory one in the sense of CEDAW's definition. In short, it reaffirms inequality in the marital relationship and as such contradicts the right to participate in the household affairs on an equal footing, something which the law in fact purports to guarantee in its article 51. Its repercussions are manifested in the following excerpt from the interview with Yasmin, a divorced middle-aged woman from Oued al-Ouliya, whose story will later be narrated in more detail:

I went to the court some time ago and I met there a divorced woman. I don't know what happened between her and her husband, but she was afraid that her husband would take away her daughters. We can say that even if a woman gets divorced she remains afraid. Even if she is divorced she's not completely free. She has children and that's why she's not completely free.

Perpetuation of the patriarchal character of society ten years after the reform of the PSC is reinforced with countless instances of public perceptions of women and children as men's wards. Aïda was an independent and educated woman living in Rabat, who on the basis of being a well-paid public official contributed significantly to her nuclear household. She had three children, two of whom were schooled in expensive private schools in Rabat, while the eldest attended university in France. During my research visit to Rabat in 2011 she wanted to open a savings account for her daughter. The clerk at one of the largest banks in Morocco, however, refused to help her, arguing that she needed her husband to sign the contract and open the account, despite that the money for her daughter's savings account would be transferred directly from Aïda's own bank account and from her salary. I chose this example of a well-situated and informed urban woman to demonstrate not only how deeply embedded patriarchy is but also the discrepancy between the so-called spirit of the Mudawwana, which according to secular feminists is one of gender equality, and the lived reality. The Mudawwana in and of itself is certainly not the cause of the clerk's refusal to allow Aïda to open the savings account by herself. However, in my interview with Stephanie Willman Bordat, the former director of Global Rights' Morocco-based office, she is correct in asserting that "the law [has] an educational function and sets norms for what society thinks is right and what's wrong." This anecdote serves as a telling indicator of the law's limited impact on the changing social reality, specifically women earning their own money, and on people's attitudes toward working women. There also seems to be a lack of harmonization of principles emanating from one law with other laws, specifically laws regulating contracts, assuming the clerk acted on the basis of discriminatory bank laws of some sort. Moreover, Aïda's agency and awareness of women's issues did not help her with opening the account; therefore, even when women know their rights, even when they are highly educated, the patriarchal state and/or its agents deny them their rights and refuse to recognize them as equal citizens.

Mudawwana's conflicting spirits

The secular feminists I interviewed often asserted that "the spirit of the Mudawwana" is one of promoting gender equality. Comparing my experience of interviewing feminist activists in 2008 and 2011 demonstrates that there has been a move away from promoting the idea that the law establishes gender equality on the basis of articles 4 and 51 to seeking to establish a culture of equality based on this so-called spirit of the Mudawwana. This is an important shift in the attitude toward the law because the former promotes the idea that gender equality is already enshrined into a formal law—a view that was also promoted by some of the Moroccan policy makers, like Nouzha Skalli and Rahma Bourqia,[21] in the international forums and elsewhere—whereas the latter falls short of this (perhaps recognizing the invalidity of the former claim) and focuses instead on the promotion of the culture of equality. This shift demonstrates the evolving pragmatism of its most vocal proponents—secular feminists—based on their disillusionment with the law itself as one that does not in fact create gender equality, justice, or fairness. Outaleb, in my interview with her in 2011, stated that after the initial excitement came the realization that the reformed "Mudawwana does not offer everything, or even let's say fifty percent, of what we [secular feminists] were requesting."[22] Organizations such as UAF and ADFM now use the Mudawwana as an educational tool in the hope that concentrating on the Family Code's spirit rather than its letter in their diverse awareness campaigns shall foster the kind of culture in which gender equality will become a lived reality before it can be translated into a fully implemented law. Many such activities and awareness campaigns were fully endorsed by the pre–Arab Spring governments as part of the task to combat negative stereotypes and discrimination against women in Morocco's proclaimed pursuit of promoting "the culture of equality" as well as "the culture of human rights" (CEDAW 2006, 15–16).

However, the Mudawwana appears to emanate multiple "spirits," depending on the ideological leanings of the discussant. For the JSO, Fathallah Arsalane said that "the spirit of the Mudawwana is one of struggle between the husband and wife," and it is in fact such perception of the law that is commonly invoked by people. Instead of this built-in struggle, Arsalane concluded that the family law should be based on

the spirit of complementarity between the husband and wife, on the brotherliness between the husband and wife. But even the program fea-

tured on the TV is divisive, this side against the other side. . . . We have
to promote the atmosphere of respect, mutual understanding, appre-
ciation of mutual understanding, and mutual brotherhood. These sort
of things should dominate; but when we only talk about dry rights and
laws . . . , this gives the opportunity for one to fight with the other.

But whereas Arsalane avoided a more thorough discussion on gender
equality, the organization's two leading women, Nadia Yassine and Yafout, launched into the debate. Reluctant to use the notion of gender
equality as something which is imported, Nadia Yassine prefers to engender the kind of path leading toward this ideal. "I think there should be
absolute equality," she told me, "but as an intermediary we have to convince people [about this] by using our own words . . . because words are
dangerous in our culture and because people are very sensitive towards
them." Many Muslim female activists use the notion of complementarity
to describe gender roles, but, in Nadia Yassine's opinion, they are in fact
talking about equality. Therefore, she concluded, Western and Moroccan
cultures are not in conflict, but there is the history of colonialism and neo-
imperialism, which renders the issue extremely delicate for people like her,
who have (voluntarily) taken up the role of an intermediary between two
cultures. For Yafout, on the other hand, the issue is not problematic due to
the origin of the notion, although that crops up as well, as it is because of
its philosophical and ideological connotations. As for the JSO in general,
for her too, the root of the problem lies in the fact that Morocco is an undemocratic country, where one institution reigns supreme. Consequently,
not only women but men, too, suffer from injustice, poverty, and disenfranchisement. The reform of the Mudawwana was, as Yafout contended,
"a unilateral despotic decision," which did not come from people and was
not written for people. The Family Code was merely "an upgrading of the
facade," which left the regime structure in place, she concluded. Therefore,
patriarchy, as an ingredient of injustice, has to be addressed in both the
public as well as the domestic spheres. Failure to do so is the reason for Yafout that the Family Code has not been able to affect meaningful change.

The struggle for the JSO is multidimensional (rather than gendered)
and involves combating negative attitudes and stereotypes toward
women, instituting activities to improve the position of women and men
within the larger society, and, finally, bringing about a democratic system. Their activities within the organization as well as on the grassroots
level are directed toward a long-term socialization (*tarbiya*) of their followers to change the prevailing misogynist attitudes toward women, in

addition to creating a politically informed and conscious population, who will be empowered to seek political, economic, and social change. For the JSO, therefore, women's liberation becomes possible only in the context of national liberation from the undemocratic monarchical and *makh-zenian* regime.

Turning her attention to women, Yafout insisted that the solution to women's suffering is in bringing about justice and not equality. (Justice is the notion which Yafout preferred to use instead of gender equality, although she acknowledged that the difference between the two is rather small.) It is here that her understanding of the issue diverges from Nadia Yassine's. "What is justice?" she asked as she offered the explanation. "That a woman has respect, dignity, to have the right to participate in all areas of society—in the economic, political, associational areas, in all fields." However, women cannot escape their unique biological role as mothers and hence, Yafout continued, "when we say equality, we don't mean this mechanical equality. We think that there are feminists who exaggerate in their demand for equality," which, in her opinion, trivializes women's roles as mothers. She explains further:

The function of women as mothers cannot be filled by anyone else. Her role within the family cannot be delegated to anybody else. The function (*wadifa*)[23] of motherhood is something that honors a woman; it's not a shame. This is the point of divergence between us and Western feminists—not all of them, but some radical feminists see motherhood as shameful. It's the opposite! Motherhood for us is a privilege, to give life to a child, to raise them, and educate them [in the spirit of] worthy ethics and principles and give them as a gift to society—to me it's an asset that we should preserve. We need to preserve this [women's right to motherhood]. This is justice. Justice means that a woman in her function (*wadifa*) as a mother is distinct from that of men, but this doesn't mean that mothers should be forbidden from politics. She can be a mother and a politician, she can be a mother and a businesswoman, she can be a mother and a president of an association. Her role at home doesn't exclude her from having a role in the public space.

In a similar manner, Hakkaoui in 2003, as in her parliament speech in 2011 against Morocco's withdrawal of reservations to CEDAW's article 16, criticized the "philosophy of gender" introduced by the reformed Mudawwana as being dangerous (reported in Mdidech 2003, 46). In her opinion it emphasizes "a mechanical equality between men and women," which does not take into account biological differences between the two. Abu-Lughod's conclusion on the pick-and-choose attitudes of Arab Islamists toward women's rights is germane:

> [W]hat is characteristic of the Islamists is that they stigmatize sexual independence and public freedoms as Western, but much more gingerly challenge women's rights to work, barely question women's education, and unthinkingly embrace the ideals of bourgeois marriage. Yet the latter three are elements of the turn-of-the-century modernist projects that might well carry the label "feminist" and whose origins are just as entangled with the West as are the sexual mores singled out in horror. (1998b, 243–244)

In Morocco too, the Islamists like Hakkaoui and Yafout are selective in their reading and applying of, essentially, Western feminist ideals. Women at the JSO headquarters giggled at the mention of men doing household chores, such as cleaning and cooking, since the wider population still considers the sight of men "wearing aprons" at home to be *hšuma* (shameful). Yafout related: "If ever his mother catches a glimpse of him doing [household work], he will never hear the end of it." However, because the JSO is encouraging women to finish their degrees and take up jobs outside the home, the help of their husbands with child rearing and household chores has become regarded as essential. Yafout and other JSO activists I interviewed spoke persuasively about their success in socializing men into this new domestic role. Hakkaoui too, in her public role as a successful politician, promotes the idea of the women's right to work and education, and she regularly speaks in favor of women's quotas while misinterpreting the notion of gender equality and speaking of it as an alien concept to Moroccan reality.

The divergence between the Islamists and the feminists on the issue of the meaning of equality is arguably rather minuscule, if it exists at all, but its resonance is nonetheless salient. The problem lies both in the semantics (particularly regarding the notion of feminism and gender equality) and, more important, in the ideological proclivities of the two movements. Simone de Beauvoir in her formative book on the construction of "woman," *The Second Sex*, argued that "[o]ne is not born, but rather becomes, a woman." Judith Butler in her interpretative essay of de Beauvoir's work explains what she meant with "to *become* a woman" and it is worth citing here because of the implication of this explanation for the overall argument. "To become a woman is a purposive and appropriative set of acts, the acquisition of skills, a 'project,' to use Sartrian terms, to assume a certain corporeal style and significance" (1986, 36). Gender is not only a cultural construct "imposed upon identity but in some sense gender is a process of constructing ourselves" (36). Therefore, gender becomes both a construct and a choice, albeit perhaps an involuntary one because becoming a woman is a "political program" contingent upon the mainstream ideological orientation of society a person is born into and attached to the demarcation of sexes at birth (47). (Butler herself extends the idea of gender as a cultural construct, contending in her book *Gender Trouble: Feminism and the Subversion of Identity*, 2006, that even sex is a construct imposed and thrust into bodies, which actually defies the XX-XY binary.) The Islamists continue to "biologicize" the social, and it is for this reason that for them women cannot escape their reproductive capacity, which decidedly distinguishes them from men and invalidates the issue of gender equality.

However, maternity as a distinct women's attribute is not disregarded among feminists or by CEDAW. Facio and Morgan (2009) compellingly argue that equality as understood by both the convention and the feminists does not entail identical treatment of women and men. Women do not have to be more like men to be equal because human rights are not androcentric, in which men would be made to be the standard of human experience. In other words, to demand to be treated like a human does not mean to be treated like a man. Equality, therefore, is not understood as the "mechanical equality" that both Yafout and Hakkaoui spoke against. In fact, CEDAW makes special provisions for maternity protection and women's reproductive rights in articles 4(2), 5(b), and 11(2). Accordingly, it acknowledges different biological gender roles. It is for this reason, authors conclude, that equality requires nondiscriminatory treatment, which is not necessarily identical because such treatment can result in discrimination against women either because of biological differences or the history of gendered power relations. "What equality always requires is that this treatment, whether it be different or identical, result in both men and women enjoying their human rights on an equal basis" (Facio and Morgan 2009, 23). Moreover, seeking justice and fairness—or equity—should not be the end goal because compared to equality, equity is a subjective notion not associated with human rights, which can have different meanings according to context and does not require state intervention (Facio and Morgan 2009). The Islamists in general, therefore, misinterpret the meanings and consequences of gender equality. Hakkaoui's own definition of CEDAW's article 16 and her statements of what gender equality implies when translated into the Moroccan context, discussed above, are at best ill-founded, if not a (demagogic) way to mislead the public for political ends.

During my stay in and travels in Morocco I realized that the law's supposed message as interpreted by the secular feminists, but also the JSO's attempt to resocialize society to accept men's domestic work, was perhaps not lost on the population entirely. If anything, I encountered strong attitudes toward the enhancement of women's legal rights. It is therefore important to demonstrate how these public debates and the official discourse on the enhancement of women's rights shape gender relations and what people themselves make of it. The following chapter will contextualize the official discourse on women's rights and gender equality as well as, at times, acrimonious discussions between the proponents of universal human rights standards and those of a culturally specific approach to rights and freedoms analyzed above and in the previous chapter.

Conclusion

Morocco's government promotes the image of Morocco in the international community as an exemplar for Muslim societies. In its 2005 MDG report it stated that the reform of the Family Code is "in the opinion of all national and international observers *a result of an innovative approach* that makes it a model for Muslim societies. It provides a legal basis and legal guarantees to the principle of gender equality" (2005b, 11). The report is, following the objective of the MDGs, using the notion of (gender) equality wherever possible, but without clearly defining it. It does, however, recognize that "achieving gender equality and empowerment is a long-term task" (24) that reaffirms the king's professed gradual approach to the project of enhancing women's rights. However, the analysis of the Mudawwana's purported goals, notably those of "doing justice to women" while "preserving man's dignity," as well as the peculiar case of Morocco's withdrawal of CEDAW reservations, demonstrate that the state does recognize, albeit tacitly, that there is a tense relationship and indeed a disagreement between the universal and Islamic human rights standards. The Moroccan state and society operate on two distinct levels, the Islamic and the universal, the public and the private, the collective and the individual, modern and traditional. In short, the reformed Family Code and the regime's discourse on women's rights and gender equality do give the impression of the country's progress, but underneath the liberal veneer, the regime reaffirms and sanctions patriarchal gender relations. Such divisions have been aggravated in the last few decades with the penetration of alternative ideologies and discourses disseminated through modern media, universal education, vocal civil society groups, and finally, the reform of the Mudawwana.

Children attending preschool, which is organized by the local women's association and staffed with single adult educated girls (December 2009).

CHAPTER 4

Twenty-First-Century Marriage: Gender Equality or Complementarity?

Popular impressions of women's rights

One of the less researched questions about the reform of the Family Code is whether reformed laws and the accompanying women's rights discourse have affected social reality and, if they have, in what ways. I always asked my interviewees and other interlocutors two questions: "Have you ever heard of the notion of women's rights?" and "In your opinion, what do women's rights mean?" I was curious to hear people's thoughts and attitudes toward the issue because locals frequently discussed the Mudawwana and, inevitably, women's rights. The presence of local women's associations, literacy classes, and numerous local cooperatives promoting women's artisanal work have created a more organized forum for dissemination of information regarding legal reforms, but also for sensitizing the public to the changing roles of women in the twenty-first century. I argue that the awareness of women's rights and the Mudawwana is underestimated by necessarily reductionist accounts of the situation, which contend that people's ignorance of the reformed law and the corruption of judges are primary reasons for the Family Code's lack of implementation (Ennaji 2011; Sadiqi and Ennaji 2006; Zoglin 2009).

My first significant observation was that people automatically started to talk about married women's rights rather than rights of women regardless of marital status, the latter of which is what I had thought my question asked. Yet even when I rephrased the question to include girls—I asked about *huquq al-mar'a wa-l-binat* (rights of women and girls) instead of merely *huquq al-mar'a*—their answers would still invariably concern married women's rights. Interestingly, answers of single girls were quite similar to those of married women and men with only a few exceptions. Mouna was a thirty-year-old literacy teacher with a law degree and the person who ran the local listening center (*markaz al-istima'a*) for women victims of violence. Her answer shows her awareness of the issue.

> First of all, . . . why did the notion of women's rights appear? Because women were denied rights; they didn't have any rights. To a certain extent in the past people dealt with women only as objects, it means like a thing and *safi* [that's it], not like a human being who thinks, is intelligent, who feels and has emotions, who's inventive, etc. Then came the demand for women's rights. The situation in which women lived has changed. The demand for women's rights came first to treat her as a human being (*bašar*), to not deal with her as an object anymore. She is a being, a human. Then came the demand for women's rights in the fields of politics, culture, and work so that she would become employed. What is important is that we should deal with women as we deal with men. We should give women the same rights as we give to men on the basis of the fact that the difference between men and women is only biological. There's no difference, for example, in thinking and in intelligence (*al-'aql*), or in emotions. This is the starting point for women's rights. That's why we say women's rights and not men's rights because women have suffered from injustice in terms of rights. She didn't have rights in the past. We should demand her rights and deal with her in the same manner as with men, to be equal.

I then asked her to give me examples of rights she thought women should get.

> All the rights. All the rights available to men should be available to women except those that pertain to biology. These are from nature, from God, and we won't intrude on those. For example, political rights, which give women the right to be elected, they have the right to be candidates, they have the right to have a job, have the right to be respected as a human being. A lot of things.

The majority of my interviewees were much less nuanced in pondering women's rights than Mouna was. Siham, a middle-aged married woman and a mother of five, explained that "women's rights give us importance, that we [exist] in society." Hanan, a mother of two young boys, understood women's rights in a similar manner. She stated that women's rights "are a defense of women, [that] we have rights. It means that there are people, who defend us even if we're not . . . ," she continued, but let her sister Habiba finish her thought: "[even if we're] not intelligent." Hanan's husband emigrated to work in France a week after their wedding, which coincided with King Hassan II's death and was thus rather than a jovial event accompanied with copious amounts of dancing and food, a somber reading of the Qur'an. (The state announced forty days of mourning, during which time all festivities were prohibited.) After the wedding, she moved to her in-laws to a village in Oued al-Soufla, about a half-hour grand taxi ride north of Tamazirt. She did not stay there for long because of constant tension between her and the other women in the family. (The relationship has continued to be strained. Habiba told me in 2011, when she visited me in Rabat, that it had been two years since Hanan's husband had come home. According to her, his family forbade him to visit and to send her money.) At the time of my fieldwork she lived in a rented apartment in Aït Ayyur, a five-minute walk away from her parents and enjoyed her freedom and an active social life. Her husband came home only once every few years, which prompted me to ask her whether she missed him. She did, she told me, but she also liked planning her day on her own and being able to go out whenever she wanted without asking his permission. This illustrates why she defined rights, which women should have, in the following way: "[Women's rights mean] that she is free, that no one controls her, that she goes out whenever she wants to and comes back whenever she wants, but within limits." Women's direct experiences shape their ideas of rights and injustices, but they are also realistic in that they acknowledge and respect boundaries of female propriety. Ghizlane, whom we met in the discussion on the issue of *wali*, defined the need for women's rights similarly to Hanan: "Women's rights mean that there are some things that are not given to women. That a woman is deprived of some things. Now a new term came, *ya'ni*; in the past she didn't have rights and now she was given new rights," but, she continued,

> if she gets married and her husband gives her clothes; she eats, drinks, sleeps; she has children; they are nurtured and they don't need anything, what else does she want? As for work, if her husband tells her [not to work, she shouldn't work] . . . A husband is created for work, and if he's not able to take care of her, then there's no reason to marry her.

People in general, like the Islamists, biologize gender and, consequently, societal roles of women and men are viewed in terms of complementarity rather than equality. Moreover, rights and obligations, too, reflect the gendered division of labor and are hence reciprocal—one's rights are the other's obligations, following the religious legal ideology of rights. Although this attitude toward rights was a common thread among women and men, it was much more apparent and emphasized in my interviews with men. Hasan, a middle-aged married man, was critical toward the institution of women's rights because

> they wanted to treat a problem, but created another one. They wanted to treat one problem, but then they created ten because if you give women freedom, you'll face big problems. A woman says that she wants to go to the *suq*, she says she wants to travel alone, she says she should go out and work like [a man].

But the husband still has the authority and hence the extent of women's rights "depends on my abilities," Hasan added. Primary school teacher Hajj was of a similar opinion when he stated that "since the man is the head of the family, he is the source of [women's] rights. It is he who gives these rights. If she does not have them it is because of the man." As such, rights do not exist independently but are instead contingent on the successful fulfillment of obligations toward the husband (and the family). In fact, some people interpret rights as obligations. Hasan, for example, defined rights of women as "the right to respect her husband and to raise her children. Well, to respect the parents of her husband and to respect herself." In a discussion I had with five men from Oued al-Ouliya, the interplay between rights and obligations becomes clearer. Hamid started the discussion on what they understood under the rubric of women's rights, explaining: "I can say that women's rights are what I should do toward my wife. What should my wife do for me. What are my rights and what my obligations. When I know my limits I shouldn't transgress them and others shouldn't breach my limits." Jamal, a physical education teacher in his late thirties, continued: "I can start with the religious issue. Rights are food, water, and accommodation. These three things. If a woman needs one of the three things it means that she didn't get all of her rights. And respect and honor," he finished. Hasan then summed up the extent of women's rights and men's obligations, stating that "women's rights mean to work for her and that she shouldn't need anything," to which Hamid added, "and she should obey you."

Rights of women, therefore, do not come without conditions, and obedience is one of the most important obligations of the woman and cannot be dismissed simply by abrogating the clause in the new Family Code. Women's rights are also not perceived as rights of individual beings but rather as rights of married women as family members. Furthermore, men seem to be concerned predominately with the impact of women's rights on their own rights, but some of my male interviewees became almost defensive when I asked them questions about women's rights. In an unusually heated debate with the *fqi*, he argued that men are the ones who are oppressed.

> The Mudawwana and the application of the law is the problem. We didn't have it in the past. They now perhaps apply the Mudawwana, and I can say that it's sometimes useless. It is the cause of problems. You asked about going to school and to work, so the woman can work but the man can't?! That is why there's a problem. Do you understand? There are many married couples where the wife works, but the husband doesn't. Since their wives have money, they try to impose things on their husbands. They impose rules on them. . . . There should be men's but also women's rights. . . . We hear about women's rights, but not men's rights. I don't know why. Has the man never been oppressed by a woman? I have seen men beaten by their wives. He couldn't do anything. There is oppression. Even in Europe women beat their husbands.

(His source of information about European marital relationships, he told me, was a TV program called *Ça va se savoir*, a French-Belgian adaptation of *The Jerry Springer Show*.) I then asked whether men had enough rights, to which he replied: "He has never had rights. We have never heard of men's rights."

"Why," I continued, "has the government not given you enough rights?" A bit cautious after my mentioning the government, he changed his mood slightly and smiled:

> By God, I don't know. I won't go into that. This issue is not my business. I won't tell you [whether it is] the state or not. We have heard about women's rights, the Women's Mudawwana, women's freedom, and violence against women. That we have heard about. We have never heard anything about men. This issue still baffles me. . . . Everything is on the side of the women, but no one mentions men, their rights, their issues. I've never heard about that. It's always only about women's rights, women's freedom, violence against women, but against men, no!

"But men have more rights [than women]," I was not yet ready to drop the issue, but neither was *fqi*.

"Where have you seen this?! Show me these rights that we have!" He was adamant, whereas Karima and his wife, Aicha, were giggling.

"They have them in the house. There's no equality between men and women because men . . ." I was quick to explain, with Karima finishing off the sentence: "Because men don't work inside the house." *Fqi* raised his voice, slightly annoyed at this point. "Where? At the beginning yes, but now she does nothing. For instance Aicha, what does she do? She just bakes bread and cooks. This is what she does. How is she oppressed? Tell me!" I turned to Aicha to ask her to comment, but *fqi* did not want to hear her answer. "No, you tell me, she knows! It is me who brings flour, vegetables, I go to work. Sustenance (*rizq*). Things pertaining to the outside [are my responsibility] and the problems within the house are her responsibility." I then tried to explain that there are also other rights which pertain to the public space, for example the right to work. "There's no work," he was firm.

> We have nothing. There is nowhere to work. . . . There are teleboutiques, small shops, but these are not important jobs. If a person gets 6,000 riyals [300 dirhams] or 10,000 riyals [500 dirhams], what can you do with that? He buys a kilogram of meat for 1,200 [60 dirhams] or 1,400 [70 dirhams]. It is nothing.

Many men, not only *fqi*, were quite defensive when I asked them about women's rights. Rather than feeling powerful they felt disenfranchised in the face of poor economic conditions and concomitant inability to fulfill their societal role and legal obligation as family breadwinners. Moreover, the pervasive emphasis on the enhancement of women's rights, while not guaranteeing men's rights, such as their right to earn a living if not to get a job in the public sector,[1] makes them vulnerable and, indeed, intransigent in their opposition to women's empowerment. Not much attention or resources are devoted to sensitizing men to women's rights and numerous women's rights organizations, national and local campaigns, and literacy classes—as the main forums for educating the public—have largely failed to explain to men why gender equality in general and the enhancement of women's rights in particular are also beneficial for them and their rights. The emancipation of women is thus regarded as a zero-sum game and a disruption to the traditional order, something that many people in Oued al-Ouliya view negatively.

Furthermore, in the discussion on gender equality or whether women and men are *kif kif* (the same)[2] it becomes clear that people in general perceive such notions as largely ideological and imported from the West. To a certain extent most people still do not think in these categories because for them men and women are clearly different. Zaynab, a middle-aged married woman who moved from Oujda to Oued al-Ouliya after marrying a local man, explained it in the following way: "A man is a man. Look, they're called 'a man' and 'a woman.' And look at winter and summer, winter is female and summer is male."[3] Zoulikha stated that "there's no equality because husbands work outside and wives inside the house. When the husband comes home he has to find food, clean clothes, everything, which means that his wife has to do everything." Rabat's senior judge and president of the Rabat's sector for Family Law, Muhammad Farchadou, too, opposes gender equality, and explained why during our interview:

> This isn't in the human nature. Not everything that a woman does can be done by a man and vice versa. There is complementarity between the two and there should be compromise, agreement between the two. This is at the heart of marital relations. *This is concerning marital relationships only.* There has to be equilibrium within the house.

He, like the Islamists and laypeople in general, perceives the (domestic) world in androcentric terms, where gender equality necessarily takes on a distorted and mechanical meaning. Complementarity, on the other hand, follows a "natural" order in which women's and men's biology determines their roles, while making them both *equally* essential for the survival of family and consequently society. For him, similarly to Yafout and Hakkaoui, biology plays a role only in defining domestic and not public gender roles. Domestic space is therefore gendered, whereas the public domain is becoming increasingly recognized as genderless.

People continue to distinguish between the Islamic law and the Mudawwana. If there is a difference between the two, Islamic principles will take precedence over the Mudawwana. Youssef, a teacher in the primary school in Taddert, recognized that the problem of "doing justice to women" lies in men's mentality, in their exploitation of the traditional moral order, in which women are expected to show modesty in front of men. He gave an example of inheritance because despite women having the right to inherit after their fathers' death, their brothers cajole them into handing over their share of the inheritance under the pretext of *hašma* (shame, modesty).

[Women] have the right to inherit, but there's deception and not, as we say, *hašma* [which prevents them from inheriting their shares]. For example, a brother has sisters and he tries as much as possible to [take away the inheritance share from them] . . . so he says: "I'm your brother. Will I give [the inheritance] to you so that you will give it to your husband?!" But really, he cuts her off not because of *hašma*, as they say. . . . They exploit this *hašma* because she's shy in front of men. This means that you violate her rights differently.

Many people "trick" the newly established system not necessarily out of unfamiliarity with the reformed law, as the prevailing discourse has it, but because people disagree with the law.[4] However, many may also think this deception to be their *right*. Men in particular were of the opinion that the new Mudawwana was destroying the inherent order of society, which is based on Islamic principles originating in Islamic law. They, rather than women, were also slightly circumspect when I approached them for an interview about the reformed Family Code. Some of those men who assented to the interview used it to "educate" me about the supremacy of Islamic law and/or local traditions over the Mudawwana. "In our Islamic heritage a person has rights in general, be it a man or a woman," started Hajj. "It is our heritage. Islam emphasizes women's rights more than the international forums." *Fqi*, for example, was firm that "no law can change Islamic law." The two of us, again, launched into a rather fiery debate about polygamy. I tried to tell him about the conditions, which the Mudawwana imposes on the polygamous husband, but he refused to listen to me chattering about the clauses in the new law.

I'm not talking about the Mudawwana. This is a new issue. I don't know why you want this. You like to apply these things. I told you, everything is in our religion, in the Qur'an. It is the divine law. We believe in God and his Prophet. The divine law. We cannot interfere in what is divine. The Qur'an is the first constitution of Islam. According to the Qur'an, you can have two, three, or four [wives] if you're able to. It's not an obligation to have four! . . . You keep talking about the Mudawwana and I can see now that one woman is against another woman. Why don't you let another woman get married even if the husband [already] has a wife? Is she not a woman? If she's forty and unmarried isn't this injustice? Do you understand? . . . There are some who have four or five wives. They have money and they live well. It's not my business if he marries someone who is eleven or sixteen. Do you understand? . . . But you foreigners have other things.

For my male interviewees, Islam not only elevates women but also provides order for society. The Mudawwana and the encroaching Western discourse on women's rights and gender equality, in their opinion, are destroying the inherent, if not God-given, and therefore natural order. But other men also recognized that women did lack rights. "Islam gave rights to women," explained Abdallah, "but they added other things, for example the right of women to work, the right of women to have their opinion. . . . But when Islam came, she was saved from disgrace and [Islam] heightened her position." Similarly to the position of the JSO as regards the reasons for the poor state of women's rights in the country, Hajj explained:

Women's rights have existed for a long time. It might be [that the reason for why they lack rights] is that the dominant culture covered these rights. Do you understand? If only our society was aware of our Islamic heritage we might not need this. I think that because we strayed away from the Qur'an that this is all new to us.

Aissam blamed the existing culture for the women's lack of enjoying their rights.

There are documents and rights, but there is aversion to applying these rights even if these documents exist. Why? The reason is culture. It's not always the man who's the reason. Most of the time it comes from women themselves. This means that we have inherited the kind of culture which says that a woman should always be under the authority of the man because we live in a patriarchal society. This means that the authority will always belong to the man even if sometimes the educational level of the wife is higher than that of her husband. He is always the decision maker.

Ali, a forty-seven-year-old man from Oued al-Ouliya, was of the opinion that while only "a person who understands the meaning of rights will have rights," the problem is nonetheless multilayered.

The government doesn't give many rights to men or women. Imagine a person who studied but can't find a job, for example. You have a BA but you can't find a job. You should get your rights. I should get my share from the government.[5]

Hamid listed a number of reasons for lack of women's rights in his region.

Because there is illiteracy in our region women still don't know their rights and obligations, neither do men of men['s rights and obligations]. . . . Secondly, the financial and economic situation of the family. Thirdly, many families are not opened to the outside world. These are some factors that make people unaware of rights and obligations of the other. This is in contrast to some other families because there are some families now who have Internet at home, audiovisual tools and other means that help them to get an insight into the outside world. This means that the culture, if they like it or accept it or not, entered their houses. The culture influences the son who is studying or the daughter who is studying and this also helps the mother to understand the outside world, the world that surrounds her. And even the father. But if the mother is educated (*muthaqafa*) and the father is educated, although there are negative sides to this as well, it helps them understand.

It is evident from the foregoing snippets that for these locals the issue of rights is not merely a problem of discriminating legislation. Perhaps more significantly, enjoyment of rights is contingent upon the ability of the state to provide employment, general awareness and understanding of rights, and cultural factors. According to people, state intervention is crucial for guaranteeing men's and women's rights as well as in spreading awareness about them, which is also of consequence for the discussion on equity (or justice and fairness) as opposed to equality. Although people's perceptions of rights and obligations continue to be more or less firmly embedded within the customary and/or religious Weltanschauung, their criticism of alternative ideologies and subsequent defense of *their* moral order attests to the community's being aware of and affected by the diverging discourse.

In what follows, I focus on three specific issues to evaluate the impact of the Mudawwana on society. These three issues will also elucidate how and why national identity is fluid, eclectic, and indeed schizophrenic much the same as both the state itself and the Mudawwana. These three issues are underage marriages, Mudawwana's articles 47 to 49, which deal with customizing one's marriage contract, and on a shift to a more companionate marriage.

Underage marriages

Feminist organizations criticize the work of judges (and indirectly the Mudawwana) because of the continuing high number of marriages with a minor, as manifested in the table below.

The number of marriages with an underage person has been steadily increasing, although the percentage of approved applications in 2011 was slightly lower than the preceding year. (The difference between registered underage marriages and granted applications may be attributed to marriages being postponed to the next statistical year or perhaps to broken engagements.) The majority of applications in 2010 came from rural areas, 56.72 percent of rural and 43.28 percent of urban applications, while in 2011 the trend was reversed. The percent of applications that came from urban areas was 52.76 and 47.24 percent from rural areas (Ministry of Justice 2011, 2012). It is important to emphasize that, as the numbers demonstrate, underage marriages are as much a rural as an urban reality.

The reformed Mudawwana condones underage marriage in article nineteen, but only when the judge authorizes it

in a well-substantiated decision explaining the interest and reasons justifying the marriage, after having heard the parents of the minor who has not yet reached the age of capacity or his/her legal guardian, with the assistance of medical expertise or after having conducted a social enquiry.

It was perhaps inevitable that what was meant by the reformers as an exception became the rule. This law was, explained Rahma Bourqia, one of the members of the king's Consultative Commission in charge of drafting the reformed law, intended as

an open door . . . for absorbing some problems, for cultural reasons. . . . If you make [the legal age of marriage strictly] eighteen it's very difficult to deal with these [cases] . . . For example, if a girl is pregnant . . . at sixteen years [of age] and the guy is willing to marry her, how can you deal with this if you don't have the law that will protect her? So, that was the reason, it was [meant] for exceptional [circumstances].

Because the law is not specific as regards the minimum age of marriage, some applications, although not many, are made for girls as young as fourteen. Judge Farchadou explained that it is the task of every court to decide about the lower age limit, which therefore differs from one jurisdic-

Table 4.1. Underage marriages

Statistical year	Number of all marriages	Number of marriages with a minor	Percentage of marriages with a minor	Number of applications for a marriage of a minor	Percentage of approved applications
2006	272,989	26,520	9.71	n/a	n/a
2007	297,660	29,847	10.03	38,710	86.79
2009	314,400	33,253	10.58	47,089	90.77
2010	313,356	34,777	11.10	44,572	92.21
2011	325,415	39,031	11.99	49,622	89.56

Source: Ministry of Justice 2010, 2011, 2012.

tion to another.[6] He believes that sixteen should be the lowest permitted age unless there are family problems and social issues, which will prompt him to consider lowering the age limit. The following excerpt from the interview demonstrates the judge's perception of his role not only as the guardian of the established moral order, but also as the authority who can mitigate such social ills as poverty:

> If a girl gets pregnant at the age of fifteen I fear for the unborn baby. If the families decided to solve this amicably, then a nice way to avoid scandals and social stigma and to give the child a family name is to allow this girl to get married. Or, for example, there are ten children in a family and the mother and father are poor. I can allow the marriage of their fifteen-year-old daughter to help the family with solving some social and financial problems.

Feminist organizations disagree with the law and criticize the work of judges who have allowed the custom of underage marriages to continue, contributing to the vicious circle of women's marginalization. I interviewed two ADFM activists a few days after my interview with the judge. I explained his reasoning for allowing some underage marriages, but Fouzia Yassine was not persuaded.

> You're right. They say this is the reason, this is their argument. But in reality this can't be an argument because the girl is young and this is violence [against her] when she is sixteen, fourteen, or twelve years old. At this age the girl should be in school . . . to be able to work, to learn a

trade and to work, and to be able to be independent in the future, to be financially independent! But if she's married young, younger than eighteen, she doesn't have a body, she can't carry a baby, she can't have a family. . . . But it is true that these problems exist—the girl is pregnant or her father doesn't have money [to support the family]. This does exist. But the state should assume responsibility for her. It should provide a socioeconomic environment in order for her to finish school.

Judge Farchadou invited some of these associations to attend one of his court sessions dealing with underage marriages and let them reach a decision instead of him. "Practice is not like theory," he said. "People like to think in theoretical terms, but reality is something different." He was disappointed that no association accepted his invitation. "I would love to see them to witness why I give the permission to marry off a minor," he lamented.

A judge dealing with family matters . . . is called to solve social problems and not to further complicate them. Giving permission to an underage girl, who was deflowered and is pregnant, is better than to risk that she and her child end up on the street. The objective is to preserve the destiny of the unborn child and bring forth into society a sound child, who is not resentful of society because he doesn't have a father. The law, social customs, and the Islamic law follow this logic. It baffles me, why shouldn't I allow this girl to get married, knowing that this won't cause her to be homeless, bringing shame upon her family, and cause the father of the child to go to prison because of his deed?! That is why we shouldn't have this very narrow conception and oppose underage marriages just because the Mudawwana says eighteen is the legal age. There are other circumstances which need to be taken into account.

One of the basic principles in Islamic law is avoidance of harm (Arshad 2006–2007), and it is evident from the judge's answer that it is harm done to society rather than to an individual that causes concern. Moreover, the Penal Code punishes sexual relations outside wedlock in its Chapter Eight, entitled "Crimes and Offenses against the Family Order and Public Morality," and article 490 more specifically with one month to one year imprisonment, placing further limitations on the work of judges as well as explaining Judge Farchadou's decision making.

The case of underage marriages is, according to Judge Farchadou, additionally complicated by the existence of the so-called *zawaj bi-l-Fatiha* (also called *zawaj bi-l-jamaʿa*). These are traditional marriages wherein the opening sura of the Qur'an, *al-Fatiha*, is recited. It is conducted by a group of people who act as witnesses, but without the presence of an *ʿadul* and without registering the marriage with the authorities. It is this type of marriage ceremony with which the Mudawwana deals in article 16 and reads as follows:

> A marriage contract is the accepted legal proof of marriage. If for reasons of force majeure the marriage contract was not officially registered in due time, the court may take into consideration all legal evidence and expertise; During its enquiry the court shall take into consideration the existence of children or a pregnancy from the conjugal relationship, and whether the petition was brought during the couple's lifetimes; Petitions for recognition of a marriage are admissible within an interim period not to exceed five years from the date this law goes into effect.

Judge Farchadou explained that when a judge refuses marriage with a minor some parents or legal guardians disregard the judgment and marry the girl off *bi-l-Fatiha*. In other words, when parents are determined to marry off their underage daughter, they will do so with or without the official stamp. The girl can then get pregnant, which will force her "husband" to plead with the court for the official recognition of marriage (*ithbat al-zawjiyya*), or else the couple may face criminal charges for having sex outside wedlock and encounter difficulties with registering the child in the Family Booklet. In the case of pregnancy, the judge therefore feels obliged to apply article 16 and register marriage retroactively. "It is better to allow the marriage in the first place and spare the court unnecessary embarrassment," concluded Judge Farchadou.

Article 16 gave an interim period of five years after the enactment of the law—thus, 2009—by which time all marriages would have to be registered. The Ministry of Justice toward the end of this period announced an extension of an additional five-year period, to 5 February 2014.[7] There has been a steady increase in retroactive recognition of marriages, which most probably also include unregistered marriages prior to the Mudawwana, followed by a sharp fall of over 40 percent in 2009 and an even more dramatic increase in 2011 by 228 percent.

There is no available disaggregated data that would separate pre- and post-Mudawwana marriages *bi-l-Fatiha*. However, the problem clearly exists according to the judge and Fouzia Yassine, who added:

Table 4.2. Retroactive registration of marriages

Year	Marriages	Retroactive registration of marriages	Total marriages
2004	236,574	6,918	243,492
2005	244,795	14,817	259,612
2006	272,989	16,832	289,821
2007	297,660	18,751	316,411
2008	307,575	23,390	330,965
2009	314,400	13,962	328,362
2010	313,356	11,856	325,212
2011	325,415	38,952	364,367

Source: Ministry of Justice 2008a, 2010, 2011, 2012.

The Mudawwana and judges aren't the only ones responsible [for underage marriages]. Among the poor, life is hard and the custom is to marry off these [girls] from distant villages. They have nowhere to go, school is far away and they don't have any money. So what will they do? They marry them off to protect them. Other laws don't protect [these girls]; the Penal Code doesn't protect a pregnant girl, it charges her with a crime. . . . And abortion is considered a crime according to the Penal Code. Therefore, when a girl gets pregnant with her boyfriend or fiancé, not just anyone . . . she can get pregnant with her boyfriend, they can have a good relationship, and he perhaps wants to marry her in the future, she won't go and abort because the law will punish her. So what do they do? The father marries her off her off to protect himself, his honor, and the honor of the family.

Underage marriages are thus inextricably linked with the notion of family honor and are as such an established part and parcel of preserving the status quo in a society that puts family above the individual. Judge Farchadou's concluding remark on the topic is potent, if defensive, about his role as a humanitarian:

I am a family judge so I should judge according to what is best for the family. What is family? The family is the nucleus of society. If the family is sound, society will be sound as well. And if it decays, society will decay as well. We shouldn't get restricted by different laws and the article 16. We have to understand the goal of the court in applying this article. This is my belief.

My interlocutors in Oued al-Ouliya gave me a similar rationale for underage marriages, that of protecting and reestablishing the status quo, while recognizing that the values are changing also as a consequence of exposure to modern media and greater mobility. Many of my interviewees recognized the age of adolescence as the critical moment in a person's, and particularly a girl's life, which can have serious repercussions for her if mishandled. Yasmin was a woman in her early forties. She grew up in France, and when she turned fourteen her parents took her back to her native Oued al-Ouliya and married her off to one of her cousins, who was eighteen at the time. She was very critical of underage marriages because she experienced it firsthand. Of this practice, she says the following:

> Parents say that if a girl is married, she has a good reputation (*mastura*). This is a mistake because the girl hasn't lived her life, [hasn't experienced] adolescence (*l'adolescence*). When does adolescence begin? From fourteen to twenty. At this age, emotions are created but parents put an end to these emotions. . . . A girl's parents say that she is protected, but they erase her emotions.

Adolescence for Yasmin is a crucial time in a girl's life because it is at this stage that her personality is developed.

However, when girls are expected to remain modest and shy, developing emotions and adolescence can get in the way of maintaining chastity. It is for this reason that particularly the behavior of girls and their whereabouts have to be increasingly monitored, and in some cases, parents do so by marrying off their adolescent daughter. Mama, the widowed daughter-in-law in my host family, was having problems with her adolescent sons and she defined such age (*sinn al-murahaqa*) as the time when girls and boys become bad and when they stop listening to parents. For her this was a new phenomenon and she explained the reasons in the following way:

> Parents don't control their children, even girls. [The reasons are] mobile phones, Internet, TV, telephone. That's what causes problems between girls and boys. In the past, even if a girl wanted a boy they would only run into each other by accident, but now they call each other through the Internet. Now there are phones to arrange to meet on the Internet.

This new era of technology simplifies encounters between girls and boys and makes their relationships (friendships) easier to hide from the eyes of the community. But this does not mean that people are any less suspicious, quite the contrary. Soukaina lamented: "If a girl goes out a lot of people talk about her and they ask, 'Where did she go, what is she doing?' . . . If you go out people will talk about you and if you stay in they will still talk about you. So what can you do?"

I asked Habiba why parents continue to marry off their daughters at such a young age. "I think that people prefer to marry off their daughters," she started to explain, "because they're afraid of the scandal if the girl [would have] an illicit relationship [outside wedlock], which is something forbidden in our society." Zoulikha elaborated on the issue by adding the religious dimension: "If you go back to our Islam, we should get married at an early age."

"But," I interrupted, "is it Islam or traditions?"

"It's Islam," she answered.

> The Qur'an says the age of puberty (*sinn al-bulugh*), which means before eighteen. We girls should get married before [we're] eighteen because girls are in puberty before they're eighteen. Islam says marry your children off because depravity (*fasad*) isn't good. It's not like in Europe. Sexual relations between girls and men (*l-binat ou-l-rijal*) are normal but in Islam no, they're not. As for Muslims, sexual relations between girls and men are forbidden, but they don't apply Islam. Many people [don't]. God knows they have relations.

Virginity remains one of the most important characteristics of young girls that both future husbands and their parents adamantly insist on, although no such requirement is placed on men (AbuKhalil 1997, El Feki 2013, Makhlouf Obermeyer 2000). John, the Peace Corps volunteer who lived in Taddert at the same time as I did, told me that it was an open secret in the community that boys become sexually active before marriage. This was tacitly accepted by many local men as something that was quite normal and biologically predetermined. Particularly adolescent and single boys visited prostitutes because this was more or less the only avenue to get some premarital sexual experience. The prostitute quarter is conveniently set next to the *suq* area in the center of Tamazirt, and although most men stopped visiting prostitutes when they got married, some men continued with their "relationships."[8] On the other hand, proof of a bride's virginity remains required by the groom's and the girl's families, whereas no proof is required of men's virginity. Whereas the event of blood-stained sheets being paraded across the village for everyone to see in order to preserve the good name of the bride's family was rare at the time of my fieldwork, demonstration of such a sheet still forms a necessary part of the morning after the wedding night (*laylat al-dukhla*). In Oued al-Ouliya this is a much more private affair, where only the mothers of the bride and the groom are presented with the stained sheet. It is also common that the mother of the bride keeps the sheet as a sort of proof that her daughter was indeed a virgin before the wedding night, reaffirming the family's honor. Where such a proof is not established, the mother-in-law has the power to force her son to divorce his bride, which results not only in village gossip but also in the girl's family losing its good reputation. The importance of a girl's premarital chastity is shown in the following example. The uncle of Habiba, whom she still calls Baba (father) because they had lived in the same household before he emigrated to France, threatened his daughters—and implicitly also Habiba and her older sister Hanan—that in case the sheet would not be bloody after their wedding nights he would strip them naked, drag them across the village, and leave them in the *wadi* for everyone to see that they were not his daughters anymore. (*Wadi* also refers to the area where people toss their household garbage and to a place that stray dogs make their home. Women and children cross the *wadi* with stones in their hands in case they are attacked by these dogs. The *wadi* area is therefore associated with abandonment and excretion.) No such drastic action was ever taken, but perhaps Baba's intention was more to intimidate and firmly establish the boundaries of female propriety.

"Still," I sometimes persisted, "with much talk about the new laws and particularly the legal age of marriage, parents would wait at least until their daughters reach eighteen years of age." A twenty-seven-year-old divorced woman, who was forced at the age of fifteen to marry a man nine years her senior, explained:

> Parents don't respect [the legal age of marriage] because a father's only goal is to marry off his daughters. If someone comes to ask for the girl, he will give her to him and good-bye to problems. Age isn't important. . . . I didn't want to get married but my father forced me. He told me it was better to marry someone I know. (Hajar)

But fears of parents are not entirely unsubstantiated. Girls of all ages can and do play an active role in presenting themselves as possible brides.

Moghadam (1998b) contends that one of the seven constraints for the education of girls is a shortage of female teachers, who could act as their role models (Spratt 1992). In Oued al-Ouliya, however, these female teachers and other employed girls functioned as a constant reminder of the consequences of delaying marriage well past the prime marriageable age rather than as role models to be imitated. If anything, their situation and they themselves were pitied and not celebrated. Singlehood caused some of these girls to feel "contempt" for themselves, "bored and lonely," "frustrated," and "emotionally empty." A twenty-five-year-old single girl lamented:

> I feel that I'm not complete because I miss the other part. When a girl is over eighteen she says to herself that her train has left her behind. For the most part in our region [girls] get married when they're still young. They are afraid that if they will not get married at this age they will never get married. A proverb says: A girl without a husband is like a cow without milk.

Girls flirted and secretly talked with boys and men on the less busy side streets and at weddings. They arranged for men to meet their eligible friends. They exchanged phone numbers and opened chat room accounts. Their resourcefulness had no end when it came to marketing themselves as potential brides. Most girls were aware that idly waiting for the "right one," refusing too many marriage offers, or finishing their studies while growing older meant risking spinsterhood.

At nineteen, Aziza was divorced, but she continued to be optimistic that despite her terrible experience with her first husband, she would find a suitable match. She had a joyous temperament that many local women regarded as boisterous and tantamount to indecent. Since she had dropped out of school before she got married, she spent most of her time at home because her father believed that the movement of girls outside the house should only be limited to necessary and sanctioned outings. Though this was a common attitude, Aziza's father was noticeably much stricter than the average father in Oued al-Ouliya. For example, he refused to allow his two daughters to rejoin school in order to gain a professional qualification necessary to work outside the home—Aziza's sister wished to pursue a degree in hospitality management—and he was adamant in forbidding them to join a trip to Todgha Gorge organized by the women's association in spring 2010 or allowing them to accompany their two aunts on their visit to Tangiers to help their sister a month after she gave birth, as was customary in the community. Women in my host family rushed to justify Aziza's father's sternness, saying that if left unchecked, Aziza's flirtatious nature would bring shame to her family. Decreasing the opportunities of meeting boys and limiting exposure to village gossip is one method parents use to prevent the tarnishing of their daughters', as well as their own, reputation. Without an almost impeccable record of good behavior there is a high risk for the girl to remain unmarried, effectively an adolescent, and hence a lifelong burden for her father and brothers.

Modern technology, however, has become the main medium for circumventing limitations on girls' movement. Most of the girls owned a mobile phone and some had regular access to the Internet from home without having to go to a public cybercafe. As a public school teacher, Aziza's father was able to get an affordable desktop computer and an Internet connection, which allowed Aziza and her sister to spend every free moment they had surfing the Web. Aziza had three aliases and over seventy male friends on MSN chat, some of whom she talked to on a daily basis and had even gotten "engaged" to.[9] She exchanged pictures with them, which showed her without the requisite *hijab*, taken in the privacy of the bathroom. (The bathroom offered the only completely private space in the house.) Aziza got "engaged" to a number of men, all of whom proposed to her almost instantaneously upon chatting for the first time. One of them even visited her in Tamazirt and bought her a fake gold engagement ring to prove his professed intentions. But it soon became evident that he was trying to abuse Aziza's status as a divorcée to get her to sleep with him and even made their wedding conditional on premarital sex. Aziza, though without a doubt wanting to get remarried and claiming to be in love, was not foolish enough to believe the man and gamble with her reputation, which somewhat invalidates the negative perception of her among the women in my field-site family. The community was small and it was almost impossible to keep a secret from the wandering eyes and curious ears. A sexual scandal could forever disgrace her family and have serious repercussions for her. Trespassing local rules of female propriety regarding Internet and phone contact with men was one thing because modern technology allows for discretion as well as, technically, minimizing physical contact, but compromising her and her family's honor by having an illicit sexual relationship was inconceivable. For Aziza, the Internet represented not only an important means for meeting eligible men but also a way to circumvent her father's authority because being a divorced woman her name was rarely brought to the attention of female matchmakers.

In this what seems to be a race against time, underage girls may even force their parents to marry them to the man they have fallen in love with. Soukaina, sixteen at the time of her marriage, got married on a whim and a few months later filed for divorce. (To do that she obtained a fake identity card showing that she was eighteen years old.) She fell in love with a thirty-one-year-old man, whom she met at her cousin's wedding and wanted to marry him without much ado. Her divorced mother Zaynab opposed the marriage because she knew his mother and disagreed with the way she was treating her children from the first marriage. (Soukaina's future husband was from the second marriage.) Soukaina, nineteen and divorced by the time I met her, pressured her mother to look beyond her reservations and even threatened that she would otherwise leave the house and do whatever she wanted, implying sleeping with him or even prostitution. It was only this that persuaded the mother to relent and allow her daughter to marry the man. Zaynab recounted:

> And so I said it's better for her to marry him than her going out and doing who knows what. And because I had sworn before I wouldn't allow her to marry this man, I fasted three days. I feel relaxed now because I wasn't the reason for her failed marriage. I told her that she was still young and didn't know him very well. But she wanted him so I told her "OK, then go and get married to him!"

Such cases are seemingly rare, but they do suggest the following underlying issues as regards underage marriages. Forced marriages are a problem,[10] but some girls are equally pleased with the prospect of getting married because they do not wish to end up like numerous adult girls who, for a multitude of reasons including pursuing education, delayed their marriage. The following chapter will discuss the importance of marriage for girls, suffice it to say here that calendar age does play a role because the community in general does consider girls at the age of fifteen to be mature and indeed old enough to get married, whereas waiting for too long can result in the girl staying single. *Fqi*'s answer illustrates this point well: "If she hasn't married by [the age of] twenty-five, what's left for her? She can start using a crutch!"

The phenomenon of underage marriages has not subsided, and it continues to be practiced in rural as well as urban areas. The large number of applications demonstrates that what the drafters of the Mudawwana thought would be a window turned out to be a gate, if not an invitation to continue with the practice even nine years after the reform. "Preserving man's dignity" reigns supreme particularly because the Mudawwana's goal of "doing justice to women" is set within the reality of "telemodernity," which poses a serious challenge to the traditional idea of family honor. Moreover, without the state offering viable alternatives to women's societal role or redefining it, marriage continues to represent the only available avenue for girls to improve their social status, become adult women, and be materially taken care of.

Prenuptial agreements and marital conditions

The reformed Mudawwana grants a couple about to get married the right to stipulate extra conditions into the marriage contract (articles 47 and 48), in addition to article 49 introducing the option of concluding a prenuptial agreement, which is separate from the marriage contract. Both of these optional provisions could be important instruments introduced by the reformers to enhance women's chances in negotiating a more secure future, in which their rights and interests, as they see fit, would be safeguarded. However, there are many problems with the content and wording of these provisions as well as with the implementation, demonstrating a tense relationship between the intended "doing justice to women" and "preserving man's dignity," in addition to the discrepancy between the rights granted by the general public to the "modern" employed woman and her "traditional" counterpart, the housewife.

Only two conditions, which can be included in the marital contract, are specifically mentioned in the Mudawwana—the monogamy clause (article 40) and the husband assigning the right of repudiation to his wife (article 89). Aside from these two examples, the law is silent on what constitutes legitimate stipulations. Moreover, the law is also unclear about what is meant by "these provisions" when it, in article 49, obliges the ʿadul to "inform the two parties of *these provisions* at the time of the marriage" (emphasis added). In other words, are the ʿadul required to inform the couple of all the provisions contained in *Title Four: Of Volitional Conditions in the Marriage Contract and their Effects* and hence articles 47 to 49 or merely of the option of a separate marital property agreement contained in the preceding two paragraphs of article 49? The ʿadul have to note at the end of the marriage contract that they have informed the couple of the options. However, there is no legal mechanism to verify whether or not they have indeed done so (Global Rights 2011). Judge Farchadou is of the opinion that the law only requires the ʿadul to mention provisions contained in article 49. His further explanation is important because it manifests the arbitrariness of interpretation and uneven application as a consequence of the law's lack of clarity or, in fact, poorly written stipulations, while giving judges much discretionary power.

> In my opinion, article 51 is the most important article put forward by the Mudawwana. It determines mutual obligations and rights of spouses, reinforcing and emphasizing the idea of equality between spouses. That is why I insist that the ʿadul here in Rabat include this article into the marriage contract. The law requires the mentioning of article 49 in the marriage contract, which talks about division of property, but on my own initiative I demand that they also add article 51 and notify the spouses about the content of the articles in order to ensure the cooperation between the two. [He then showed me an example of a marriage contract used in his jurisdiction, which contains reference to both articles.] This means that future spouses are informed about both articles, 51 and 49.

The ʿadul in my field site however, informs the couple only of the provisions contained in article 49 and only those couples, where the bride is a civil servant. "I inform civil servants," he told me, "specifically civil servants. But when one is a civil servant and the other isn't, then it's not . . ." The ʿadul did not finish the sentence, but his statement merely reflects his understanding of the community in which he lives and works, and hence also the general opinion of the people in the community (and elsewhere in Morocco) as regards housewives' entitlement to co-ownership of assets bought during marriage. (The vast majority of married women in Oued al-Ouliya does not work outside the house.) It is here that the power of discretion is manifested clearly. In Judge Farchadou's words: "A judge who is dealing with family matters is not only a judge but should also be a guide (muršid), psychologist, teacher, sociologist, etc. because we are called to solve social problems and not to further complicate them." Therefore, Rosen's analysis of judges' intentions in delivering judgments, in which the social background of the person and her identity matter, still resonates today (Rosen 1980–1981, 1998). Judges (and the ʿadul) are looking for a "cultural consistency" rather than a "legal and logical consistency" as is done in the West, but such a practice is nonetheless "far from arbitrary and unbounded" (Rosen 1998, 18; Zoglin 2009). It is for this reason that the ʿadul only informs civil servants because it is they, rather than housewives, who are able to buy assets. In his opinion, therefore, civil servants should have the right to co-own or split assets in case of divorce.

Locals as well were of similar opinion. Zoulikha was quite knowledgeable about the new Family Code and explained article 49 as follows:

> The judge can give future spouses a separate paper, on which they write down assets of the woman and assets of the man. Assets of the woman if she is working because a woman who is employed has assets. First, she gets a salary, a monthly salary, she can have a car, a house before she got married, which she bought with her own monthly income. This exists for those wives and husbands who work as civil servants.

The term used for housewives in Morocco is *galsa f-dar*, which in its literal translation denotes a woman who is sitting or staying at home. The most revealing instance of the potency of this expression was given during the interview with Judge Farchadou. I wanted to ask the judge whether the contribution of housewives to households was recognized in case of divorce; however, my assistant phrased it as follows: "*Ila kant l-mara ghair galsa f-dar, ma katdir walu . . . ,*" meaning "If the woman only stays at home, she doesn't do anything . . ." Such interpretation of housewives' work, or rather lack of it, neatly summarizes numerous conversations I have had with Moroccans across the country and exposes the idea that employed women or female civil servants are entitled to many more rights than housewives because of their pecuniary contribution to the household.

In addition, the opinions were also split as regards assigning the level of hardship to women's household work and men's work outside the home. Some women and men were of the opinion that women work much harder than men do and that their work is much more significant. This is not only because, as Boutayyeb put it, "housework, honestly, is tiring," but also because, in Hajj's opinion, women's work "is unpaid and very essential for the upbringing [of children]. The woman who stays at home here is not paid for what she does, but she is the foundation of everything." Others, such as Hanan, however, disparaged women's work:

> No, [men's work outside the house] is not like women's work. She stays inside the house in the shade, she turns on the ventilator [a ceiling fan] to be cooler.[11] If she's tired she sleeps, not like the poor man who works in the sun, he stays in the sun until he gets burnt and when he comes to his

wife she asks him if he brought her something. If he didn't she would tell him to leave. It's not the same.

Moreover, the word *work*, or *khidma*, was not only used when work was remunerated; some also used it to refer only to civil servants' jobs.[12] During a formal interview with Khalti Ftouch, I asked her how many of her children worked. She answered: "Three of them work and one . . . well, we can say that all of them work because [Hicham] also works. . . . One of them, *tbaraka llah*, is a teacher, the other, *tbaraka llah*, is an engineer, the one who died was a teacher, and another one works for a company." What is interesting is that, first, she included her dead son among those working, although this is understandable because civil service is highly regarded in Oued al-Ouliya as in the rest of Morocco. Second, it is significant to note that Khalti Ftouch used *tbaraka llah*[13] for her two civil servant son, but not for Hicham, who "merely" worked for a private company. Moreover, she did not mention her daughter Karima, who worked full-time as a literacy teacher, teacher in informal education classes, and a tutor to neighboring children. I later asked Karima why her mother had not included her among the working children, but she merely shrugged her shoulders and said that she must have forgotten about her. Many of my educated single friends, who were teachers in the local private school, kindergarten, or literacy classes, told me that they were unemployed despite working in these institutions twenty hours and more a week. Their type of work was seasonal in many ways because it did not give them a steady income—they received a salary only during school time—and it did not come with health insurance, paid holiday and sick leave, or a guaranteed pension like the work of civil servants. Moreover, the community in general did not value their work as "prestigious" in the same manner that they appreciated the jobs of civil servants. Many girls thus treated their work as giving them something to do in the unexciting Tamazirt and an opportunity to earn a bit of extra money for their families, but mostly for their pocket money to buy credit for their mobile phones, clothes, and other accessories. (Habiba was one of the exceptions because she gave all of the money earned to her family and kept whatever her father gave her.)

Aissam was of the opinion that giving material value to women's housework was a new (but welcomed) development initiated by women's associations:

> I think that the issue here is that associations that defend women started being aware. It is now said that women's work as housewives should

be given value. For example, imagine that there's no wife and we hire a maid. We give her a salary, which means that this work inside the house is paid. We should give value and importance to such work because it makes things easier for someone who works outside and it simplifies his circumstances.

However, recognizing the value of housework is not a recent campaign led by women's associations. An old customary right has existed in the southern Souss region. *Haqq al-si'aya wa-l-kadd*—the right to the fruits of one's strivings and hard work—continues to be applied by some judges at local courts when wives during divorce procedure petition the court for recognition of their contribution to the household (Global Rights 2008, 2011). Article 49 stipulates that in the absence of a prenuptial agreement "recourse is made to general standards of evidence, while taking into consideration the work of each spouse, the efforts made as well as the responsibilities assumed in the development of the family assets." Judge Farcha-dou explained:

> The wife can sue her husband in case of divorce in order to get her share of his wealth because of her part in taking care of the household. This is called *al-kadd wa-l-si'aya* [hard work] that the wife does. She has the right to ask for [her share in assets] because she helps with managing the household budget, she creates serenity within the family, and this helps her husband to increase the finances.

However, the problem with recognizing housewives' contribution to the prosperity of their households is complicated by the fact that most brides live at their in-laws' house, and the assets bought during marriage normally comprise of a few pieces of bedroom furniture. Therefore, in most of the cases I encountered or heard of, divorced and widowed women returned to their father's house with barely a suitcase of their possessions, containing jewelry and clothes, and sometimes empty-handed. Azzeddine, who lived in his father's house with his young family and the families of his two brothers, seemed perplexed when I asked him about his opinion of spouses dividing marital assets in case of divorce:

> What [does the couple] have that they can divide? They don't have anything to divide. What do they have? . . . If she wants to divide the cyber-cafe with me *bismillah* [go ahead!]! . . . Perhaps a trader can build a house, but we can't do this!

The issue is further complicated by the fact that in order for the labor within household to be recognized, the wife has to present evidence of her contributions. The nature of the work is such that only the women-in-law (or other women within her household) could function as reliable witnesses because it is they who have seen her at work, which may be problematic if they take her husband's side.

However, perhaps the root of the problem lies in the fact that the vast majority of my interviewees, both women and men, and those (newly) married, single, or divorced were not familiar with either the provisions contained in article 49 or articles 47 and 48. Many of them also did not believe me when I tried to explain that the law does not discriminate between housewives and those on a salaried wage of a civil servant. Karima, who had a degree in Islamic law and worked as a literacy teacher and as such participated in numerous USAID-training seminars where the Mudawwana was also discussed, was not convinced that I could possibly be right despite discussing these specific articles with her on numerous occasions. "You do know [that the issue of prenuptial agreements] only applies to working women?" she contended when we discussed my questions for the interviews with locals. She thought that asking interviewees about their knowledge of the issue was irrelevant in that region "because women are only *galsa f-dar*" and therefore not materially contributing to households. Literacy teachers and their personal opinions should not be disregarded because they are for many women an important, and sometimes the only, source of information regarding the reformed law in particular and women's rights more generally. They can act as an intermediary between the law and the community, but one that may in fact omit information or subject it to their own (mis)interpretation. Women in general attributed to female civil servants many rights, which they as housewives were not entitled to; but at the same time many of them, and particularly those educated, also recognized that the married woman's job in Oued al-Ouliya was that of a homemaker, creating a classic catch-22 situation.

I interviewed Najat, a twenty-four-year-old woman without much formal education, who signed her marriage contract a few weeks prior to our interview. (It is customary in Oued al-Ouliya to sign the contract well in advance, sometimes even a year before the actual wedding celebrations.) The bride normally resides at her father's house until after the wedding celebrations, which is when the community considers the couple to be officially married rather than after the signing of the contract.[14] I was particularly interested in talking to Najat because I wanted to hear about her experience with the *'adul*. She was quite critical of the procedures, saying that she and her fiancé spent much time waiting for the judge, who according to article 65 (III) must authorize two 'adul to draw up a marriage contract. (It is not insignificant to note that the judge in Tamazirt was not a specialist in family law, but rather a "general practitioner.") "And when we got tired of waiting, we went to the 'adul [directly]. . . . We came to him and he told us to wait [outside] until he fills out the papers. We came back after lunch to sign and that was that," she added. They both signed the contract, the 'adul recited *Surat al-Fatiha*, and the ceremony was over. When I asked her whether she knew of the possibility to conclude (sign) a prenuptial agreement, she told me that she was not aware of this option, further manifesting that the 'adul was selective, if anything, about which couples to inform based on his own personal reflection of what was expected in this community. Having said this, it is also quite probable that even if Najat had known about the prenuptial agreement and despite her approval of the division of marital property after I had explained the article to her, she would not conclude it. She said she had known about her right to stipulate conditions but thought it was not necessary to do so. "I didn't want to. I saw that I didn't need conditions and I didn't put them [i.e., add them to the document]," she explained.

Another common reason women did not use the opportunity to enhance and protect their rights[15] is because signing the contract was more or less a family affair. Malika was a teacher in kindergarten, but her working days were coming to an end because she had signed the marital contract a few months before my arrival to Oued al-Ouliya. Her husband, Tariq, was three years younger than Malika, who was twenty-four at the time of my arrival, and also her maternal cousin. During a formal interview with both of them I asked about their experience with the signing of the marriage contract.

> [The 'adul] simplified everything for us. They didn't ask us many questions because they knew our fathers. They asked them [the fathers] outside if they agreed with everything. They said yes. They didn't ask us a lot of questions. They shortened the procedure for us. They asked if everything was acceptable and they [the fathers] told them that everything was acceptable.

Not only did the 'adul interact more with the couples' fathers than with the couple themselves but they also did not follow the procedural duties of the 'adul "because they know us, *safi* [and that's it]," Malika reiterated. "They told us: 'Do you have everything you need? Did you talk to each other about this?' We told them yes and he told us to just sign and we signed without asking him anything specific. Azzeddine gave a similar account:

> He only says: "Do you know him, do you want to marry him?" "Yes" [and he concludes by saying:] "*'ala sunnati llahi wa rasuli, bismillah*" [according to the sunna of God and the Messenger, in the name of God] . . . Five minutes. There's not much [to it]. . . . *Aslan*, the girl here doesn't go to the *'adul*. She stays with her mother or somewhere else. Usually we bring the *'adul* home. We either bring them or we go to the wife's house. *Ya'ni*, the wife isn't present at that time. Her father, who's her *wali*, is. After that she comes in to agree with [the marriage]. Before this she was informed that he'll come to her. [Because] there was a relationship before they signed the contract, they [could] agree upon the day when they would do the contract.

A day after the interview, when I came into his cybercafe to check my e-mail, Azzeddine started to talk to me about the issue of the *'adul* not informing future spouses about the different options contained in the Mudawwana. He did not think that it was feasible for the *'adul* to explain the entire law to the couple because it would take him the whole day, while there are other couples waiting to get the formalities out of their way. When I contended that the *'adul* could at least inform the couple of the various options beforehand and instruct them to read the Mudawwana, Azzeddine agreed with me and concluded that the *'adul* could then ask the couple whether they had any questions for him to explain the law to them. Unfortunately, Azzeddine concluded, the *'adul* did not take his time to do that.

Perhaps not surprising is the fact that most of the divorced women or women in difficult marital situations, such as those married to immigrants or polygynous men, I talked to embraced the right to stipulate conditions. Aziza did not want to get married when she was sixteen because she did not like the man, but her mother persuaded her father to allow the marriage. (Aziza's mother often said to me that she regretted her insisting on her daughter marrying the man as, she was contrite, she had not known better at the time.) Aziza was also entirely left out from negotiations with her in-laws and the signing of the contract. It was her father who acted as her *wali*, since she was still a minor and it was he who brought the marital contract home for her to sign. She stayed with her husband for eight months, after which she returned home because of daily physical and emotional abuse that she underwent almost for the entirety of their living together. She welcomed the right to stipulate conditions "because I had a bad experience. I didn't have to do anything, wasn't present at anything and didn't know anything. There was no mutual understanding between us and he didn't respect me. He beat me."

Nouzha, a thirty-four-year-old divorced woman, also approved of the new right. She married a man when she was twenty-three. She did not know him before and, as it often happened, a neighbor brought the man to her house and soon they were married, although not for long. Nouzha left him after six months because he was beating her, smoked hashish, and drank alcohol. During the interview, she expressed her wish to get re-married, but this time she would insist on writing down her conditions.

> I'll write down as a condition religion. Someone came to propose to me some time ago, but I didn't accept him because he said that he wanted his wife to go out naked, to take off the *hijab*. I refused him because of this. I told him that I pray at *fajr* (first morning prayer), I fast every Monday and Thursday, I will not take off the *hijab*! My first condition for the husband is religion. Secondly, he should trust me. He should want what I want. If we want to do something we should agree upon it. Not that he'll take one road and I'll take another.

Women certainly expressed prudence, which might not have been present at their first marriage, either because they got married before the reform of the PSC or because they did not think that writing down conditions would be pertinent for a number of reasons. "Because," pondered Zoulikha, "if the experience failed it's better to put conditions the second time." Oral arrangements can be forgotten and witnesses hard to get. As one proverb, often repeated by my interviewees, says: "When we live in peace and harmony, we write; and when conflicts and quarrels start, then we read what we wrote," and hence people seem to be slowly accepting the idea of the significance of recording their oral agreements.

The local *'adul* told me that in his career as an *'adul* he had neither come across such an agreement nor was he ever asked to prepare it for a couple. Available national statistics show that, for example, in 2007 out of 297,660 marriages registered only 900, or 0.3 percent, of the couples also signed a prenuptial agreement. In 2009 and 2010 the number was even lower: among 314,400 marriages registered in 2009 only 487, or less than 0.2 percent, agreed on the mutual management and distribution of marital assets, while in 2010 the number dropped to 139, or 0.04 percent of married couples. In 2011, the number of cases slightly increased, but it was still lower than 0.2 percent of all newly married couples who decided upon the division of marital assets (Ministry of Justice 2008b, 2010, 2011, 2012). I was not able to find out what the figures were with respect to stipulating extra conditions into the marriage contract because it appears that they do not exist in the same form that the statistics on prenuptial agreements do. However, my inquiry among newlyweds leads me to believe that the overall number must be extremely low. None of my interviewees, and certainly not women, included such stipulations even if they knew about the option. The research done by the Maghreb branch of Global Rights (2011) on marriage contracts in the three North African countries of Morocco, Tunisia, and Algeria corroborates my findings. They found that out of 75,173 marriage contracts, which their assistants reviewed in Morocco, only 1.9 percent included such clauses (10). Among the most frequent stipulations placed by brides were her right to work outside the home and continue with education after marriage, her right to visit and care for her family, a monogamy clause, and the right to choose the place of residence. Interestingly, many of the recorded clauses were included by men, such as requiring that the couple lives with his parents or that his children from the previous marriage reside with the couple. The law is, again, unclear as to who has the right to stipulate extra conditions, although the intention of the drafters, I was told by Rahma Bourquia, was to give women the opportunity to extend their rights. Some of these clauses, Global Rights found, were in fact violating the law and others the constitution. Stipulations, such as demanding that the wife renounce her right to work outside the home or abandon her formal education after the wedding are denying women their right to education and employment guaranteed by article 13 of the 1996 constitution (and article 31 of the post–Arab Spring 2011 constitution). Yet, in my field site such a right is not recognized. Boutayyeb, Taddert's primary school director, for example, said to me: "Moroccan law doesn't allow girls after they get married to continue their studies at the level of middle or high school. It doesn't allow her!"

Moreover, some grooms in the Global Rights sample renounced in advance their legal obligation to pay their wives financial maintenance (*nafaqa*), expenses paid during the legal waiting period (*idda*) following repudiation, divorce, or annulment of marriage (if it was consummated), or refused to give their wives a share in marital assets upon divorce.

One of the often invoked reasons against either the prenuptial agreement or stipulating extra conditions into the marriage contract is that such demands demonstrate bad faith, while the brides display their bad intentions and lack of modesty. Ali, for example, explained it in the following way:

> The word splitting (*al-taqsim*) is shameful for people to say at the beginning because will I want to get married [to her]? I will think that the woman wants to break up. It's shameful to mention this at the beginning. Why? Because I will think that the woman has something on her mind, that she wants to get divorced. . . . Even if the *ʿadul* asks the man [*sic!*] what they decided upon the woman can't say "we split."

Girls in Oued al-Ouliya I spoke with normally did not utter a word during family negotiations, if they were present at all, let alone speak up during the signing of the contract to demand their rights to be written down. The *ʿadul* confirmed that he asks girls if they consent to marriage in order to establish that they have not been coerced into marrying the groom; however, girls and women I talked to asserted that there was not much they could actually do or say. Many were ashamed to speak up, but even if they would attempt to say something, the repercussions could be disastrous, not only because shameless brides could lose their fiancé but because showing impertinence by disrespecting local rules of female propriety could diminish their chances of ever getting married. Rumors about rebellious and immodest girls spread fast and their names as available potential brides could forever be erased from the lips of women matchmakers if girls challenged the elders. Mudawwana's goal of "doing justice to women" can be perceived as violating customary norms of women's modesty. Therefore, the problem lies not in that the girls were not present at the signing of the contract; on the contrary, all of my interviewees assured me that the bride's presence is *daruri* (necessary). Instead, the girls' presence is a mere formality and understood as their consent to marriage.[16]

On the other hand, I also heard women criticize the younger generation of girls, who, they argued, were only after money and as Mama concluded, "[Girls] don't put conditions [because what's important to them is that] he has money. She doesn't care about anything else." Hence, Global Rights is right in raising the question of "how much of this opposition is to conditions per se, and how much is really against women in particular stipulating conditions to protect their rights" (2011, 10).

A similar conclusion can be reached for the absence of and resistance of the *ʿadul* to inform the couple of their right to conclude a prenuptial agreement. Many people opposed such a contract because, as mentioned above, it implies bad faith in the manner of "are we getting married or divorced?," which is what I often heard from my interviewees when we discussed the matter. Yet, my interlocutors were not consistent in their reasoning because they, too, insisted on the bride's *wali* being present during the signing of the marriage contract under the pretext of protecting the girl in the event of marital discord. People therefore do contemplate the possibility of divorce before the couple is even married. Families are, more than anything, pragmatic in marriage negotiations to assess that the would-be marital candidate for their daughter or son is an appropriate match in order to avoid the all too frequent divorce.[17] Furthermore, families' prudence is also demonstrated by the fact that they and the ʿ*adul* insist on the father's presence (or of some other male relative) during the signing of the contract to reaffirm that the girl has *asel* and that she is protected. Therefore, the issue with both extra conditions and a prenuptial agreement is that they create a new reality and a new method for the girl to protect her rights, contravening the family and challenging the established customs and traditions.[18]

Perhaps the most widespread opposition to signing a prenuptial agreement is that it, as mentioned above, shows bad faith on the side of the bride and her family. Azzeddine explained why:

> No one would accept this idea. You treat [marriage] as a business. In a way [it means that] you come to your wife to ask her: "How much do you have? That's what I have. . . ." I want to get married, I bring her a paper and tell her that I have these assets. "What do you have?" We'll agree to do something. This is necessarily like buying and selling. That's not marriage anymore. Buying and selling. I bring my money and construct a building, then we'll say that we divide it.

The idea of a separate document, in which spouses can divide their marital assets, must have been on his mind even after the interview because he initiated a conversation with me the next day. At the end of our conversation in his cybercafe, he stated bluntly: "I don't agree with [dividing the assets], so what do you do then?"

Because there is no model marriage (or prenuptial) contract, which could be disseminated to all judges and consequently their ʿ*adul* across the country, the content of the contract varies from one jurisdiction to the other as does the interpretation of articles such as 47, 48, and 49. Judge Farchadou instructs his ʿ*adul* to merely read the contract to the newlyweds without interpreting it (or the specific articles included in the contract) based on their own ideological persuasion as they had done in the past. While the reason for his instruction is undoubtedly to avoid biased misinterpretations, his directive is nonetheless not void of problems. The articles are read to the newlyweds as they are written—in classical Arabic and in convoluted legal jargon—regardless of whether or not his clients are versed in the language or the legal lexicon. This practice represents an enormous obstacle, especially in a country where in many areas literacy does not extend beyond 50 percent, and based on my observation even such figures are in fact too high, and in areas where people may not even be Arabic speakers such as in Oued al-Ouliya. Moreover, particularly in the summer season, which marks a high wedding season, signing of a marriage contract becomes a quick formality, in which neither the ʿadul nor the families want to devote more time than is necessary to discussing the piece of paper in front of them. As far as families are concerned, negotiations regarding the bridewealth, rights, and other particulars were discussed properly and in much detail well in advance, and it is the family, after all, which shall guarantee and protect the rights of the bride rather than a piece of paper or the Mudawwana.

Despite the Mudawwana extending the rights of brides (and, evidently, grooms) through prenuptial agreements and a customized marital contract, the options are rarely used. True, many people do not know about the clauses or misinterpret them; yet it appears that the fault lies not with the people but with the state. Institutions and agents in charge of implementing the law have largely failed in informing the public about the possibilities and rationale behind them. Without clearly defined laws regulating both options as well as the responsibilities of the ʿadul with respect to informing the couple (and their families) of the articles, without having recourse to independent legal advice before signing, and without a uniform model contract used in the country as a whole it is inevitable that the application of these three articles is arbitrary and weak. The law with its many loopholes allows for significant discretionary rights of judges and the ʿadul, who apply the law according to their own beliefs and personal assessment of the situation in the pursuit of maintaining the (patriarchal) status quo.

Marital relations in flux

Finally, how has the Mudawwana, with its multiple spirits provoking debates and "introducing the principle of democracy within the family" (Rahma Bourquia, interview), affected marital relations? Or, to what extent was the reform merely reflecting social reality? The evaluation of these questions is not clear-cut, and it is further complicated by the multitude of clashing discourses and, essentially, divergent social realities. The observation that Moroccan society is changing is no breakthrough revelation, but how does this change apply to marital and gender relations? One such evolution is the broadening of the meaning and the length of the engagement period. The newspaper *Aujourd'hui le Maroc* reported in 2002 that "there is a high proportion of divorce among couples who have been married between two and five years because 20.8 percent of them divorce subsequently" (Al Oumliki 2002). This percentage, however, "tends to lower the longer the period of marriage, until it reaches the lowest point of one percent among those married for over twenty-nine years" (Al Oumliki 2002). Sometimes the reason can be the "disproven" virginity of the girl, or the bride seeking divorce on the grounds of domestic violence or an antagonistic relationship between her and the family-in-law, but oftentimes locals admitted that it was also because weddings ensued too soon after the first meeting. *TelQuel* (Achehbar and Lamlili 2006), for example, corroborated this claim in the article about single people in Morocco, concluding that the rising divorce rate in the country was also a consequence of society not allowing the couple to get to know each other intimately before the wedding. Dating in the sense of a prolonged romantic and sexual involvement outside of wedlock continues to be condemned. However, one result of the technological modernization and migration is also the inevitability of the encroachment of "foreign" styles of living—both Western and wider (urban) Arab, as can be seen in the Egyptian and Lebanese influence exerted through pop culture, albeit a much more conservative trend coming from the Gulf states can also be observed in the *Ikhwanization* of some people's sartorial preferences and their attempt to establish a new and imported moral order. (As stated in Chapter 2, both "Westoxication" and "Eastoxication" can be equally found throughout Morocco.) This certainly has had an impact on the local customs, but it remains uncertain which direction it will follow, particularly when it is contingent upon the overall degree of conservatism of the family as well as the specific social milieu in which one lives.

For now, the marriage customs have changed, for the prolonged engagement period has become the established part of the marriage process. Those families who can afford it throw an engagement party, which functions as a sort of rehearsal wedding party. This is a much smaller affair than the ostentatious wedding itself, organized for both families to get to know each other and to bring gifts to the bride. But its purpose is also to notify the community that the girl is engaged. As a result, the couple is allowed to spend some time together even in public, although almost always accompanied by a friend or someone from the girl's family. Engagements therefore have, in many respects, become a socially sanctioned way of dating. Many relationships break up during the engagement, but whereas divorces have legal and other consequences engagements usually do not. I met and heard of many girls who had been engaged a few times, but broke off the engagements because of incompatibility or falling out of love. As such, protracted engagements, which can last for over a year, are one strategy to pragmatically address and prevent the reported high rate of divorce, ensuing within the first years of marriage; but many people also tacitly recognize a "modern," or in Abu-Lughod's (1998, 2005) words, a bourgeois model of marriage—the companionate marriage.[19]

However, such a shift toward a marriage based on love is not void of conflict. I discussed differences between marital relations in the past and in the present with my female and male interviewees. Despite the majority of them evaluating these changes as progressive, some of them nonetheless looked back at the time of their parents' or their own youth with a sense of nostalgia. Abdelouahid, an old man, who partook in one of the discussions I had with men, said that when he was younger, there were fifty-three people living in the house and only one had the authority. Commenting on power relations in the family, he said that "in the past men ate meat and gave women only the sauce (mrka)." His reflection also shows the extent of women's demureness, something which, according to many of my interlocutors, has been largely lost among the younger generations. They ruminated on marital relationships of the past as being based on gender harmony, where everyone knew their role and place, without challenging them. Ali, for example, compared his marriage with that of his parents: "In the past [my father] didn't mention his wife's name; now if I want to call her I should call her by her name, Souad. My father has never called my mother by her name, he always said to her 'Here, this one (ahiya, thah), where are you now?'" Hasan, too, criticized contemporary women, saying:

> In the past, your wife could live with forty people in the same house.
> Now she says she should live independently from the others. . . . Women
> in the past were patient, even if you only brought her something once
> every three months she was quiet about it. But now she says that she
> wants to buy new things every day. It's too much, you can't imagine it!

Life and relationships appeared much simpler in the past than they do in the "schizophrenic" twenty-first century. But such a view of marital harmony may also be a consequence of spouses rarely talking to each other, even at home, and women never contradicting their husbands or men in general. In other words, locals think of companionate marriage as not only based on love but also on conflict. Zaynab used the word *'ayb* (shameful) to describe what was meant for a wife to contradict her husband, even if injustice was done to her:

> In the past, there was no conflict (*sda'*) between spouses, but now there is. In the past when spouses had problems, the wife didn't return to her father's house even if her husband had beaten her, as it was shameful (*'ayb*) to do so. Now, he only says one wrong thing and the woman returns to her father's house.

In a similar manner, Khalti Ftouch, perhaps alluding to the marital relationships of her own two sons, defended the patriarchal relationship of the past, arguing that the younger generation of women had too much power, exceeding that of the husband:

> Wives today control their husbands. The poor husbands are cornered. Wives do what they want to and control everything. They don't care about their husbands. If he wants to say something, she corners him. He can't say anything. If he breaks up with her, she demands their home and he has to rent a house. He's forced to do so even if he has children.[20]

The move toward a more companionate marriage, which challenges the old patriarchal power relations, may be the reason for people to think of marital relations as disharmonious and necessarily disrupting the "traditional" gendered power relations. Notions such as *tafahhum* (mutual understanding) and *tašawwur* (mutual consultation) have become key notions for many of my interlocutors in describing a successful marriage, and it is these two notions that accompany the move toward a companionate marriage (Abu-Lughod 2008). Many girls talked to me about love, and when I started to teach them English and asked them what words in English they knew they would giggle and say, "I love you." (The word *hello*, however, was unknown to them.) Soap operas and pop music certainly influence their perceptions of alternative relationship models, but some women also remained realistic in what they expected from marriage.

Hayat, a teacher in Taddert's kindergarten, thought that although love was important, it might not be easy to find. "What happens if you don't find the person who you'll fall in love with first? Are you going to stay single?" she asked. Love, therefore, though desired, is not necessarily a requirement for a successful marriage; rather, it is mutual understanding, and that transcends love. For Hamid, *tafahhum* "is a difficult word. It means love, to understand and respect each other." Azzeddine as well, mentioned "respect" as the underlying principle of mutual understanding. Khalti Ftouch, despite her criticism of wives' assertiveness nowadays, was positive about the importance of mutual understanding between the spouses. In her opinion, *tafahhum* means that "they understand each other, they are good to each other, and that they love each other. Their intention is the same." Perhaps the most elaborate definition of mutual understanding was given by Mouna.

> It means that they should think alike. The ability to discuss, for example if there's a problem, there will be a discussion so that one will know the point of view of the other. This is my opinion and this is your opinion and at the end we'll arrive to one opinion, which will be beneficial for both of [us]. Mutual understanding means that one mind shouldn't control the other mind. The wife's point of view shouldn't be the only one or the husband's point of view shouldn't be the only one. Finally, mutual understanding is a dialogue. The ability to make decisions in the form of consulting one another, cooperation between them, discussion and dialogue between them to arrive at one opinion about everything, not only on a specific subject but everything concerning their lives.

Thus it is mutual understanding that reigns supreme in the idea of companionate marriage, but mutuality does not give rise to equality because husbands retain their power to completely disregard their wives' wishes, if need be. One such example is the question of whether women should be allowed to finish their studies or work outside the home after they get married. A typical answer of female interviewees is summed up in by the following response given by Zoulikha:

> It's allowed if spouses agree upon it [before the signing of the marital contract]. If her husband wants it, it's possible. . . . Even if she wants to [work outside the home or continue with education], if her husband doesn't want it, she can't go [to work or school]. In Islam, if the husband doesn't approve (*rida*) of [his wife] going out, [she] shouldn't go out. . . .

When you go to your husband,[21] even if you had a job before, if he tells you to quit your work you should quit it. But you have to agree upon this before signing the marital contract.

(Women also mentioned this "agreement" between future spouses as one reason for not resorting to their right to stipulating extra conditions into their marriage contract.) Mutual understanding therefore implies that the wife has a greater say in the decision-making process, but the final decision still hinges on the man's role as the patriarch. Though writing about Lebanese families twenty years ago, Joseph's words resonate with the situation in much of contemporary Morocco. She writes that "the patriarch sees his wife . . . as [an] extension of himself. He speaks for them, makes decisions for them, reads and expects to be read by them. The patriarch conflates his will with the will of the family" (1993, 461). And women in my field site as well as in other areas I visited and researched in a similar manner continue to conflate the will of their husbands with their own will.

Although women, as the above example shows, tacitly recognized such power relations, it was men who were much blunter in stating this fact and related it to obedience. Hamid admitted that the laws of the reformed Mudawwana were not applied at his home "because in my house there's still the authority of the man even though the Mudawwana came to fight against it." *Fqi* explained the link between obedience and mutual understanding in the following way:

Obedience is necessary for the understanding between the husband and wife. If there's understanding, everything will be good. This exists among Muslims, Jews, and Christians alike. Without mutual understanding, the Mudawwana can exist or not. Mutual understanding is the true foundation of human [relations].

I then asked him about his definition of obedience. "It's a lot of things," he replied. "Even singers sing about it, it's not just in the Qur'an. The woman should obey her husband. The man works and suffers outside, and when he gets home, he should find a nice atmosphere rather than [one that] makes him nervous." I felt a bit cheeky at this point, as our interview had already gone on for more than an hour and *fqi* had not thrown me out of his house, despite the fiery dialogue, so I asked him whether men also had to obey their wives. After all, I concluded, would not this be equality? "Equality?" he was astounded by what he was hearing. "How is this equality? If the woman doesn't cause problems, will he cause them?" Karima interrupted and asked him the question again. "What do you mean the husband?" he was still annoyed by the question. "That isn't obedience. It's God who stated that the woman has to obey the husband. I can tell you the Hadith, so don't discuss it with me! What is obedience? It is a matter between the husband and the wife."

Yet, most married women interviewed, both young and middle-aged, felt more empowered compared to their mothers. According to them, their husbands give them money to manage some daily household expenses, which was something unimaginable in the time of their mothers. It is adult male members of the family who do the bulk if not all of the food shopping at the weekly *suq*[22] and small locally owned grocery stores and who deal with buying furniture and other large or more expensive items for the house. However, Latreille is right in contending that although men "officially conclude economic transactions[,] [this] should not conceal the fact that those transactions may be initiated or overseen by women" (2008, 622). Zakariya, the head of my host family, always consulted his wife (and through her the other women in the house) about groceries and bigger purchases such as furnishings.

Contemporary women or brides have more power within the house compared to married women in the past, which can lead some of them to pressure their husbands to move to a rented apartment on account of their strained relationship with the in-laws. Mutual consultation gives them a sense of agency and relative power over not only financial issues but also their marital life, and thus should be interpreted as a feeling of empowerment and recognition of the enhancement of women's rights compared to their mothers' situation. However, matters pertaining to the macro level of households, such as women's work and movement outside the house, continue to be controlled by and contingent upon men's approval. Therefore, division between public and private spaces remains relevant. The private, domestic sphere appears in this context to be much more flexible and prone to change than the public space. It is the behavior outside the house which determines the honor and the reputation of the family, and thus women's movement has to be much more closely supervised.

It is true that women assessed their situation to be better compared to that of their mothers or the previous generations, but an analysis of their answers and my observation of marital relations reveal a continuing pattern of inequality and social deprivation for women. My observation is corroborated with the data from a Ministry of Health Survey, conducted

Table 4.3 Women's decision-making abilities in comparative perspective

	Percent of women deciding by themselves about their own health	Percent of women deciding by themselves about everyday purchases for the household	Percent of women deciding by themselves about visiting family	Percent of women deciding by themselves about all of the included possibilities*	Percent of women not participating in any of the possibilities included in this table
Age					
15–29	13.6	10.4	22.2	7.2	55.3
20–24	27.3	22.2	34.6	17.0	34.8
25–29	39.9	36.3	47.0	26.9	22.2
30–34	51.9	46.4	57.6	38.0	13.3
35–39	60.4	54.5	64.8	45.1	10.2
40–44	64.6	60.2	69.6	50.6	5.8
45–49	66.1	62.7	69.7	52.6	5.5
Marital status					
Single	20.7	16.1	28.4	10.9	46.7
Married	56.5	52.5	62.2	43.1	8.2
Divorced	67.3	61.4	70.1	56.0	14.2
Milieu					
Urban	49.0	45.0	54.3	35.5	24.9
Rural	31.4	26.5	39.3	22.2	24.5

Source: Ministry of Economy and Finances and UNIFEM 2008.
*I did not include all the options as presented in the original table.

in 2003 and 2004 (in Ministry of Economy and Finances and UNIFEM 2008). Generally speaking, the older the woman the more she was able to decide by herself regarding various aspects of daily life. Marital status also impacts the decision-making powers; hence, single girls were much less likely to participate in the process or act more autonomously. Moreover, rural women were less likely than urban women to make decisions independently.

Many women I interviewed also felt uncomfortable with the increase in their rights. Fatima, an older, illiterate woman, explained that when her mother-in-law had still been alive, she had been used to consulting with her. However, despite Fatima learning about the Mudawwana's clause on "the consultation on decisions concerning the management of household affairs," she could not bring herself to follow the stipulation because she was not accustomed to discussing matters with her husband. She therefore asked me whether she was obligated to apply the law, fearing that she was doing something wrong.

Furthermore, women like Hanan and Nadia, who by and large run their households because their husbands work abroad or live with the second wife, did not consider themselves to be the heads of their family. They were dependent on the money sent to them by their husbands, which was sometimes contingent upon their relationship with the in-laws, as the case of Hanan discussed above related. As de facto single women, their behavior and outings were also under increased scrutiny of the community and their families. Moreover, they had to take over men's responsibilities, such as buying groceries and going to the *suq*. De Haas and van Rooij (2010) convincingly argue that long-distance migration of men from the Todgha region, an area close to Oued al-Ouliya, left their wives as temporary heads of households, resulting in an increase in their wives' responsibilities, something that women themselves did not perceive as a positive experience. The authors conclude:

> Women have been pushed to assume responsibility for entire families, and to intervene in domains and processes that were not formerly in their sphere of influence. As this new role is generally not assumed out of free choice, it should not automatically be equated with "emancipation" in the meaning of making independent and conscious choices against prevailing norms on gender roles. (60)[23]

Whereas *kif-kif*-style empowerment may be a goal among Westernized urban elite women, women in Oued al-Ouliya did not feel it was in their interest or ambit to tread into men's territory. By the same token, they did not want men to take over their responsibilities. Each one of them is suited to perform her or his duties on the basis of their biological differences, which explains the laughter I inspired when I talked about the division of labor in my own household. Women often rebuked me for my husband doing, what they perceived as, women's household work because in the context of Oued al-Ouliya it was shameful for men to do "women's work" and vice versa. In a similar manner, during my discussion with Aissam on gender roles in Europe, he shook his head disbelieving what he was hearing and finally asked: "And your husband is OK with cleaning the house?"

Conclusion

The discussed cases of the *wali*, underage marriages, and extended marital contracts show that the Moroccan general public is torn between the available binaries of modernity versus traditions and Islamic law versus universal human rights standards, much the same as are Moroccan women's rights activists and the regime. For many people "doing justice to women" implies injustice to men and, consequently, the family as the core of society, particularly in the absence of a system that would safeguard the rights of all, women and men alike. The unjust economic and political system denies men their rights, such as the right to employment, leading many men to question and indeed oppose the pervasive discourse on the enhancement of women's rights.

Moreover, Lynn Welchman is right in concluding that in the Moroccan Family Code "the principle of *qiwama* [authority] is construed as not necessarily gender-specific and indicating care and support rather than hierarchy" taking into account the lived-reality of many people (2011, 17). However, local practices diverge significantly from the postulates of the law. My ethnographic material demonstrates that authority continues to be perceived as not only gender-specific but also contingent upon seniority and, as the following chapter will further argue, marital status. While care and support are the underlying principles of and the justification for male authority, they are predicated on the continued significance of honor for the identity and the survival of the family. It is ultimately this idea of family honor that requires hierarchy in gender relations. For the time being women's rights and gender relations remain firmly embedded in the patriarchal family ideology.

Finally, this chapter dispelled the myth of ignorance about the law, which many politicians and activists have been pointing their fingers at as one of the main reasons for the nonimplementation of the Mudawwana. The reality, however, shows quite a different picture. People's criticisms, their strong opinions, and their willingness to discuss the Family Code and its individual provisions demonstrate that the public is far from ignorant or indifferent to the issues emanating from the reformed law.

Girls from informal education classes at their class trip in Todgha Gorge (April 2010).

CHAPTER 5

Rural, Educated, and Single

In 2006, *TelQuel* ran a cover story on bachelors in Morocco entitled "Céli-bataires ou bikheeer" ("Single and Doing Weeell").[1] The authors report that singlehood is a new and growing social phenomenon in the country. On the cover of the magazine is a suggestively dressed woman with a wonton expression on her face, stepping into, I speculate, her apartment with a man whose face we do not see but whose hand is on her buttocks. Reading the title of the cover story printed on the side of the picture, while looking at the photo, may give the reader the impression of single women as loose, immoral, or even prostitutes. The article concentrates on urban female and male singles, who have either been unable to get married as a result of financial and other constraints or have chosen to focus on their careers, despite the enormous societal pressure put on women in particular to conform to the general expectations. A large part of Moroccan society, rural and urban alike, continues to disparage single women "as if," write the authors, "for a woman there is no salvation outside marriage. It is a belief more firmly rooted and even shaped by the education of a Moroccan girl" (Achehbar and Lamlili 2006, 43). Sociologist Mustapha Aboumalik, who was interviewed for the article, explains that the recognition of such life choices is contingent upon the approval of other people. It is for these reasons that among women (voluntary) singlehood is largely an educated urban and upper-class phenomenon because their families and the circle of friends may be more open to alternative (or "American," as the authors regard them) lifestyles. "But," ends the article,

> rest assured, dear singles, not everyone hates you. Not least because you're great consumers, with thick wallets, and the impulse to buy still

very much alive. For, you're all the designated customers for banks and their revolving loans, real-estate agents and their fully equipped studios, car dealers and their two-seat convertibles, telephone operators and their unlimited plans, fast-food chains and their maxi menus, cosmetic labels and their miracle cremes, fitness and diet programs, cosmetic surgeons and their Botox, travel agents and their special "singles" tours, night-clubs and their regulars tables . . . And after you consumed, bought, traveled, rejuvenated, and beautified you will finally find the right fit. Because did you seriously think that in Morocco you can escape marriage? (44)

For the urban, educated, and middle- to upper-class singles, delay-ing marriage may be a personal choice that their parents, as well as the surrounding community, either willingly or begrudgingly accept. These urbanite singles may indulge in such a life that "offers an extraordinary sense of freedom, difficult to find anywhere else" (38). What about edu-cated girls from provincial and conservative areas, who despite their edu-cation, cannot enjoy the spoils of getting a well-paid job, of moving away from their parents into a singles apartment, whose families and commu-nities cannot conceive of them as autonomous individuals, and who, un-like the woman in the *TelQuel* photo, cannot pursue relationships out-side wedlock, either for having a moral issue with dating or for being aware that their communities have eyes and ears planted everywhere? (It is true, as *TelQuel* reports, that having illegitimate children may even be overstretching the boundaries for the otherwise liberal urban singletons. Having said that, some do circumvent the interdiction by getting married with the aim of getting a child and soon thereafter divorce [43–44].) The gap in the public perception of singlehood between urban and rural areas can further be seen in the jargon applied to describe a single person. In the urban parlance a single man is called *zoufri* and a woman *azri*, meaning unmarried, whereas their female rural counterparts are called *ba'ira* and without a masculine equivalent. The meaning of *ba'ira* is much more value laden than *azri*, not least because it denotes "a spinster, past the expiry age and henceforth almost impossible to marry" (43). The word is taken from the Moroccan peasant jargon, describing an infertile land, impossible to plough. Such semantics exposes differences in ideas of female singlehood based on social class and locality, as well as adding nuance to the meaning of the social exclusion of rural educated single girls.

Education of girls and boys, of course, is essential. However, does edu-cation necessarily cause a linear progression from disenfranchisement to empowerment? This chapter shall demonstrate that while there are many successful examples of women fitting in this model, there are also many who failed to make it onto the success story wall of fame of the development community.

The importance of education?[2]

Amartya Sen perhaps more than any one economist-cum-development academic influenced the thinking and policies of major international development organizations concerned with poverty alleviation and, concomitantly, the empowerment of women in the Global South. In his book *Development as Freedom* Sen writes that even "the limited role of women's active agency seriously afflicts the lives of *all* people—men as well as women, children as well as adults" (1999, 191). What the development community needs, he argues, is "to take an agent-oriented approach to the women's agenda," because it is such agency that can play a decisive role in "removing the inequities that depress the *well-being* of women" (191). According to Sen and the wider mainstream international development community, the well-being of women is shaped by their ability to get an education, work outside the home, earn a living, have ownership rights, and be recognized as active managers of households. There is, we are told, an almost organic correlation between these aspects, following the perception of progress as linear modernization with a guaranteed outcome and success—women's empowerment and gender equality. Sen explains:

> These different aspects (women's earning power, economic role outside the family, literacy and education, property rights and so on) may at first sight appear to be rather diverse and disparate. But what they all have in common is their positive contribution in adding force to women's voice and agency—through independence and empowerment. For example, working outside the home and earning an independent income tend to have a clear impact on enhancing the social standing of a woman in the household and the society. Her contribution to the prosperity of the family is then more visible, and she also has more voice, because of being less dependent on others. Further, outside employment often has useful "educational" effects, in terms of exposure to the world outside the household, making her agency more effective. Similarly, women's education strengthens women's agency and also tends to make it more informed and skilled. The ownership of property can also make women more powerful in family decisions. (191–192)

Women's power is therefore defined as "economic independence as well as social emancipation" (192). This in itself has become the manifesto of many women's rights and poverty-alleviation campaigns, repeated ad nauseam. Education in such campaigns has become the principal (and) most effective means to engender the apparent linear progress. One such report, entitled *What Works in Girls' Education: Evidence and Policies from the Developing World*, summarizes that the overall conclusions of the impact of educating girls on families, economies, and nations "are straightforward: educating girls pays off *substantially*" (Hertz and Sperling 2007, 1; emphasis in original). The authors recognize four major areas of educational benefits: more education means a higher salary and a faster national economic growth, as well as more productive farming; more education means smaller, healthier, more educated, and happier families; more education means lowering HIV/AIDS infection rates; and, finally, more education means more empowerment for women. How do such optimistic and straightforward digests translate into the Arab world and, more specifically, into Moroccan provincial hinterlands, if at all?

Official education

The literacy rate in Oued al-Ouliya is low, especially among women. According to local statistics from 2004 (Monoghrafia Jama'at [Oued] Al-Ouliya),[3] which are based on the national General Census of Population and Habitat 2004 (*Recensement général de la population et de l'habitat 2004*), 49.4 percent of women were illiterate. A different report written by the local administration on the development of the community in 2009, however, concluded that the rate is in fact much higher at 77 percent.[4] This makes it higher than the national illiteracy rate for women in 2004, which was 54.7 percent and higher than the national average for rural women at 60.5 percent.[5] I would agree with the adjusted percentage for reasons that I will address later.

The perception of local teachers is that the literacy rate among women in the community is improving as a result of numerous literacy classes targeting adult women and greater awareness among parents regarding the importance of education for girls and boys. Ninety-nine percent of local girls between the ages of six and eleven are attending school.[6] However, a director of one of Oued al-Ouliya's four junior secondary schools,[7] whom I shall call Mudir Rachidi (Director Rachidi), stated that particularly among the girls the dropout rate after finishing basic primary school remains relatively high.[8] It is important to note that all community data showing school enrollment indicate that there are fewer girls than boys attending school at all levels, including preschool. There are many reasons for this, suggesting hard living conditions on the one hand and poor infrastructure coupled with the lower priority still attached to the education of girls. Sending girls to school is a recent development as even in the not so distant past the large majority of girls in this community did not attend school of any kind—formal or the *kuttab* (Qur'an school)—or completed only a few grades. During my fieldwork I noticed that in many families the educational level of their daughters varied significantly; some families had illiterate older daughters, while the youngest one(s) had a university education. Such was the case in my field-site family as well as in that of many of our neighbors'. The reason for this discrepancy, I was told, is that fathers at first were not aware of the benefits of sending daughters to school, but that gaining awareness finally influenced their decision to send one of the younger daughters to university, while others at least to primary school. However, in some cases the age difference between the illiterate and educated sisters was almost negligible to be able to conclude that change in awareness from one year to the other would have had such a profound impact on the father's decision. (Particularly when people's general attitudes toward social change and modernization are fairly intransigent, as demonstrated in the previous two chapters.) In my field-site family, the age difference between the two youngest sisters, Karima who had a degree in Islamic law and Zakiya who was illiterate, was merely a year and a half. If awareness raising was indeed the reason, I was interested to know, then why did the father send only his youngest daughter to school? Why not her year-and-a-half elder sister also? Some parents in the development literature reportedly make a strategic decision regarding which of their children they should send to school, to the effect that they are putting "a large premium on picking a winner" (Abhijit and Duflo 2011, 88–89). Children are considered to be parents' investment for old age. In Oued al-Ouliya, it is not just *any* child who may get picked to pursue postsecondary education; rather, it is most likely a male child who is thought of in terms of an investment. Hamid, for example, asserted: "In Morocco, and especially in this area, my son is like an investment. When he finishes going to school he has to get a job." Such perception is implicit in the legal designation of the man as the family breadwinner in the reformed Mudawwana, placing an onerous responsibility on him at a time when well-paying and secure jobs in public service are hard to get, and migration abroad for young people is severely restricted. Abhijit Banerjee and Esther Duflo, however, found that in Morocco

> parents believed that each year of primary education would increase a boy's earning by 5 percent, and each year of secondary education by 15 percent. The pattern was even more extreme for girls. In the view of the parents, each year of primary education was worth almost nothing for them: 0.4 percent. But each year of secondary education was perceived to increase earnings 17 percent. (2011, 88)

Without much context with respect to where in Morocco the two academics conducted their survey and who was included in their sample, it is dangerous to attempt to draw optimistic conclusions from the limited information they provide. Perhaps not insignificant in this context, albeit over fifteen years old, is the information contained in the 1995 *Morocco National Survey of Family* (*Enquête nationale sur la famille*). The survey reports that 72.1 percent of people in rural areas regarded girls at the age of seven to be much more "useful" for households than boys (Ministry of Economy and Finances and UNIFEM, 23). Children's usefulness was reversed from age fifteen through twenty-five, with 52.4 percent of respondents describing boys as more useful in contrast to 24.5 percent for girls (23). Such usefulness is measured in the individual's contribution to household, which, arguably, with respect to girls represents their ability to assist in household chores, whereas boys become useful for their families once they can financially contribute to their families' budgets. Gender roles therefore are ascribed at birth but implemented at school age. I suggest that fifteen years after this survey took place the ideology of gender roles, at least among provincial families, has not changed much. Girls, regardless of their educational level, are expected to get married, bear children, and manage the household, which is something that school does not teach them. It is true that having educated daughters is an asset because, according to locals, educated women take better care of their children's well-being. But being "educated" or "aware" (*waʿiya*) is frequently associated only with being able to read and write, which is understandable considering that most of the girls' mothers never attended formal education. Touriya, a thirty-seven-year-old married woman, who dropped out of school in grade four because of her responsibilities at home, explained why education is important:

[Education is important] in order to understand because educated people aren't like the ones who didn't go to school. . . . They go to school and can take responsibility for themselves, not like those who aren't educated. They're not the same. . . . The one who goes to school is aware (*wa'iy*), he knows everything, he knows the road, he knows how to use the telephone, he knows everything.

When I asked my interviewees to talk about their image of an ideal woman, not one mentioned education as a characteristic of such a woman, whereas being a good wife and a mother who is patient, modest, pious, whose voice is rarely heard, and who is honoring local customs were frequently identified. Therefore, while it is certainly wrong to sneer at the progress that Morocco has made in terms of female education since the end of the colonial era, it is nonetheless necessary to discuss the issues of quality and quantity, if not the importance of, education for women. Youssef complained about the intransigence of people in the region. "People here are a bit traditional," he said, repeating the statement in French to emphasize his remark.

Ya'ni, they are still a bit traditional. The father, for example, prefers his daughter to get married than for her to go to school. For example, a girl is intelligent, she works hard. . . . I experienced this. I taught in a region called [Ksar], and I taught there an intelligent and hardworking girl. *Ya'ni*, we say *tbaraka llah 'alayha*! But then I heard that she dropped out. I met her on the street and asked her: "Why did you drop out, *binti* [my daughter]?" She told me: "It's my family." I said to her: "Why?" and she told me that they didn't want it. I was very harsh to her mother: "Why did you make her drop out?" She told me: "No, that's enough for her." *Ya'ni*, her idea is that the girl should [get married] . . . But for me this is a mistake. Girls should have what boys have. A girl, too, can go and achieve a certain level. Maybe even higher than the level of boys.

Reasons for girls leaving school are abundant. One of the girls I interviewed stated that the reason she dropped out after finishing grade seven[9] was because "education in our region is not organized and men in the region do not let girls study. They stop us on our path." Some parents do not see the value of educating their daughters beyond primary school, like the parents in Youssef's example, because it is still customary in the region to marry girls off at a young age. A few of the older girls (in their mid-twenties) attending informal education got engaged during my fieldwork, after which they stopped coming to afternoon classes. I asked them why they dropped out when the wedding was not for another six months. All of them explained that these were the last months of intense learning for wifehood, and they had no time left for school. Marriage and responsibilities associated with it, therefore, outweigh continuing education.

Another prevalent reason for the high dropout rate among girls, which to a certain extent speaks of girls' position and purpose in society and explains their "usefulness" for families, is to help their mothers with household chores. Since most of these domestic tasks take place from the morning until mid-afternoon, when girls are normally in school, it is common for parents to withdraw them from school. Whereas nothing similar is expected or even encouraged from boys—hence their "uselessness" for the household at this stage of their lives—girls from a young age are reared into following their mothers and other women in the household. They imitate women's work at first, slowly assuming more and more responsibilities until finally they can do their chores independently and like a *woman*. Many girls take over domestic responsibilities from their mothers and start, effectively, managing the household activities or help their neighbors with such seasonal work as making a yearly supply of couscous or harvesting wheat and barley, while their mothers merely assist them. Come spring, classrooms in informal education were mostly empty, and teachers complained about girls not taking education and the program seriously. Harvesting and accompanying activities can take up a whole month, and household commitments take precedence over any other activity, even school.[10]

Finally, families tend to be big, and thus older daughters help their mothers with raising their younger siblings, resulting in girls leaving school prematurely. A girl who dropped out of school after finishing basic primary level explained to me her reason for leaving:

> My mother had small children and there was no one to help her with household chores. My mother wasn't able to do housework and raise children at the same time because it made her tired. I couldn't see her in such a state because she is my life and I love her very much.

Fertility rates have decreased dramatically in rural areas from 7.0 children in 1975 to 2.7 children in 2010, and many young women were firm believers in small families, having three and at the most five children (HCP).[11] In the past, however, some women in Oued al-Ouliya gave birth to as many as seventeen children,[12] and therefore teaching their older daughters how to do housework in order to assist and sometimes even take over their household commitments was essential because tasks in the household economy were, and continue to be, rigorously divided among the individuals. It is still a common practice to send daughters to primary school, after which they stay at home, help their mothers with household work, and wait to get married. This is the practice particularly with the older daughters, whose educational background may significantly lag behind that of their younger siblings. This might have been the fundamental reason for the discrepancy in the educational attainment of women in my field-site family as well as the other neighboring families where older sisters were in charge of taking care of their younger siblings since an early age. Arguably, getting them educated was not a priority in a multigenerational and multiunit household of oftentimes twenty and more people, where work, despite being divided among a number of women, was constant and based on the active participation of everyone. Moreover, being the youngest one in the family also implies that she will likely have to wait for her turn to get married until all of her older siblings are married. Marrying off children is expensive not least because wedding parties can last up to a week—although nowadays it is mostly a three-day affair—during which time the families of the groom and bride can host separately up to five hundred guests.[13] Therefore, sending the youngest daughter to school could be a strategy to give her an alternative in case she is "too old" by the time it is finally her turn to get married.

Yet, reasons for girls (as for boys) leaving school prematurely and poor literacy skills should also be sought outside of the typical paradigm of "unrelenting traditions," such as the ones discussed previously. In my field-site community children did not devote much time after school to practicing what they learned or were supposed to learn in school. Most mothers and other women in the house could not help them with schoolwork, although those parents who could afford it, paid a local educated girl to tutor their child. (But evening tutoring was usually done in a room full of women and children, with the cacophony of voices and the TV synchronized at full blast.) Grade repetition was commonplace, as well as one of the reasons for children to drop out either before finishing basic primary level or immediately thereafter. The Moroccan state only allows children to repeat one grade twice, after which they are expelled. In fact, this was the reason for some of my interviewees dropping out of school before they could finish primary school. Many children also left school because they simply did not like it, while their parents did not appear to mind their children's decision.[14]

Perhaps an even more urgent problem with primary education in a rural setting such as this one is the poor pedagogical performance of teachers.[15] Many children complained that their teachers beat them with sticks, and for some this was the reason to either play truant or to drop out of school permanently. Furthermore, some teachers did not come to work regularly, which led to unfinished curricula at the end of the school year. But Oued al-Ouliya is no exception. Teacher absenteeism, inadequate teaching methods, and their general poor performance are topics addressed by a growing body of (development) literature concerned with the quality rather than quantity of education in developing countries (Banerjee and Duflo 2011; Kenny 2010; Galal et al., 2008). Teachers, according to Mudir Rachidi, can be insufficiently trained in pedagogics and didactics as well as not being educated beyond high school baccalaureate level.[16] Many people defended the system whereby one could become a primary school teacher without a university degree or, as was the case in the past, without a teaching certificate. Their explanation was that the problem of substandard teaching performance was not in the educational level of teachers but in the fact that there was no pedagogic training on a continuous basis available to these local teachers. The approach to teaching is mostly traditional, akin to the format of the Qur'an school. It involves writing on the blackboard, while pupils passively copy what is being written into their notepads or their little boards and mindlessly repeating the material after the teacher. Rote memorization of material is also required from students when learning for exams, be it Arabic, French, geography, Islamic studies, and even subjects in the sciences. But such a method of "learning" merely reflects the overall teaching approach and fulfills what is being expected from pupils, while largely failing to teach pupils problem solving and analytical skills and neglecting to encourage creativity or innovation. This, too, has serious repercussions for the overall economic and social development of the country. Whereas the state invests large amounts of its budget into expanding education, it fails to pay much attention to the quality of both instruction and learning.

Poor schools and substandard public-works infrastructure as well should be taken into account when discussing education in Oued al-Ouliya. Whereas primary schools are quite numerous—there are sixteen for the community of twenty-four *ksour*—there are only four junior secondary schools and one senior secondary school, the latter of which is situated in Tamazirt. Supply, it seems, follows the decreasing demand for higher educational levels. Several *ksour* are ten or more kilometers away from the nearest junior and/or the one senior secondary school, and there is no other means of transportation except for the occasional grand taxi, which costs at minimum five dirhams (less than a dollar). This can present a significant strain on the family budget, where, for example, a seasonal construction worker earns about 50 dirhams (approximately six dollars) a day. Schools themselves are poorly equipped, drafty, without proper doors and windows, with teachers resorting to making their own posters and painting letters and numbers on the walls of lower grades. Even in the private primary school, teachers complained that books came with CDs but they were not given a CD player, or could not listen to the CDs, leaving them without an important pedagogical tool. Moreover, with the school day broken into morning and afternoon classes, during which time children have to return home for a lunch break, it is hard for parents living some distance away to justify continuing education for their children, and particularly for daughters. Some girls also reported being harassed on their way to school, in addition to schools being coeducational, which causes concern among some parents when rumors about the purported immoral behavior of particularly adolescent schoolgirls spread (Schaefer Davis and Davis 1989). In 2005, however, USAID's Alef project together with the Entraide Nationale (National Service) started the initiative called Dar Taliba de Qualité (Quality Girls' Dormitory), establishing boarding schools for girls in different locales across Morocco's poorer and rural areas. One of them is situated in the center of Tamazirt. It houses and feeds girls from remote *ksour* who would otherwise be denied education beyond primary level, along with providing further tutoring and psychological support.

Despite the problems associated with how many years of schooling suffice for girls, locals considered the event of girls finishing primary school to be a great leap forward particularly when compared with the educational level of their mothers and in many cases also their fathers. The middle-aged to older generation of women rarely attended school, and of those that did, a great majority did not continue beyond primary level, which in the past was only five levels rather than today's six. However, whereas parents and the community regard girls as literate and indeed educated after a few years of primary education, their actual ability to read, understand, and write—or rate of functional literacy—can be quite poor (Wagner 1993). Without much incentive to practice in order to retain this skill, many also lose it as years go by. Or, as Jennifer Spratt,

Beverly Seckinger, and Daniel Wagner concluded in their 1991 study of functional literacy in Moroccan children, lack of visual stimulants in one's environment may lower a person's chances to become household literate. Books and magazines are too expensive for people to buy, and rural areas such as Oued al-Ouliya lack many of the visual stimulants of urban areas that would prompt people to use acquired reading skills in their everyday life, via billboards, advertisements, and street signs. Moreover, despite most households owning a satellite dish with a wide range of Arab and foreign channels, including the Saudi-run MBC group, which shows foreign films and series with Arabic subtitles, few people in the community watched them. Instead, persons of all ages and educational backgrounds preferred to watch Moroccan and other Arab TV channels, which broadcast in or dub movies and soap operas solely into various Arabic dialects, or they tuned in to religious channels, which broadcast in literary Arabic.

Four years of formal schooling is sufficient for many Arab countries, including Morocco, to regard a person as literate, whereas, for example, the Canadian government only records a person as literate after completing nine years of formal schooling (Agnaou 2004). However, Spratt, Seckinger, and Wagner are right in asserting that "some persons may learn to read through informal means, and others may reach high school with minimal reading skills" (1991, 180–181).[17] The issue of literacy and statistics is further complicated by the difference between school-type and household or functional literacies[18] and the fact that "years of schooling" became the national measure of literacy. Wagner, a professor of education and a literacy specialist who designed the USAID Moroccan Passerelles program, thus quite correctly concludes on the basis of his study conducted in Morocco that "many of the literacy skills called for in everyday life may not be acquired even after four or five years of formal schooling" (1993, 205, 2009; Spratt, Seckinger, and Wagner 2009). What literacy statistics do represent, therefore, is the quantity, or the number, of years spent in school rather than the overall quality of people's learning. Being literate in Morocco means being able to read and write in Standard or literary Arabic, which further complicates the issue of recording individuals as literate after four years of attending school in Berber-speaking communities such as that of my field site.[19] Some teachers in Oued al-Ouliya also complained that textbooks were based on the environment and experiences of urban children, which made it harder for rural children to learn new words and understand concepts, since the examples they are presented with include more or less abstract ideas such as eating a pizza or swimming in the sea or a pool. Although Wagner's study of literacy in

Morocco concludes that "Berber monolingual children essentially caught up to their Arabic-speaking peers by the fifth year of primary school" (1993, 181), the question of whether children can actually *read* and *understand* what is written remains. For Mudir Rachidi, at least nine years of uninterrupted schooling are necessary to equip children with lifelong literacy skills. So far his goal to persuade parents to allow girls to finish at the minimum junior secondary school has been hampered by, what he argues to be, a tenacious grip of local traditions, some of which we have previously discussed and others that will be discussed further.[20] However, without much supervision of teachers' work from their superiors and from the educational ministry, coupled with inadequate infrastructure, it should not come as a surprise that the overall success rate of children's performance and retention in primary school is rather poor. While this is a problem affecting both girls and boys, girls are at a further disadvantage because of their different future societal roles from boys and general gendered expectations.

The current state of local education explains the more critical evaluation of literacy rates contained in the 2009 community report mentioned at the beginning of this section. But it also questions the overall national success in lowering illiteracy rates in the country. I spent much time in the women's association sitting in classes during informal education and as an English teacher and time and again I was surprised at how little these girls retained from their time spent in school and from what they learned in the informal education class. Therefore, lowering standards to a level that considers an individual literate after four years of schooling suggests a country's preoccupation with numbers in order to fulfill certain expectations emanating from the international development agenda, such as that of the MDGs. Rather than indicating the true quality of the educational system and persons' literacy skills, literacy statistics are being employed to improve the country's international standing.

Adult literacy classes

People in Oued al-Ouliya are becoming increasingly aware of the value and purpose education holds not merely for children but also for adults. Numerous and consistently growing literacy classes have been organized by the various local women's associations and mosques and have been offered for the past decade to women and at first also to men. Their popularity is a testament to what could be interpreted as successful awareness raising about the importance of education. In literacy classes women learn not only how to read, write, and do simple mathematics but are also taught about religion, family health, family planning, women's rights, and the new Family Code. The purported aim of the government, which provides teaching material for teachers and learners, is to include women in the development of the country and instill in them values of patriotism and of being a good and responsible citizen, as well as fighting religious extremism. The literacy curriculum is a top-down political campaign, designed in much the same way and for similar purposes as the reform process of the PSC. Perhaps Sharabi is right in arguing that literacy campaigns in the neopatriarchal Arab state are a means to bring the newly literate "closer to authority and its controls" (1988, 95). He asserts that these literacy courses are not meant to introduce learners to the "intellectual texts," which could lead them to question the authority, but rather enable the reproduction of the regime-sanctioned discourse (95). It is functional illiteracy which for Sharabi is the "invariable product of all anti-illiteracy campaigns" (95). Fatima Agnaou comes to a similar conclusion, arguing that although adult literacy courses have the ambition to empower women, the fact that they were planned as "achiev[ing] nationally defined needs and interests" (2004, 115) led to neglecting women's strategic needs and differing socioeconomic determinants. As such, she concludes, they only "reinforce women's illiteracy and dependence" (165). K. R. Kamphoefner (1996), writing on the education of low-income Cairene women in the mid-1990s, on the other hand, concludes that a successful literacy program must be tied to the immediate needs of women within households rather than to their participation in the labor market. It is true that the adult literacy curriculum in Morocco strives toward the state-defined and approved empowerment. As such it disseminates the urban elite perspective of a "modern" wife, with the aim to enhance the image of Morocco as a progressive and liberalizing country; yet, such an urban elite definition of a modern wife does not always resonate in rural areas, where promoting women's formal employment and men's sharing of household chores is largely disregarded, if not derided.

The women's association in Taddert organizes sewing, cooking, and computer classes for women. This may be interpreted by authors such as Agnaou and Sharabi as locking women into their traditional roles as housewives. However, teachers themselves argued that classes and workshops are designed to modernize and not to disrupt this traditional and ruralized version of the ideal housewife. The message teachers convey to participants is that women have to be literate in order to help their children with homework, to be able to read food and medicine labels, to be able to count in order to go shopping alone if need be. In this rural context, this is believed to enhance their role and status within the family without transforming it into, what is perceived to be, a man's role. Many women participants listed being able to better understand religion and its precepts as their primary motivation to join literacy classes; yet, what they obtained was much more than that and considered an (un)intentional side effect. Since learning about the Mudawwana is part and parcel of these government-initiated literacy classes, the Family Code has become a synonym for not only women's rights but also a kind of catch-all manual on how to become a "modern," more "up-to-date" mother and wife. In my discussions on the Family Code with women participants in literacy classes, women told me that the law is also about how to raise their children properly, how to improve their health, about the importance of hygiene, the education of both boys and girls, and their crucial role in meeting these new standards.

These literacy classes have therefore had the more or less unintentional effect of becoming the only public forum for women to voice their opinions, to hear about their rights and about the new methods of managing the household. The status of women participants in literacy classes has improved compared to other illiterate women in the community as the new "literates" have become one of the main agents and sources of information regarding women's rights and the family legislation. Other women now seek their advice in health and family issues, which has had as a consequence a greater recognition of the existence of the Family Code. In short, these literacy courses have raised women's awareness and contributed to the improvement of their own self-image. It is true that they are not designed to challenge the established division of gender roles by failing to equip them to take up jobs outside the home and have not enabled them to question the regime, but most of the female course takers would argue that they would not want to do any of that, regardless. The emphasis of these literacy classes appears to be on gradual progress, which is customized to fit the vagaries of local life, rather than to subvert patriarchal relations.

Informal education program

A further option for girls and women to improve their educational level and increase their knowledge was offered by the governmental initiative called informal education (*tarbiya ghair nidamiya*). This program was targeting girls who left school at an early age or before finishing a certain level and aimed at reintroducing dropouts to school. In Tamazirt, informal education was carried out by Taddert's local women's association. In the 2009–2010 school year, adult girls and a few married women, ranging in age from ten to thirty-five or so, from diverse educational levels, from the functional illiterate to those possessing up to ten years of formal education, attended these afternoon classes. The daily schedule consisted of Arabic, French, mathematics, in addition to occasional weekend activities such as learning how to sew, bake, use a computer, and navigate the Internet. After taking an exam at the end of the year and upon passing it with a satisfactory mark, a girl could be reintegrated into formal school. Ten-year-old Asma was one such "success story." She moved to Oued al-Ouliya with her parents from a remote High Atlas village, where she had attended school for only a few months before her father withdrew her because of the distance between the school and her home. Tamazirt's primary schools had rejected Asma on the basis of her illiteracy and for being a few years older than the other beginning students. She commenced informal education, where she was the youngest one, and after two years of attending it she successfully passed the exams to enter formal primary school.

Motives behind joining informal education, however, were usually less ambitious, and Asma was the only "success story" I heard of in my field site. One of the participants told me that she was attending afternoon classes "because times have changed and everything has changed. I know I cannot regain my childhood, but I know I can regain knowledge because knowledge doesn't recognize age." Indeed, girls did want to improve their reading and writing skills and learn French, and given their family constraints and obligations, informal education offered a perfect opportunity for this. All classes and most of the activities and supplies were free, and classes always took place in the afternoon. Such a schedule was designed to give girls sufficient time to finish their household responsibilities; but pragmatism in respecting local practices with the aim to reintegrate more girls into school also tacitly reinforces the strict division of labor and complementarity of gender roles.

Nonetheless, one of the main motivational factors among girls joining the program appeared to be boredom, resulting on account of parents and society in general limiting girls' movement outside the house. Sitting at home, in the words of one of the girls, made her feel "useless, like having a brain tumor and like I'm not able to do anything." Another girl concluded that since participating in the informal education, she was "not forced to spend [free time] at home, watching TV or sleeping." Moreover, it was not only the belief of many locals that a woman's place is at home, but it was also a consequence of there not being (m)any communal places for girls and women where they could go to be away from their families, such as women-friendly cafés or youth clubs. Informal education represented for many of the girls the only alternative to sitting at home and the only permissible way to change their daily routine, leave the house, and catch up with their girlfriends, rather than a way to get a school certificate.

The presence of diverse possibilities to obtain basic education in the community is noteworthy, and it has certainly contributed to the rising reputation of education, if not to the overall literacy rates. However, education has also disrupted what is regarded as the established customary status quo, which, to a certain extent, has had as a result retraditionalization as a strategy for locals to cope with "modernization." While schools are available and on the whole relatively inexpensive (at least for children living closer to them), the issue today is not whether to send children (girls) to school but for how long. The question that arises is, how useful is education considered to be for girls after completing a certain level? While Banerjee and Duflo report:

> People who are comfortable with reading are more likely to read newspapers and bulletin boards and to find out when there is a government program available for them. People who go on to secondary education are more likely to get a formal-sector job, but even those who don't are able to run their business better. (2011, 82)

I argue instead, that the reality for many educated girls and boys in Oued al-Ouliya, as in the wider MENA region more generally, is quite different from the standard development literature conclusions, which fail to take into account diverse family and state socioeconomic factors affecting lifestyles of individuals. The (Nasserist-style) social contract, whereby the state promised educated youth employment in the public sector, has long been void. Jobs in the growing informal sector are oftentimes presented as the only alternative to these young adults despite rarely meeting their expectations or needs and it is this topic that I now turn to.

Is employment important?

Big expectations and even bigger promises of human and national development came with the winning of national independence in the MENA region. Governments such as those in Egypt and Morocco instituted universal and free educational policies and in their drive to modernize their countries made the impossible-to-keep promise to all those with high school and postsecondary diplomas a job, at least for the time being, in the expanding bureaucratic apparatus. Perhaps it was this discourse, too, that contributed to Karima's father's decision to educate her, thinking that it would ensure her a spot in this high-salaried, secure, and well-respected sector. (As Alan Richards and John Waterbury [2008] write, public sector wages in the region are approximately 25 percent higher than those in the private sector. And although this is true for starting salaries, Boudarbat [2005] contends that because the wages in the private sector are increasing at a higher rate, the wage gap between the two sectors narrows over time. Despite this, many people associate public service jobs with job security, additional social benefits, and prestige.) It was inevitable that the social contract would be breached, not least because of the dramatic demographic growth experienced in the region as a whole. As a consequence, the public sector could not absorb the increasing number of educated employment seekers, coupled with the structural adjustment measures dictating the slimming down of the government sector. Despite this, many Moroccan graduates and their parents continue to prefer waiting for a spot in the government sector even if that causes longer-term unemployment and subsequent protracted adult adolescence as well as financial dependence on family (Boudarbat 2005; Boudarbat and Ajbilou 2007; Martin-Muñoz 2000; Singerman 2007).

A number of families in Oued al-Ouliya allow their daughters to move to the city to undertake studies, but many also require them to return back to the village immediately after they graduate. Nour was one of my neighbors, living just around the corner from us in a traditional adobe one-story house, which revealed without stepping inside that the family was rather poor. She was thirty years old and the fourth of seven children, only one of whom—the eldest brother—was married. Her mother was severely ill, taking many painkillers and other prescription drugs, which put a strain on the family budget, while her father was too old to work. These circumstances required six of the seven children, girls and boys, to work outside the house to make ends meet. The oldest and the only illiterate daughter took care of the house and her ailing mother. When Nour finished her bachelor's degree in Arabic language she hoped to be able to find a job and a husband in Tangiers, while living with her maternal aunt. Yet, despite being looked after by a senior and trustworthy member of the family, her father and brothers demanded she return to Oued al-Ouliya immediately after graduating. At first she worked as a literacy teacher at Taddert's women's association, and when the community opened a pre-school she took up teaching children. She earned 300 dirhams a month (approximately 36 dollars) during the school year. As any private informal sector job, hers, too, did not come with social benefits, such as paid vacation, sick leave, or a pension fund. Most of the money she earned she contributed to the household budget and the rest she kept as her pocket money to buy clothes and an occasional phone card. At the age of thirty, Nour, like many of her peers, knew that her chances of getting married were diminishing rapidly. But until she gets married, her brothers, two of whom are younger and much less educated than she is, control her movements, professional opportunities, and aspirations. Age and education do not entitle a girl to more independence and do not expand her rights when one's gender and to a certain extent also marital status determine the individual's capacity to control and direct her life choices. Nour is one of the increasing number of educated girls in this community who try to put their education to work, while they are waiting to get married, but failing to either become (economically) independent or a *complete woman*.

Finding a job in Tamazirt can be an enormous challenge for men let alone for girls, who are not supposed to build a professional career, but are expected to get married, become housewives, and mothers. Informal education and literacy classes offer one such opportunity to the educated girls as they are not only beneficial for girls and women participating in them but also for teachers. These are all local (unmarried) girls, like Nour, with various university degrees—in Islamic law, civil law, Arabic, Islamic studies, French, geography—who because of the societal expectations, family pressure, and the higher cost of living in urban areas returned to the community after finishing their degrees. As shall be discussed later in the section on the importance of marriage, these girls are to a large degree considered too old for the marriage market, and thus working for a wage gives them not only a purpose in life but also provides a bit of pocket money and helps their families financially. On the basis of their education, availability, and the fact that they are willing to work for a low wage, they are recruited by the local associations, mosques, and the private primary school located in Tamazirt to teach either children in (pre)school, girls in informal education, or adults in literacy classes. None of the local educated girls taught in government schools within Tamazirt, but the situation was reversed in the private primary school, which in the school year 2009–2010 was staffed by only local and unmarried female teachers and one male teacher of science. One of the reasons for such a divide is that for teaching in public schools one needs to not only pass a national government teacher's exam but also complete the *stage*, or the compulsory professional training period, which normally takes place away from the family.[21] One of these national exams took place during my fieldwork and my female educated friends, who traveled to Agadir, Oujda, Rabat, and Meknes to take it, reported that tens of thousands of applicants participated in the exam nationwide, hoping to be selected for one of the relatively small number of positions offered. None of my friends passed the exam, which to them did not come as a surprise because of the large number of exam takers, insufficient amount of positions offered, and, in their opinion, the corruptibility of the examiners. Particularly this last reason poses a significant impediment for poor rural girls with no connections or money. In short, these girls lack social capital, which is understood here as established networks and opportunities available to individuals. Such social capital could, in the right context, help girls with putting education to work and have as a consequence improved material as well as psychological conditions of that person. Significantly, Silver and Miller link social exclusion with the indicators of social capital "taking account of associational membership, social network involvement, democratic inclusion, and access to rights" (2003, 8, 12). A practical example of how lack of social capital affects exclusion is offered by Shana Cohen in her book *Searching for a Different Future: The Role of a Global Middle Class in Morocco* (2004), in which she analyzes professional, political, and social opportunities available to young and educated Casaouis (Casablancans). Cohen's female informants, like the single persons in *TelQuel*'s article opening this chapter, drive cars, eat out, interact with the opposite sex without being defamed or fear of being seen. Cities offer individuals a greater plethora of lifestyles, behaviors, and ideologies to choose from without necessarily standing out. However, despite the much less monochromatic lives compared to their rural counterparts, many of Cohen's female and male interviewees complained about their low wages[22] and jobs and many shared the frustrations of or were among the unemployed graduates (*diplômés chômeurs*). They, too, much like the urban youth elsewhere in the region, are socially, economically, and politically marginalized, but compared to educated single adult girls from Oued al-Ouliya and other similar economically depressed areas, they have at least two important advantages. Their middle-class and urban environment enable these young adults much less conformist lifestyles and, as Mounia Bennani Chraïbi (2000) argues, a chance to develop more fluid and transient identities. She calls the urban youth "cultural innovator[s] who [are] busy with the reconstruction of [their] image" (144). Moreover, living in a city such as Casablanca offers them considerably more opportunities to look for and ultimately find a suitable job with a decent wage (or use connections to do so) and a chance to climb the social ladder as initially promised by the social contract. Doris Gray is right in concluding that "social class often outweighs all other factors with regard to a person's personal and professional opportunities. . . . Professional opportunities for educated women from the urban middle or upper class are superior to those of rural men or women from a lower social class" (2008, 135–136). Moreover, in a recent online newspaper article, Siham Ali (2010) reports that urban Moroccan single men are increasingly looking for wives who wish to continue working outside the home after the wedding because of the rising cost of living.

In contrast, expectations for girls in Oued al-Ouliya do not deviate much from the traditional gender roles regardless of their education (or perhaps on account of education). Many men and their families continue to prefer and some indeed demand from their wives to be *galsa f-dar* despite possible economic hardships. Youssef, for example, explained the situation in Tamazirt. "There are some [girls] who achieve a certain level, she gets a bachelors degree. When she gets married, *yaʿni*, this marriage becomes an obstacle for looking for a job. They say: '*Safi*, the wife belongs to the house.'" I asked him if men want an uneducated wife and he replied:

No, they say, "*Safi*, what she has learned is enough for her. . . ." The majority of young people now say that a girl should be educated. They want her to be [educated], but to look for a job, [no] . . . There are some who want a public servant, but they are different. They go directly to a public servant woman, but if [a girl] is still in school, *yaʿni*, he won't think of [wanting to marry] a public servant. . . . He's thinking: "If she still wants to go to school, will I provide for her, will I forget about myself in order for her to go to university? I won't!" Because, for example, if she wants to pursue her studies at the university she won't be here [in Tamazirt as well as being away from the house], so he would have to [marry] a woman who's a bit older [and who has already finished university]. But to this he says no. If he wants a public servant, he'll go directly to a public servant and if he wants someone for the house, he will look for someone who's educated or not [it won't matter to him whether she is or is not educated].

Pursuing university education indicates that a girl will be past her prime marriageable age. Younger and therefore less educated girls are much more in demand because they are less likely to want to look for a job after the wedding. However, it is not only men who prefer to marry a housewife but their families' preference as well. When Habiba finished university, a man from the village of her sister's family-in-law, who had been patiently waiting for Habiba to graduate, finally asked her mother for her hand. Habiba often fondly talked about him as, after all, he had waited three years for her and had promised her that he would find her a job after they got married, which was her most important condition. Sadly, the often invoked *duruf* (circumstances)[23] prevented her from accepting his repeated proposals. He lived in a large family with a small farm, where tasks were divided according to gender and age, and not personal choice or educational level. Habiba envisioned that her job outside the house could cause endless conflicts between her and the other women in the family because, she concluded, they would not accept her lack of contribution to household chores. In fact, the demand for brides increases when the household loses daughters to another family. When I asked my neighbor and brother of Nour, Abdallah, why he was still unmarried, he replied: "One gets married if there's no one who'd take care of the house. [It's good to get married] when it's empty and there's no one to do housework at home, but now, thank God, there are still girls [at home]." Household economy depends as much on men's financial contribution to it as it does on having a sufficient number of women who are able to manage the household. Missing one set of hands can ruin the balance and the division of labor within the household. "People can be good," Habiba concluded, "but their *duruf* can be bad."

Women marry into a family and their relationship with the rest of the womenfolk becomes as important as their relationship with the husband, if not more, because they spend more time with the women-in-law than with their own husband. Habiba is aware of this, and her education as well as determination to continue working outside the house after the wedding have prevented her from either accepting marriage proposals or caused her suitors and their families to change their minds. More recently, an educated man asked Habiba to marry him and he, too, accepted her condition to continue working outside the house after the wedding.

However, whereas Habiba's mother accepted the suitor, his family rejected Habiba without meeting her or her family on account of her higher education and determination to work after the wedding.

Girls from Oued al-Ouliya do not have the advantage of living in Casablanca or the "useful" part of Morocco, where they could look for a better-paying and respectable job, if possible, in the public service. Instead, they have to settle for a life in a rural setting working in the informal sector, where they earn between three hundred to eight hundred dirhams (approximately thirty-six to ninety-six dollars) per month. Jobs in the public sector and particularly teaching jobs in public schools, since the government sector in the community is not large, are admittedly the most sought-after jobs for these young graduates. The community perceives such jobs as respectable and not compromising girls' reputations, but they also come with important social benefits. The jobs of the educated single adult girls, on the other hand, come with no benefits and they can, to a certain extent, be compared to seasonal jobs of agricultural and construction workers and hence do not have the prestige attributed to public servants. Therefore, the work of these educated girls is mostly not appreciated by their families, despite their contribution to the family budget, and local women constantly remind them of their societal role, which they have yet to fulfill.

"A woman without a husband is like a cow without milk!"

Marriage, I thought, was constantly on everyone's lips. It is that sort of preoccupation that even tourists cannot escape. Strangers in shops or taxi drivers would invariably inquire about my marital status or express concern about my older sister's singlehood, while thoroughly disregarding her professional success or the fact that such a lifestyle may be entirely her personal choice. The most important news and sometimes the only information of substance from my friends in Oued al-Ouliya I get normally involves engagements, weddings, and pregnancies.

But why is marriage so important for girls? Marriage equals societal adulthood and hence independence from the girl's father and/or brothers. Legally, too, with marriage a woman assumes greater rights as well as greater responsibilities, which in and of itself is a symbol of adulthood. For many girls, the prospect of not living under the authority of the male members of her family is understood as liberation, if only for a brief moment. A twenty-three-year-old single girl described her situation as follows: "I'm a girl myself and I have problems with my family. I hope that my dream of becoming a woman will come true. I ask the moon when my sun will rise to remove the darkness of the night, loneliness, and deprivation of my freedom." This poignant description may sound like an extreme or even exaggerated case, but many girls likened their life at home to being "in shackles or in prison." Girls, irrespective of their age and educational level, have to submit to their fathers', brothers', and oftentimes also to their mothers' authorities. Indeed, many girls complained about the troubled relationships with their mothers. Not only do mothers make their daughters work hard at home, in some households so much so that they themselves are almost entirely relieved from completing chores. Moreover, mothers act as extensions of their husbands in disciplining the daughters and limiting their movement outside the house, particularly when fathers are absent from for a large part of the day, or indeed for most of the year, when they work away from their families. I heard of a few cases where girls willingly accepted the first marriage proposal because of the strained relationship with the mother even if, or perhaps because, that meant that they had to move to a remote mountain village without familiar faces and any of the amenities that Oued al-Ouliya offered, such as electricity, running water, and countless teleboutiques. Elizabeth M. Bergman (1994) analyzed Moroccan Arabic proverbs and found some that expressed the idea that the mother-daughter bond has "built-in tensions," in a similar way as the relationship between the mother-in-law and her daughter-in-law later on in life would have. It is indeed this relationship between the bride and her mother-in-law that is "the most intense and long-lasting" (210–211). Many young brides complained about their demanding and even vicious mother- and sisters-in-law. However, contrary to single daughters, brides can in time, with hard work, patience, and bearing children, win quite a lot of influence over their husbands as well as their single and divorced sisters-in-law. Kandiyoti is right, therefore, to contend as follows:

> Woman's cycle in the patriarchally extended family is such that the deprivation and hardship she experiences as a young bride is eventually superseded by the control and authority she will have over her own subservient daughters-in-law. The cyclical nature of women's power in the household and their anticipation of inheriting the authority of senior women encourage a thorough internalization of this form of patriarchy by the women themselves. (1988, 279)

In my host family, to a certain extent, even the mother-in-law had to adapt to the unwritten rules of the wife of her youngest son, who was the head of the family. She had to sweet-talk her in order not to lose her favor and consequently her son's. It is therefore not surprising that very few girls thought that demanding an independent household from the in-laws was a good strategy on their part. (But some brides did require their husbands to rent an apartment away from his family as a consequence of a severely strained relationship with the women-in-law.) A twenty-one-year-old girl wrote that she would choose to live with her husband's family "so that one day when I have a son he wouldn't leave me like when I wanted to live separately with my husband."

In Chapters 3 and 4 I discussed the significance of protection for women. It is the family that has a lifelong responsibility to protect a girl if and when she fulfills her obligations toward the family. But marriage, too, means protection (*sitr*) because "no one will protect a girl except her husband," as one of the girls wrote in the survey I conducted on the importance of marriage. A married girl is considered to be *mastura*, or having a good reputation. Both words, *sitr* and *mastura*, are derived from the same root letters. A married girl therefore is one whose good reputation is protected because, as locals told me, marriage is necessary for the girls "to remain chaste."

Unmarried girls often complained of their lack of purpose in life saying that their only occupation for the time being was "to stay at home and pass time." One twenty-four-year-old girl concluded that because most adult girls were unemployed they should at least make an effort to look for a husband. Married women also liked to remind particularly the older girls that at their (st)age they really should not be overly concerned about finding "Mr. Right," but should instead gladly accept the first man who asked for their hand because there may not be many more coming. Some other women even went so far as to suggest that girls should accept the proposal of an already married man.

Marriage in Oued al-Ouliya is the only modus operandi available to a girl to become an adult and a respected member of society. Furthermore, girls told me that marriage is "the rule of the Prophet," "the rule of life," "marriage is half of Islam," and "the one who doesn't carry out his rule, doesn't belong to [the Prophet]." In a religious sense, therefore, marriage is an obligation. Socially, getting married and bearing children fulfills women's purpose in life and within society, where gender roles continue to be reciprocal rather than equal. Legally, marriage is the only permissible way to have a sexual relationship and, consequently, to have children. For girls in Oued al-Ouliya, who are not in school and are not working, but also for those employed, marriage also offers an escape from the mundane and sequestered life. But above all, marriage is perceived as a natural progression of life. Many girls who failed to achieve this next step felt that they let down not only themselves and their families but society and God as well.

The first step for girls to gain power is to get married. Failing to do so, their position as an unmarried daughter shall decrease proportionately as their sisters-in-law increase. Therefore, positions of power in the hierarchical family system are not only dependent on gender and age but also on the marital status, whereas the educational level of a person and particularly of girls does not appear to have a significant importance. It is such an understanding of the patriarchal system in Morocco, reinforced by the state, its laws, ideologies, and institutions, in addition to poor regional distribution of economic opportunities available particularly to educated women, which importantly affect the lives of educated single adult girls in provincial areas.

The problem with education and delaying marriages

Education, though undeniably important, can have serious and not altogether positive consequences for girls living in conservative and economically depressed areas. Particularly university education can seriously diminish the likelihood of girls getting married because in order to get a degree girls have to move to a city, where they normally cannot be supervised by her community or family. Their reputation can be tainted in the eyes of the people, who assume that female students living on campuses drink, smoke, have sexual relationships with men, and even prostitute themselves, which makes the cover photo of the *TelQuel* issue, reporting about the phenomenon of urban bachelorettes and bachelors discussed at the beginning of the chapter, all the more disconcerting. A women's magazine called *Nesma* ran an article in March 2010 (Al-Saaidi) about female students living on university campuses, acknowledging the stereotype of female students held in Oued al-Ouliya. Contrary to these stereotypes the magazine reports that many students are forced to live on campuses because of lack of financial means to pay for a higher rent elsewhere. The article portrays these female students as hardworking individuals who are likely to take up visible professional positions in the future. A director of one of the female student dorms told the reporter of the article that, contrary to popular belief, living on campus offers a much more secure and supervised environment for the female students. It provides diverse amenities, such as a library, cafeteria, TV room, and other leisure facilities; and a health center; all of which enable students to concentrate on their studies.

But negative stereotypes about educated provincial girls nonetheless abound. My educated friends confirmed that some girls do indeed lead such a life, but they are few and far between and therefore female university students do not warrant such a negative image.[24] The problem appears to be with trusting girls, as many people question their good behavior when not under the omniscient eye of not only their family but the whole community, even if no hard data about the girls' misbehavior have ever been presented to them. Women in general continue to be associated with enormous sexual powers leading to societal destruction or *fitna* (chaos) compounded with the idea that women lack good judgment.[25] Gynophobia incorporated into folktales, such as that of Aicha Kandicha and proverbs, and disseminated as such serve as the basis of these entrenched beliefs. Many people continue to believe the stereotype of a wonton female student, and it is for this reason that many parents demand that their daughters rent, together with their girlfriends, a room somewhere in the city and away from the campus. My friend Habiba and her female roommates, all students at the university in Meknes, after a year and a half of having to deal with exploitative and malicious landladies, decided to move to campus much to the dismay of their families. It was only after Habiba's parents visited her and saw by themselves that she lived in a decent all-girl dormitory that they accepted her decision. More often than allowing girls to study, however, men propose to girls before they move to the city to pursue higher education, or parents and brothers decide against their daughters and sisters staying in school.

One widely held assumption asserts that girls who stay in school longer get married later, which is a development, we are told, worth celebrating. Boudarbat and Ajbilou, for example, conclude that in Morocco "the schooling of women has improved their status, which had a net effect on the delay of marriage and on when couples choose to have children. Prolongation of studies is another factor that contributes to delaying marriage" (2007, 21). This is usually corroborated with statistics demonstrating a link between improved education of women and an increase in average age at first marriage. In Morocco, the average age at first marriage in 2010 was 26.6 years for girls—25.6 years for rural girls and 27.4 for urban girls—and 31.2 for boys. This is a jump since 1960, when girls on average got married at age 17.5—rural girls at 17.2 and urban girls at 17.5—and boys at 24 years (HCP).

Furthermore, since 1960 the illiteracy rate in Morocco has decreased from 96 percent for women and 78 percent for men over the age of ten, to 54.7 percent for women and 30.8 percent for men in 2004 at the last national census.[26] The average age at first marriage for girls in Oued al-Ouliya is according to national statistics quite similar to the national average, being 26.1 years in 2004. Such trends in delaying marriage have prompted many, like Boudarbat and Ajbilou, to conclude that there has been "a *disappearance* of early marriage to which women were subjected in the past, which often interfered with their education" (2007, 21; emphasis added).

However, as the previous chapter demonstrated, underage marriages not only continue to be practiced but are indeed on the rise in Morocco's urban and rural areas. I also met or heard of a few girls as young as twelve who were at the time of my fieldwork engaged to be married. Particularly memorable was a meeting with a twelve-year-old girl at her aunt's house in Tamazirt, which I visited with Aziza. It was late morning on a school day and the girl was there with her toddler brother and her mother, who did not seem much older than I. The atmosphere was jovial, as the girl had just gotten engaged to her twenty-one-year-old cousin living in Spain. The women teased her about her fiancé and asked her whether she missed him. The girl, visibly uncomfortable under the involuntary spotlight, shyly retreated to a rather dim spot in a corner of the room. When I talked to Karima later that day about the situation, she reacted somewhat matter-of-factly. She explained that parents jump at the opportunity of getting their daughter married to an emigrant, and they give their word by engaging their girl even at such a tender age. They may wait for a few years until the girl is fourteen or fifteen, Karima surmised, and then bribe the judge to allow the wedding.

Moreover, not getting married at a young age is not necessarily a consequence of a progressive shift in people's perceptions of physical and emotional maturity of the girl but is rather considered to be a failure and is ascribed to various *duruf*, such as unsuitable matches or having insufficient funds to marry off all of the children. While all of these reasons are certainly to blame, continuing education and therefore the girl's advanced age and her ostensibly compromised reputation also contribute to her diminishing marital opportunities. Delaying marriage, in short, is not an empowering act but is instead regarded by locals as a personal failure, particularly when it leads to the inability to get married at all. Therefore, drawing conclusions about progress solely on the basis of statistical analysis is necessarily wanting, if not dangerous. Chant is right to conclude that

> the numerical bias in the GDI and GEM, as well as with any other quantitative measures, can also occlude important dimensions of meaning and quality. Meanings are not easily transported across cultures or classes such that while higher female income shares are commonly equated with more gender-sensitive development (and, by implication, less likelihood of female poverty), for poor women earning income can compound heavy burdens of reproductive work and thereby undermine well-being. . . . In terms of quality, the privileging of numbers in the GDI and GEM can make for some spurious interpretations of "progress." (2006, 210)

UNIFEM as well cautioned in its 2002 Biennial Report on gender equality and the MDGs against misleading statistics:

> [T]he empowerment of women does not just depend on the elimination of numerical gender disparities. It is possible to equalize the enrollment of boys and girls in school at a low level for both, a situation that empowers neither. Equality in deprivation does not represent a genuine fulfillment of Goal 3 [promoting gender equality and empower women]. (2002, 6)

A further complication with drawing conclusions solely from looking at national and other statistics in the case of marriages in Morocco is the fact that prior to the reform of the Family Code, as in 2014, many marriages were not registered and therefore did not feature in official statistics. This pertains particularly to rural areas where *zawaj bi-l-Fatiha*, discussed in the previous chapter, continues to be practiced. This is compounded by the problem of recording births in rural areas, which, I was told, was unsystematic in the past, resulting in individuals being assigned random birth dates in their Family Booklets. Unfortunately, I was not able to find out how the national census in 2004 was carried out, but I can conclude with reasonable confidence that the recorded average age at first marriage in Oued al-Ouliya is, if anything, aggrandized, much the same as literacy rates.[27]

Women's empowerment is continually linked with countries' economic development and the Moroccan government has picked up on such a discourse and promotes it at international forums.[28] Yet, statistics showing a positive correlation between education and delayed marriages,

MDGs, and proponents of the idea of education as a panacea for empowerment of women and lifting them out of poverty overlook two important qualitative assumptions: the impact of staying in school on a girl's marriage opportunities as well as youth and particularly female unemployment and/or underemployment. The national census of 2004 shows that in Oued al-Ouliya, 36.1 percent of girls between the ages of twenty-five and twenty-nine were single. The statistics, regrettably, end with this age bracket; however, in comparison, on the national level in 2009–2010, when the National Demographic Survey took place, 61.4 percent of girls between the ages of twenty and twenty-four were single, and 28.9 percent between the ages of thirty and thirty-four (Lahlimi Alami 2010).[29] Data showing the educational level of these girls is not available; however, based on my findings, many of the girls who continued beyond junior secondary school did so on account of turning down potential suitors and some in fact stayed single well past their legal age of majority and have remained so to this day.

Moreover, "[e]ducation," argues Moghadam, "plays a key role in the advancement and employability of women" (1998b, 34). However, as she rightly concludes, there remain many impediments preventing women from fully participating in the economic development as well as fully realizing their capabilities. Unemployment and underemployment are serious problems among the youth in the Arab world. Boudarbat and Ajbilou (2007), again, report that the higher the education level of a person in Morocco, the more likely it is for that person to be unemployed. In fact, the situation has deteriorated for those with university education, causing many to question the usefulness of education. Unemployment of the educated youth in Morocco twenty years after the institution of SAPs, which at the time was perceived as a natural outcome of government contraction of public service jobs, has increased. In 2010, 25.3 percent of university educated women in Morocco actively looking for a job were unemployed, while the percentage was slightly lower for those with some education, but still high at 22.1 percent (HCP). This is a region-wide phenomenon. ILO reports that MENA has the highest youth unemployment rates in the world at 23.3 percent, compared to the worldwide rate at 12.1 percent (Elder et al. 2010). In addition to this, while the share of women in the tertiary education in many Arab countries exceeds that of men,[30] this has not translated into better employment opportunities. In fact, the ILO report writes that "[d]espite education gains, the labor force participation rate of young women in the Middle East increased by less than 2 percentage points between 1998 and 2008, while in North Africa the rates actually decreased from 25.2 to 22.9 percent" (Elder et al. 2010).

In Oued al-Ouliya education does not improve a girl's chances of getting a well-paid and respectable job; nor does it lead to personal and financial autonomy. There is a general scarcity of civil servant jobs not only in Oued al-Ouliya but in Morocco as such. Most of the educated girls find work in the private informal sector, where they are underpaid, without the job security, and other benefits including prestige, which come with being a *muwaddafa* (public official). As such, their work outside the home is mostly not highly regarded, and local married women, many of whom are much less educated and have never held a job outside the house, take pity on them and constantly remind them of their own superiority. Unmarried girls, therefore, often complained about their lack of purpose in life even if they were working outside the home, lamenting that their only occupation for the time being was to pass time.

Why, then, do some parents and their daughters nonetheless decide to go to university? The importance and benefits of education have become mythologized as the panacea, the only universal solution that cannot but bring personal, familial, as well as national success. Habiba's father, despite himself being illiterate and regardless of her oldest brother's tenacious protestations against sending her to university, decided in favor of Habiba getting a university education because he was convinced that education would change her, as well as the family's situation, for the better. He bought into the promise of the government that higher education means upward mobility, much like it has for the Moroccan and other Arab elites, which took over governments in the postindependent states. "I thought I will change something in my life if I get a university degree, but I think this is a false idea," Habiba concluded. She, as other friends of ours who pursued education on the basis of a similar belief, cannot improve the financial situation of their families simply because there are not enough well-paying jobs for men, the family's main providers, let alone for girls. Furthermore, abundant stereotypes of female students on campuses increase community pressure against sending girls away to study, and thus parents believe that making concessions is necessary—while they will allow their girls to go study in the city as a temporary arrangement, living away from the family beyond the required time to finish the program is inconceivable even if the reason is to find a respectable job. Living on your own is not unheard of, but it is stigmatized and thought of as inferior to the shielded family life, in addition to rent in the city being expensive and even prohibitive for large families with only a few sources of income. Without having any guarantees that the girl will be able to find a respected, stable, and well-paying job, families cannot afford to allow their girls to try their luck away from them in the city or risk family honor to be questioned by their local communities.

It is important for policy makers and the development community to look beyond statistics and juxtapose them with the consequences of delaying marriage and education for girls. Girls or their parents, who choose school over early marriage, experience what Singerman (2007) calls wait adulthood. As discussed in the introduction of this book, Singerman focuses on the reasons for and consequences of delayed marriages for men. However, whereas these young educated urban male adults in her sample *delay* adulthood because of unemployment or underemployment, which leads to the (temporary) inability to pay for the marriage and to be considered as a realistic breadwinner and hence a husband, the girls in Oued al-Ouliya face another difficulty. These girls are not merely delaying marriage as much as they are, in effect, waiving marriage in the hope to help their families financially and, more generally, to change their lives for the better. Many girls are in fact presented with only two options: that of getting married or going to university. Delaying getting married as a consequence of pursuing education makes them to a large extent ineligible once they finish their studies because they are educated, past their prime marriageable age, and have a suspicious track record of their propriety because of living on their own. Many girls explained that men and their families prefer younger and uneducated girls because they are impressionable and innocent as compared to girls who are older, were exposed to coeducation when in adolescence, and who experienced living in a city away from their parents. "Educated girls," said Habiba, "are more conscious than other girls and they always ask their husbands to [give them] their rights." For some people, such empowerment and, in fact, "doing justice to women" violates the idea of "preserving man's dignity."

Finally, waithood, or in fact spinsterhood, makes these girls not only financially but also legally dependent on their families, rendering them de facto as well as de jure minors well into physical adulthood. The failure to address the rights of individuals, analyzed in Chapter 3, gains a practical importance when discussing the rights of single adult girls. Ann Elizabeth Mayer (2007), for example, has written about the conception of Islamic women's rights as human rights in the Universal Islamic Declaration of Human Rights (UIDHR), in which no provisions are made for unmarried women. This is understandable, since in Muslim countries, including Morocco and hence my field-site community of Oued al-Ouliya, girls are not only expected to get married but are required to fulfill their religious and societal duty. In such a scheme autonomous women in the form of unmarried adult *girls*, who are not answerable to either their male kin or that of their husband, are not envisaged. Recognizing eighteen as the legal age of responsibility does not indicate personal independence from family authority, which is evident in article 198 of the Mudawwana. This article obliges the father to provide for his daughter not only until the age of twenty-five, if she pursues further education, but "until she can earn a living on her own or until her maintenance becomes incumbent upon her husband." This article did not have in mind provincial areas like Oued al-Ouliya, where not only underemployment and poorly paid (seasonal) jobs of educated single adult girls prevent them from living independently from their families but, more significantly, customs and the notions of shame and modesty require girls to live at their father's house and under the authority of their male kin until they get married. Women's rights to protection becomes a facade for paternalism. In such a system only marital status can legally and societally empower women. This leads me to suggest that the Mudawwana does not deal with gender relations but rather with marital relations and, more importantly, with married women's rights and not women's rights per se regardless of marital status. In other words, the new Family Code seeks to remedy the status of married women only, whereas many single girls of legal age remain under overpowering control of their families not only because of the local customs but also because of the law itself. At the heart of the reformed Mudawwana is the preservation of the established and traditional patriarchal system, in which the family dictates the roles, life choices, as well as behavior of its members. In practice this indicates retraditionalization of society and gender relations within it.

Moreover, denying legitimacy to gender equality on an ideological basis has salient repercussions for women's position and image in society. Emphasizing biological differences between women and men, as is done by the JSO, the PJD, and conservatives more generally, translates into undue division of public and private space. Women and men are increasingly perceived as having access to equal rights in the public domain (where their roles are much more overlapping, and this can be seen in women taking up positions of authority, such as those of ministers, CEOs of companies, university deans, judges, etc.), however, their reproductive organs limit their rights and dictate their obligations in the domestic domain, which in turn defines women's (as men's) principal function in society. Becoming a *complete woman* does become a political program as de Beauvoir warned. Such definition of gender based on biological differences is detrimental to single adult girls, who because of their failure to fulfill their assumed biological *duty* cannot enjoy the same rights as (married) women. Womanhood is defined by marriage and the ability to reproduce, not by legal age. Since having children outside of wedlock is not only heavily frowned on but also criminalized, single adult girls by their very nature cannot be treated as *complete women*. As such, their public role is generally not contested, whereas their position at home remains largely unchanged despite positive gains in the realm of education, employment, and other civil rights and freedoms.

Conclusion

Neither the laws, the reformed Mudawwana, societal attitudes, nor the current state of Moroccan economy allow girls from politically and economically marginalized areas such as Oued al-Ouliya to put their education to work to become autonomous individuals and empowered in the process, as is assumed by the development, as well as feminist, campaigns. On the contrary, liberation in the context of Oued al-Ouliya, but also Morocco more generally, implies becoming a *complete woman*, which for the time being can only be achieved by getting married and giving birth to children. The status of single adult girls is neglected, and the pervasive women's rights discourse, adopted and promoted by the Moroccan state, fails to adequately address their fragile situation and improve their legal and societal status.

Conclusion

One of my research trips to Morocco was in the tumultuous spring of 2011. I expected the atmosphere in Rabat to be jovial and hopeful, particularly among the feminist groups, because the king announced constitutional reforms and invited civil society to actively participate in the drafting of the promised new political and social order. After all, their activities focus principally on ameliorating strategic gender needs, and therefore a constitutional reform enshrining gender equality represents an important step toward this goal. What I found, however, was a feeling of things falling apart. The judge in Rabat, whose profession is frequently being criticized by the feminist groups, was defensive in his answers, taking much time out of his, undoubtedly, busy day to explain to me his rationale behind his and other judges' rulings on, for example, underage marriages. Some of the interviews with women's rights activists, feminist and Islamist alike, were palpably more emotional than anticipated and when compared with those conducted on my previous research trips. There was a sense of antagonism, which was directed against those who held ideologically opposing Weltanschauungen as regards what modernity entails, as well as a strong need to defend one's position vis-à-vis the "Other." (Both of these are not new developments by any means, but they appeared to me to be noticeably intensified in 2011.) This was evident in the interviews with the secular feminists, who know that their status as a minority urban and francophone voice makes them particularly vulnerable and exposed to verbal attacks in a conservative society. They at times were critical of my attempt to situate myself outside the politicized debates and interpreted what I thought was my attempt at Weberian objectivity as falling in the trap of the alleged double discourse of the Islamists. In addition to this, the rivalry among the secularist feminists for limited funding and leadership further contributed to their already weak position vis-à-vis the Islamists. JSO women, too, were asserting their voices within the male-dominated organization, as well as defending the righteousness of their voices within a liberalizing state. Both movements, however, appeared to be leaving little space to the possibility of recognizing the legitimacy of an alternative discourse, be it religious or secular, if not an atheist, one. The intransigent promotion of one's own agenda as the only solution for Moroccan women shows that while the regime may indeed be stretching the boundaries of freedom of speech such shift toward greater tolerance has yet to occur among the civil society groups, the very symbol of a liberalizing society. As argued in Chapter 2, both of these movements assume that education in the sense of resocialization of Moroccans will transform their ostensible false consciousness and invariably bring about an ideologically homogeneous nation-state.

All of these conversations and those with ordinary people informed my analysis of the Family Code—its content as well as the meanings. In contrast to what is widely believed among the activist and the international human rights and development communities, I argue that the Code itself does not revolutionize gender, marital, or family relations. Instead, the reformed Mudawwana provides women and girls who are about to get married (but not single adult girls) additional legal *options*, rather than grants them *rights*, to ameliorate their position within the family. The right to choose to get married without a *wali* is one such example, as are the options to stipulate conditions in the marital contract or to decide upon comanagement of marital property. Although the drafters of the Family Code intended these inclusions to enhance the rights of women, they are still only options and not rights granted to women, which their *wali* and the *'adul* would have to automatically respect. The actual recognition as well as the exercise of these options are contingent upon the woman's family and the social milieu in which she resides and not on the law itself. The argument can hence be made that judges merely operate within the sanctioned discriminatory legal system for which the survival of the family and its rights are situated above those of its individual members. Justice Minister Mustapha Al-Ramid's statement on national TV following the suicide of Amina Filali in March 2012 that the judge merely acted upon what is permissible by law[1] reinforces this argument. It also underpins the conclusion put forward by Judge Farchadou that judges are called upon to solve social problems with the aim to avoid the decay of the family and consequently society. According to Willman Bordat, the family and penal legislations are "more [prescriptive] of an ideal . . .

than reflective so [they're] not responding to people's social reality and [they're] not giving people real solutions to real problems." Within such a system, "doing justice to women" cannot but be read as being in opposition to "preserving man's dignity."

During my time in Morocco it became clear to me that although corruption of judges and other court personnel in charge of implementing the Mudawwana certainly impedes the impact of the reformed law on society,[2] the problem is much more nuanced. Illiteracy and the general ignorance about the law are the two most frequently cited causes for the lack of implementation of the law besides the oft-mentioned corruption of judges. However, in Chapters 3 through 5 I demonstrate that even in marginalized areas such as Oued al-Ouliya, where illiteracy rates are higher than the national average, the majority of women and men are nonetheless aware of the reforms even if only in a cursory manner. More important than the issue of illiteracy, however, is that there is a culture of silence cloaked in the notion of female modesty, which perpetuates and condones discrimination against women. In such a society, gendered discrimination or indeed violence is perceived as a private matter. ADFM's Shadow Report (2007) on Morocco's implementation of CEDAW principles informs us that the vast majority of women who had at first filed a complaint of gender-based violence with the judicial and police authorities, later turned to counseling and legal assistance centers of NGOs because of the failure to implement laws and lack of harmonization of rules, legal philosophies, and procedures. The 2012 Global Rights' report on domestic violence in Morocco corroborates these assertions and relates that the police either do not respond to phone calls or mishandle cases of gender-based violence, oftentimes even by implying that women are themselves to blame for provoking violent behavior. Thus, rather than blaming women and their ostensible ignorance of the existing laws or lack of skills to navigate the system, reports such as these reveal that women are denied access to justice and just treatment by the authorities. As Bordat and Kouzzi conclude, "Under the . . . circumstances, in which laws are either not applied, are unclear, or have gaps, awareness of them is insufficient; knowledge alone is not power and does not effect change" (2009, 20). I contend that in a functioning system—where access to, for example, lawyers, legal counseling, social workers, informed police, and medical staff is established and their help not subject to personal prejudices—individuals do not need to know the ins and outs of the law in order to be able to enjoy legal protection. What they need to be made aware of is that services that help them understand their rights and pursue their legal options are available to them. In Morocco, no such infrastructure exists in (m)any areas, further marginalizing women and denying their already circumscribed legal rights. In other words, access to justice in Morocco is severely curtailed by the lack of available infrastructure, personal preconceptions, and patriarchy rather than people's lack of literacy skills.

Moreover, as demonstrated in the discussion raised in Chapters 3 and 4 on the issues of *wali* and prenuptial agreements, the impact of patriarchal relations is so pervasive that women are refused help and/or support from the *ʿadul* and judges in charge of implementing state laws. This is not necessarily due to them being corrupt, since it can be attributed to their personal prejudices and the vagueness of the law, which allow for flexibility in interpretation and application. While judges and the *ʿadul* liberally apply their discretionary rights in interpreting the law, people trick it. Both acts can be read as strategies to reconsolidate societal patriarchal status quo, which could be violated if justice, in the sense of the drafters of the reform, was done for women. Such resorting to bypassing the law by some leads me to two salient conclusions. First, people need to be aware of the Family Code reasonably well enough to know how to deal with it in order to avoid legal sanctions for breaking the law, as for example when marrying an underage daughter without the judge's authorization. As such, the argument most often put forward that the Mudawwana's lack of implementation is a consequence of the general ignorance of the law is necessarily simplistic. Time and again I was told by Moroccans I spoke with that the Mudawwana should be treated in a flexible way and that local traditions and customs overpower it. The current reformed Family Code allows for such freedom in interpretation because, as Willman Bordat rightly contends:

> From the legal point of view [the Mudawwana] is not that well written. . . . That's coming from the American perspective where our laws are really detailed and every single word has to count and be precise. And every single thing needs to be included in the law. . . . So, from the technical standpoint, just in terms of the language, the law gives a lot of discretion to the judges to apply it in the way they want to because there are a lot of provisions that are grey, that are not clear, loopholes, and total gaps of things that are not addressed. . . . What the law hasn't addressed at all is the financial relationship between spouses and the distribution of property after divorce, which is a major problem [because it violates women's] economic rights and their financial security during marriage and upon divorce. . . . There is one article in the law which talks about

this and it is unclear. In the European Civil Codes on this issue you're talking about entire chapters just on that topic, with hundreds of articles. That's not a topic that you can address in one article.

I conclude therefore, that the Mudawwana is in fact implemented. However, because of the imprecision of the articles, its application differs from one jurisdiction to the other, depending on the socioeconomic, customary, family, and geographical idiosyncrasies of the community, court personnel, and its clients. And second, substantive law is becoming increasingly recognized by Moroccans as the law that needs to nonetheless be respected, if only after one tricks it—as in the case of retroactive registration of marriages *bi-l-Fatiha*. This in and of itself is significant, especially considering the feminists and their belief that outlawing gender discrimination by way of reforming the legal order is the first step to the amelioration of women's position within society.

The psychological impact of the reformed Mudawwana is the one characteristic of the law that is acknowledged by its proponents as well as opponents. What is germane is that whether emanating a spirit of equality or a spirit of conflict, the underlying topics, such as the definition of gender inequality or injustice, continue to be mulled over in public. Feminist activists in addition to the majority of the women I spoke with in Oued al-Ouliya regard the reform as the defining moment, if not the key document, of the struggle for women's rights and overcoming the spiral of silence by generating continuous debates. It is such debates that are contributing to the reassessment of national, local, and personal identities, as well as testing the durability of certain taboos, such as having sex outside of wedlock and the personal autonomy of individuals.

Having said this, while the impact of the (spirit of the) Mudawwana ten years on should not be disregarded, its effect needs to be measured against the developments brought by better education, globalization, restructuring of the world economy, immigration, technology, and access to modern media. I argue that it is these, rather than the reformed Family Code, which are the main vehicle of and for change. The emergence of (satellite) TV, mobile phones, and the Internet, in addition to their relative affordability and expansion, are beginning to challenge gendered boundaries of propriety even in smaller and marginalized communities. Girls in particular are avid consumers of such technology, as it allows them to circumvent family, sociolegal, and geographical limitations; yet at the same time it brings with it new dangers to compromise their and their family's name as well as their future. Moreover, girls' migration to cities to pursue higher education represents a further challenge to the conservative ideology of female modesty because it licenses the modernist claim to personal autonomy and freedom. A twenty-year-old girl, who was studying to become a film producer and whom I briefly met in Ouarzazate, explained the trouble with modernity. "Women got more rights, but with more rights comes freedom, and with freedom comes more responsibility. And it's better that women know less." By such reckoning, freedom can be burdensome rather than liberating because it expands a woman's personal responsibilities toward the collective. In the kind of society where malicious sexist stereotypes and gynophobia abound, it should not come as a surprise that the only tool in the hands of the families to reverse this trend is to forbid girls to experience freedom from family authority. In practical terms this has resulted in many families and/or would-be husbands with their families preventing girls from pursuing higher education based on the assumption that a girl's freedom would negatively reflect on their own honor.

The discussion that invariably accompanies the agenda of the enhancement of women's rights is therefore a discussion about people's conceptions of modernity, which stands in contrast with the entrenched local traditions. As such, it is necessarily a debate about women's protection. As analyzed in Chapters 3 through 5, this is a physical as well as an emotional protection, which the girl is entitled to if and only when she fulfills her customary obligations toward the family.[3] Modernity increased the opportunities of being tempted by "immoral" behavior and circumventing her obligations, particularly for those girls going to universities in Morocco's larger cities. In this transition state, modernity with encroaching materialism and greater mobility of people, which leads to greater freedom from the watchful eye of the family, offers increased autonomy to individuals. However, the post-Washington consensus state dismantled or indeed failed to develop social services, which could otherwise act as an alternative to the despotism of family "protection." Individuals, and particularly those most vulnerable in society—children and unmarried adult girls—are therefore forced to entrust themselves to the family. Judges and the ʿadul, too, can be implicated in the perpetuation of such a system when they, under the pretext of protecting the girl, allow underage marriages. For them, the only other alternative to authorizing a girl to get married is for her to be dishonored, expelled by her family, and consequently end up on the street. Instead of questioning and criticizing the current state, which does not provide other and more humane alternatives, judges and the ʿadul perpetuate the vicious circle of women's marginalization. It seems inevitable that promoting aspects of modernity, such as education, employment, and autonomy of women, without addressing the underlying causes of the persevering neopatriarchy and social inequality conveys a rather bewildering and dangerous message to people living especially in more conservative, socially, and materially deprived provincial communities such as Oued al-Ouliya. The reform of family legislation is therefore merely a drop in the ocean, one minuscule aspect of overhauling the larger social, political, legal, and economic discriminatory system(s), which cannot but fail in bringing about significant amelioration of the position of women in society if on its own.

With a disproportionately young population in Morocco one has to ask how the concept of social deprivation and marginalization relates to them. Educated single adult girls from provincial areas serve as an example of the necessity to rethink political, legal, economic, and developmental strategies of the country. What makes their position less advantageous than that of their married female and male counterparts? Material poverty in Morocco among both men and women, irrespective of the household type they live in, remains high despite numerous statistics demonstrating that it is declining. Lahcen Achy's (2010) report written for the Carnegie Endowment regards Morocco's experience with poverty reduction as a lesson for the Arab world. He is right in concluding that Morocco has achieved (numerical) poverty reduction, but in doing so it has neglected human development. However, Achy's conclusion that the issues of social exclusion and lack of human development are primarily problems of material poverty and illiteracy, rather than situating them within the context of persisting systemic patriarchy promoted principally by the state and its agents, is necessarily wanting. Engagement with gender, the impact of local traditions, neoliberal policies promoted by the state, and reaffirmation of patriarchal gendered relations are more or less ignored in his analysis. (Achy, for example, negates the impact of local traditions on sending children to school and, again, blames poverty for it.)

The issue of material poverty is much more multidimensional than manifested in statistics based on monetary measurements. Material poverty was certainly a concern for many families in my field-site community. Other families, however, lived a seemingly comfortable rural middle-class life, and my field-site family was one such household.[4] Khalti Ftouch's oldest living son, Ahmed, resided with his wife, Buchra, and four daughters in Khemisset, a town in the northeastern part of Morocco. He was a government-employed engineer, suggesting that as a white-collar worker he was earning a decent salary. Despite Ahmed living in a different city with his family and supporting his two daughters in Spain, he was sending a monthly allowance of 1,000 dirhams (approximately 120 dollars) to my field-site family.[5] Furthermore, the youngest son, Zakariya, was a public school teacher. As such, I was told, he earned 6,000 dirhams (approximately 720 dollars) a month, though I was not able to verify this sum. In fact, more significant than the real sum of his salary is the wealth ascribed to public school teachers. Their house was comparable to those of families whose members emigrated abroad. It was renovated with new tiles and several salons furnished with Moroccan-style couches rather than being equipped with merely a few blankets or *ponges* (mattresses) thrown on the exposed cement floor. They also had a computer with an Internet connection, a landline, and other amenities, such as a washing machine and a tiled bathroom with a Western-style toilet that no one ever used.[6] In addition, Karima worked outside the house but kept the earned money for herself, implying that the family did not need her money. (She only contributed to the household budget for various *munasabat* [festivities] to help with the cost.) Despite my field-site family's rather comfortable financial position within the context of the community, the women frequently indicated that the family was poor compared to some other families, whose members worked abroad. Those families, they often emphasized, were *labas ʿalayhum* (wealthy, doing well) and not them.

Quite early into my fieldwork I noticed that materialism in terms of both owning and showing off one's assets was an important aspect of self-definition for particularly the younger and middle-aged married women. This was illustrated to me during the *ʿAid al-adha* (Sacrifice Day holidays) in November 2009. The Khemisset family came in their somewhat exhausted 1980s Mercedes-Benz, which for the next ten days took us everywhere, even to visit neighbors around the corner. The plump forty-something-year-old Buchra one day out of the blue decided to show all the family her Spanish and Moroccan credit and debit cards, in addition to a couple of boxes that contained, as she stressed, only a fraction of her jewelry. There was also much boasting about their seventeen- and twenty-year-old daughters and their Spanish residency permits, which they had obtained so that the older sister could take courses in hospitality training, while the youngest one accompanied her to find a job and a husband. Moreover, living in a "Moroccan modern house" rather than in the "rural-type of residence,"[7] owning multiple electrical appliances and a car, as well as wearing a heavy load of golden jewelry to numerous *munasabat* is an idiosyncratic quality married women pursued because their femininity and good repute have been established and they are taken care of. Being poor for most of the married women I associated with was thus expressed in the lack of possessing consumerist goods rather than in social deprivation. A male director of one of the local women's organizations I was introduced to as a researcher of women's rights did not lose time with the usual questions about my research and origin. Instead, before I could make a comment on gender relations in the community, he quickly delimited the state of women's rights vis-à-vis men's and criticized the twenty-first-century woman, saying that she "only wants a TV, a DVD player, a satellite dish. And we [men] have to fulfill their needs, but the problem is that there aren't any jobs in this region." (Interestingly, DVD players were more or less in the house for the appearances. I only saw individuals occasionally rerun wedding DVDs, yet possessing a player was deemed a necessary amenity.) Adeline Masquelier's (2005) conclusion on consumerism in rural Niger resonates with my field-site findings. She argues that "consumption [in an era of economic collapse] must be understood as a strategic practice of identity-making that anchors consumers—and their detractors—in an other, better world" (63). Modern rural girls in her field site aspired to "prosperous domesticity," where they expected "to be showered with market-bought goods" regardless of whether their husbands were poor seasonal workers or public officials (74). Being married, protected, and with a more or less secure position as an honorable woman in society, the emotional needs of women in Masquelier's community and in my field site seem to be fulfilled. They were recognized as *complete women*. Living in a rural community, where uniformity is celebrated while individualism is restricted, ownership of modern consumerist goods is the only means to define and enhance their social standing, as well as to differentiate themselves from the other married women. (Interestingly, a parallel can be drawn with the 1950s American housewife [Friedan 2010].)

Spending three weeks with the Khemisset girls drew my attention not only to the wide gap between the life experiences of urban, somewhat spoiled, girls and their rural counterparts, but also to the depth of social deprivation of my girlfriends in Oued al-Ouliya. Single adult girls, and particularly those with education, perceived poverty less in material terms—or nonownership of market-bought goods—than they did in being socially marginalized. A few weeks before my final departure my girlfriend Nour and I sat in front of her mud-brick home talking about me leaving the village soon. I then sighed with sorrow for my stay was coming to the end. Nour, however, would have none of it and chided me for thinking that I could possibly have anything to be sad about: "What are you sighing about? You have a PhD and a husband" were her only words, which said more about her situation than mine. Nour and my other educated single adult girlfriends often commented on my ability to travel and do research without asking my husband or, when I was still single, my family for permission. They, on the other hand, first and foremost lack authority, if not the right, to decide about *their* life choices or to act upon *their own* aspirations. Lack of substantial financial means is, without a doubt, an important aspect contributing to their social deprivation and marginalization, but even girls living in fairly well-off households[8] were not in the position to decide about their own career choices or place of residence. In fact, some of the girls from well-off families with their fathers, brothers, or uncles living abroad were worse off in terms of personal autonomy compared to those in materially more vulnerable households. The girls from *labas ʿalayhum* families did not have to work or study (or were not allowed to do so) because they were financially provided for until they would get married.

It is true that married women to a large extent are not autonomous in the same manner as I am, yet homogenizing the experiences of women and disregarding the impact of the marital status on the legal and social position of women is oversimplifying the problem. According to the local ideology, single girls regardless of their educational and socioeconomic background are not yet complete women; neither is their protection secured or their good reputation verified. They, furthermore, are also much more stigmatized as married women and their personal autonomy as well as legal rights much more restricted, if not nonexistent.

Moreover, concentrating disproportionately on who heads households, rather than looking at inner-household power relations and at the effect of family as well as state patriarchy on different categories of women irrespective of the type of household, necessarily distorts the overall evaluation of the assumed progress of Morocco. Repeating the mantra of the importance of education while only paying lip service to the significance of implementing real and meaningful legal, political, economic, and societal reforms only perpetuates the vicious circle of social exclusion and marginalization of certain categories of women and social classes. Local customs and traditions, discussed in Chapters 3 through 5, are an impediment to women's rights and justice, but they do not exist in a vacuum, independent from the larger state structures—namely, patriarchy and the overall political and economic ideologies. In this liquid modernity, where no one model has been able to grow firm roots, the struggle for the contemporary Moroccan identity is carried out by an array of actors. Such polarization contributes to the schizophrenic character of Moroccanness, well captured in the *TelQuel* article introducing the subject matter of Chapter 2. However, opening the public space to such ideological debates as is represented by the question of what contemporary Moroccan national identity is leaves the regime much leeway to further entrench the neoliberal state, in which the plight of the youth is not adequately addressed, if not forgotten, as the case of the educated single adult girls from provincial areas discussed in Chapter 5 manifested.

Hester Eisenstein (2005) is right in contending that contemporary feminists the world over have internalized the neoliberal agenda in promoting such economic policies as privatization, shrinking of the welfare services, and applying a wide range of other austerity measures in the countries of the Global South. The enhancement of women's legal rights, the promotion of education, and integration of women into the labor market are regarded as panaceas to economic and personal development. In doing so, however, feminists and the development communities have failed to address the shrinking or, in fact, the nonexistence of the welfare state, which could protect women from being exploited as cheap labor or from being denied the protection of their families for acting as autonomous individuals. Moroccan secular feminists as well as the conservatives, who operate within the state, are careful in presenting their women's agendas as nonpolitical battles, viewing the domestic space as the key to women's oppression. Morocco, after all, is still an authoritarian state. JSO in this respect may be regarded as an exception, which is attributable to their expulsion from the sanctioned political space and can therefore afford to be more vocal in their criticism of the regime. Their ambiguous stand regarding gender equality, gender roles, and the position of personal autonomy within the rights discourse, in addition to the schism along gender lines within the organization discussed in Chapter 2, however, does not inspire confidence that their involvement in mainstream politics would in fact engender an alternative agenda to the existing one.

Without a legal system that recognizes, protects, and expands rights of individuals as autonomous beings, one that actively combats misogynist attitudes, without the kind of economic policies and the overall human development, which integrate marginalized women and men from economically depressed areas, neither improved education nor a (weak) reform of family legislation will help ameliorate the position of Moroccan adult girls specifically and women and men more generally. The debate about the Mudawwana and its failure to significantly broaden the rights of Moroccan women regardless of their marital and socioeconomic status is therefore necessarily a debate about the persisting state patriarchy, sanctioned and indeed promoted by the regime.

Appendix

Information about the interviewees in Oued al-Ouliya

Abdallah Twenty-four years old and unmarried. Finished middle school and works as a TV technician. He lives around the corner from my field-site family and is one of Nour's brothers.

Aissam Thirty-eight years old and married with three children. He works as a primary school teacher, with a B.A. in Islamic law. When I first met him in 2008, in Ifrane, he was still the director of the USAID Passerelles literacy project for Tamazirt. As part of his position, he did a lot of training on the Mudawwana. In Ifrane he gave lectures about the literacy course (and hence the reform) to the other regional directors and literacy teachers. He is very knowledgeable about the reform but also very eager about the literacy project. During the interview with him in Oued al-Ouliya two years later, Aissam demonstrated that he was au courant with the law and women's rights more specifically, but he also acted as a very articulate source of information in explaining the "whys" of people's behavior and attitudes toward issues arising from the reformed law.

Ali Forty-seven years old and married with three children. He finished middle school and works as a technician/assistant for the community administration.

Aziza Nineteen years old and divorced without children. She dropped out of school after finishing middle school because she got married. She was seventeen at the time. Aziza stayed with her husband for two years before she returned home and filed for divorce on the grounds of physical and emotional abuse. She lives at home and is unemployed. I spent much time with her and her sister at their home and hence developed a close relationship with both of them. Aziza sometimes used me as an excuse to leave the house because her father was very stern and only allowed her to leave the house if she had some business to attend to.

Azzeddine Forty years old and married with one child. He finished middle school and co-owns with his brother one of the cybercafes in Taddert.

Boutayyeb Fifty-four years old and married with four children. He finished the first year of high school and is the director of Taddert's primary school. He was very reluctant to do the interview with me, and when he finally agreed to it he was very defensive about *his* culture that was being eroded by *my* culture.

Fqi   Fifty-five years old and married without children. He finished first year of middle school and works as a faith healer, which he explained means to cure people with spirituality and herbs. The interview with him was extremely animated.

Ghizlane   Twenty-one years old and engaged. At the time of my fieldwork she was finishing high school and preparing for her baccalaureate exams (required to graduate from high school).

Habiba   Twenty-four years old and unmarried. She has a B.A. degree in English and teaches English at Tamazirt's private primary school.

Hajar   Twenty-seven years old and divorced. She dropped out of school at level five of primary school at the age of fifteen to get married, but she divorced soon thereafter because, as the rumor went, she was not a virgin. Hajar was attending informal education at the time of my fieldwork.

Hajj   Fifty-four years old and married with four children. He has a B.A. in sociology and works as a primary school teacher.

Hamid   Forty-eight years old and married with five children. He has a high school diploma (a baccalaureate in the French/Moroccan system). He is the elected president of Oued al-Ouliya and the director of the local women's association. He is the maternal uncle of my two neighbors, Abdallah and Nour.

Hanan   Twenty-nine years old and married with two children. She dropped out of school in the third year of middle school and is a housewife. Her husband works in France. She is the older sister of Habiba.

Hasan   Fifty years old and married with four children. He finished primary school and is a manual worker. He was one of the very few men I interviewed who was of the opinion that there are situations when it is justifiable to beat the wife.

Jamal   Late thirties and married with children (he never told me how many). He is a physical education teacher at one of the local primary schools.

Khalti Ftouch   In her seventies, but no one knows her specific age. She is widowed with seven children. She is illiterate and the matriarch in my field-site family.

Malika   Twenty-four years old and married, but at the time of my fieldwork she still lived at her father's home. Malika asked (or perhaps made a condition) for a long "engagement,"[1] and over a year passed between the signing of the contract and the wedding—not because she was hesitant about getting married, quite the contrary, she could hardly wait to be Tariq's wife and give birth to children, but because she loved her job as a teacher in the kindergarten. She "agreed" with her husband that after the wedding she would stay at home.

Mama   Forty years old and widowed with two children. She finished primary school and is a housewife. She was married to Khalti Ftouch's eldest son, who passed away soon after the birth of his second child.

Mouna   Thirty years old and unmarried. She has a B.A. in law, works as a literacy teacher, runs the local listening center (*markaz al-istima'a*) for women victims of violence.

Najat Twenty-four years old and recently married. She does not have much formal education, but she would occasionally come to informal education classes. Until the wedding, Najat lived with her two brothers because both of her parents had died when she was a child. Her two brothers arranged the marriage for her.

Nadia Thirty-two years old and married with one child. She lives alone in a rented apartment because her husband married a second wife in 2009 at the instigation of his parents, who never accepted Nadia as his wife. After finding out about her husband's second marriage, she wanted to divorce him, but the judge refused it (on the grounds that she doesn't have any valid reasons to divorce him). When I asked her about her feelings toward the situation, she told me that she had reconciled with her husband and the idea of a polygynous marriage because, despite everything, "it is better to be protected." She finished four years of primary school and is a housewife. Nadia is Siham's sister and Aziza's aunt.

Nour Thirty years old and single. She has a degree in Arabic language and works as a preschool teacher. She is Abdallah's older sister.

Nouzha Thirty-four years old and divorced without children. She attended literacy classes and is a homemaker.

Siham She said she was born in 1973 but added that it was unclear if that was her actual birth year. She is married with five children and Aziza is her daughter. She finished five levels of primary school. She is a housewife.

Soukaina Nineteen years old and divorced without children. She was sixteen at the time of her wedding. Soukaina dropped out of school before finishing primary level and she occasionally attended informal education classes during my fieldwork. Her mother is Zaynab.

Tariq Twenty-one years old and married to Malika. He finished middle school and is a construction worker.

Touriya Thirty-seven years old and married with three children. She finished the fourth level of primary school and is a housewife.

Yasmin Forty years old and divorced with four children. She spent her childhood in France with her parents, who withdrew her from primary school at the age of fourteen to marry her off to her cousin back in Oued al-Ouliya. She was very critical of local customs, such as marrying off underage girls, and was quite bitter toward her parents, who still live in France and who took her passport away so that she would not be able to join them.

Youssef Forty-seven years old and married with three children. He has a high school diploma and works as a primary school teacher.

Zaynab In her late thirties and married with five children. Soukaina is her daughter. She is originally from Oujda and moved to Oued al-Ouliya after she married an older man from there. He is her second husband.

Zoulikha Over the age of thirty and married without children. Her husband was in prison in France at the time of my fieldwork. She has a high school diploma and is a housewife who lives at home because her husband is unable to provide for her.

Notes

Introduction

1. All names of people and places referring to my field-site community are pseudonyms.

2. Bennani 2007.

3. Under the abrogated Personal Status Code *khul'a* divorce was one of the only options that a woman had in order to seek divorce from her husband. During my fieldwork many women still thought that this was their *only* option if they wished to dissolve their marriage. In 2011, 18.08 percent of divorces were by compensation.

4. As will be shown in Chapter 2, Islamist women I interviewed refuse to call themselves feminists because of the term's ideological overtones, but they nonetheless share many of the fundamental ideas of feminism.

5. In a personal interview with Merieme Yafout, the former president of the JSO's women's section, she, too, calls them liberal feminists, whereas Nadia Yassine, the daughter of the late JSO's founding father and spiritual guide (*mursid*) shaykh Abdessalam Yassine, doubts that there is a genuine feminist movement in Morocco. Instead, she calls the women partisans (*nisa' muhazabat*).

6. This became particularly acute during the One Million Signatures Campaign to change the Personal Status Code in the early 1990s, when the conservative forces such as al-Tajkani, an independent Islamist *'alim*, and Abdelillah Benkirane, the Secretary General of the PJD who became prime minister in 2011, denounced secular feminists behind the campaign as apostates and a threat to Islam and the Moroccan family. See Buskens 2003; Salime 2011.

7. *TelQuel*'s journalist Sonia Terrab in 2009, for example, wrote an article on violence against women in which she exposed the level of unresponsiveness of the state institutions and their staff to women victims of domestic violence seeking protection, despite the reformed Mudawwana. It has to be emphasized, however, that there is a general misconception about the content and nature of the Family Code, as this law does not deal with gender-based violence. In many ways, the "spirit" of the Family Code (if it indeed is one of greater gender equality, as will

be explored in continuing chapters) contradicts the letter and the tone of the conservative Penal Code, which, if anything, is much more bluntly concerned with preserving female modesty even in cases of sexual and physical assault.

8. MPI went beyond measuring poverty on the basis of income only. This index was developed in 2010 and includes numerous aspects of deprivation, such as education, child mortality, nutrition, and available infrastructure or access to services.

9. For a very insightful analysis of the "marriage crisis" in urban Cairo during the British protectorate, with a similar outcome to today's delayed marriage crisis, see Kholoussy 2010. For a comparative view of youth struggle for social adulthood in Niger, where men delay marriage, much like in MENA, due to unemployment, bridewealth inflation, and the increasing consumerism of girls and their families, see Masquelier 2005.

Chapter 1: Ethnographic Reflections

1. Interestingly, statistics contained in the 2004 national census show a much smaller number of inhabitants than the community monograph, which is also dated 2004. The latter reports approximately 26,000 inhabitants. Throughout, I will note other instances of such discrepancies in data.

2. Harris, in fact, reported about forty-odd *ksour*, while de Foucald reckoned there were thirteen. Despite the inconsistency regarding the number of *ksour*, it is fair to conclude that the settlement is an old and established one.

3. Naciri (1986) reported of a drought between 1979 and 1986, which caused the drying up of wells and traditional underground water tunnels, called *khattaras*, used for the irrigation of the palm groves particularly in the region of Tafilalet for centuries. People who relied on agriculture were forced to sell their land, leading to building houses on what used to be productive land.

4. Khalti means (my) aunt; however, the expression is used to address older ladies.

5. The family always introduced me to other people as being a Frenchwoman (*faransawiyya*) or introduced me to other people as being from France, despite knowing that I come from Slovenia. Particularly in this rural setting, where many people were uneducated and lacked traveling experience, France was among the very few countries they heard of through the stories of numerous locals who emigrated to France to find work. France, in short, symbolized the outside world, and I was an outsider.

6. It was interesting for me to see how my being from Eastern Europe or, even more tellingly, from the Balkans, did not in any way play a role in their conception of me; neither did my affiliation with the University of Oxford, two aspects of me that usually drew attention of people in the West. What defined me much more decidedly was that my father was a medical doctor and my mother, who is a retired nurse, drives her own car. Such emphasis on social attributes of my parents is understandable. Europe for the women in my field site is *Europe* and although they have heard of communism (although not socialism), their knowl-

edge of geography, history, and political terminology is almost nonexistent and hence not tainted with such ideological divisions as the "free" West and the "repressed" East. My father being a doctor, in addition to my mother driving a car and earning a pension, in the context of this village is something that unequivocally denotes an urban family of a higher social class. Being their daughter, hence, meant that I grew up in a privileged household, leading a privileged life. How family background defines a person, rather than her own achievements, will be further explored in Chapter 3.

7. I should note that I am generalizing about married women and I am not emphasizing their level of education in the same manner that I do for single adult girls. The reason for this will become obvious in the following chapters. Suffice it to say here that I am indeed aware that there are differences between the educated and uneducated women; yet these seem to be facts that make a difference in the statistical sense rather than genuinely affecting women's overall societal status in Oued al-Ouliya. Being married and a mother determines their position within society much more crucially than does being educated or not.

Chapter 2: Politicization of Gender

1. Academics, too, have written about this dichotomous state of mind in Morocco and in the Arab world more generally. See, for example, Daoud 1994; Sharabi 1988; Skalli 2006.

2. Vincent Crapanzano in his study of the Hamdasha religious brotherhoods defines *jnun* as "a race of spiritual beings" and explains that they "are not necessarily evil or harmful. They *are* whimsical and arbitrary, capricious and revengeful, quick-tempered and despotic—and therefore always potentially dangerous" (1981, 138–140; italics in the original). He deals eloquently with the subject of *jnun* particularly in his chapter on the theory of Hamdasha therapies, which are applied to treat physical as well as psychological illnesses thought, or indeed explained, to be caused by *jnun*. While living in Oued al-Ouliya, I was surprised by the frequent conjuring up of the parallel world of *jnun* to explain deviations in the behavior or health problems of individuals, in addition to witnessing the utilization of various forms of therapies by the local *fqi*, whom we shall meet in the following chapter, and Khalti Ftouch. Both educated and illiterate people alike used their services.

3. For a general regional overview of how modernization, understood here as the postcolonial establishment of nation-states and consequent socioeconomic changes, affected MENA societies and women in particular, see for example Abu-Lughod 1998; Keddie 2007; Moghadam 2003a. For a more country-specific study of the effect that modernity has had on societal and gender dislocations, see Abu-Lughod 2008; Adely 2012; Ghoussoub and Sinclair-Webb 2006; Ossman 2002.

4. Kandiyoti's notion of "patriarchal bargains," which describes the nature of gendered division of labor, corresponds to Valentine Moghadam's patriarchal gender contract (1998b, 8–11).

5. One such example is the May 2012 physical assault on a woman in Rabat over wearing "a short modern dress," as one journalist wrote for the online newspaper Magharebia, by a group of men described as Salafists (Saadouni 2012).

6. In a similar manner, my host mother in Fez, Lalla Jamila, as I called her, told me that pedophilia and sexual and physical violence against women were something new, unreported in the "old" Morocco. We will come across similar accounts of the so-called glorified and perfect past throughout this book. Interesting to note here, however, is the mentioning of pedophilia. Lalla Jamila did not define pedophilia, and in hindsight I should have pursued the topic in this direction. What constitutes pedophilia in a country where marrying off girls at the tender age of thirteen is still carried out in some parts of Morocco, in addition to the Salafist shaykh Muhammad bin Abdelrahman Al-Maghraoui sanctioning marriage between an adult man and a girl as young as nine years old in 2008? It is true that both the act of marrying off and getting married to a minor, in addition to the shaykh Al-Maghraoui's *fatwa* are condemned, even laughed at by many people in the country, yet it does show that the questions of sexual maturity and consent are far from being resolved.

7. The predecessor of USFP was *Union Nationale des Forces Populaires* (National Union of Popular Forces—UNFP). It was established in 1959 as a splinter party from the Istiqlal (Independence) and it became the main opposition party. In the 1970s the party further branched off into USFP. PPS was a successor of the Moroccan Communist Party, which was established in 1943, but banned several times after the independence. PPS itself was established in 1974. Interestingly, their ideological leanings did not prevent them from joining a hodgepodge of a coalition government led by the country's Islamist PJD party in 2011.

8. Egyptian socialist women in the immediate post-Nasser era experienced similar setbacks. See Al-Ali 2000.

9. For a few excerpts about single mothers and "bastard" children, see Bargach 2002, 166.

10. The distinction between the "official *'ulema'*" (also called the *'ulema'* of the *makhzen*) and the "independent *'ulema'*" is that whereas the former work under the authority of the Ministry of Endowments and Religious Affairs, the latter operate independently from the state. It is these independent *'ulema'* who function as the think-tanks behind the Islamist organizations (Salime 2011, 5–6).

11. The term *Ikhwan Muslimin* means Muslim Brothers. People in Morocco do not necessarily refer to the Egyptian Muslim Brothers but instead use this term loosely to describe the very socially conservative religious men, who can be identified by wearing a *kufi* (skull cap), long beards, and *jalabiyya* (loose and long shirt-like garment, typical of the eastern part of the Middle East and Arabian Peninsula). These men are sometimes also referred to as *rijal tabligh*. I met a few in my field site and my "meetings" with them were characterized by awkwardness, since I at first was not aware of the fact that they would not shake a woman's hand, let alone look me in the eye or sit in the same room even if there were other people there. On one occasion, the mother of my friend Habiba warned me that her brother was coming for a visit. He adhered to such strict religious ideology, ran a sex-segregated household, and, according to Habiba, he forced his wife to don the *niqab* (full-face veil typical of the Arabian Peninsula). Habiba's mother told me

fairly authoritatively that I, by no means, should try to come into the hallway to greet him or to shake his hand. In fact, she said, it was better for Habiba and myself to stay in the living room with the TV on and the door shut.

12. Morocco's prime minister Benkirane in a speech at the Chamber of Councillors on 17 June 2014 asserted that the lights went off in Moroccan homes when women joined the workforce (Charrad 2014).

13. This seemed to have been Yassine's way of expressing disagreement. After her father died in December 2012, she and some other leading women, such as Merieme Yafout, left JSO for good because of irreconcilable differences between them and the leadership.

14. Although women form half of the membership of the JSO, according to Nadia Yassine, they have never been represented in the highest council of guidance. They are consulted by this council, but women have no ultimate and equal say in the decision-making process.

15. Brand (1998) reports that out of twenty-nine women's organizations in existence in 1989, sixteen were established after 1980.

16. The literature seems to be somewhat confused about which women's organization was the pioneer of Morocco's secular women's rights agenda. Nikki Keddie, for example, in her book *Women in the Middle East: Past and Present* writes that the ADFM was "the first women's organization independent of a political party" (2007, 145). Keddie also wrongly reports that ADFM spearheaded One Million Signatures Campaign. Laurie Brand (1998), too, situates the ADFM as the first politicized women's organization to be established in 1985, followed by the OFI and the UAF two years later in 1987. Baker on the other hand (rightly) writes that Jbabdi's UAF "was the first political organization in Morocco to be established outside of one of the political parties" (1998, 270). The confusion is clarified by the organizations' webpages. *8 Mars* became the mouthpiece of the UAF, which was established in 1983, followed by the ADFM in 1985 (⟨http://www.adfm.ma /spip.php?article439 and http://www.uaf.ma/an/file.php⟩, both accessed November 2011).

17. Salime defines such "movement moments" as "turning points in the trajectory of the Islamist and feminist movements," which allowed her to study these movements in relation to each other rather than comparing them.

18. In 1970 Ester Boserup published what has become a seminal work among development workers and students called *Woman's Role in Economic Development*. In it she used gender as an independent variable in measuring the impact of women's subsistence agriculture on the development of national economies at the time when women's domestic work still tended to be underreported or omitted from national statistics. She furthermore argued that modernization of African countries affected women and men in a profoundly different way. Her work became the inspiration for the Women in Development (WID) approach furthered by mostly American liberal feminists. Both Boserup's ideas and WID are based on modernization theory, which promotes a Weberian model for development of societies based on imitating Western linear transformation from agrarian to industrialized society. Educating women will, according to WID, engender an educated workforce and subsequently lead to the development of national economies.

19. Nadia Yassine in the interview explained that the JSO is certainly advocat-

ing for smaller families. However, rather than making a political issue out of it, which is what, according to her, the WB is doing by telling people that "[they] have no right to have [children]," the JSO uses the Qur'an as the starting point. "My father wrote in the *Tanwir al-mu'minat* [The Enlightenment of Female Believers]," she explained, "that nothing in the religion says that we must be like rabbits. But it's different to say it from our culture, to convince women to have a very small family [in order] to be able to give them proper education. This is our *ijtihad* for the future."

Ijtihad, or progressive reasoning, is an important concept in reformist modernist Muslim thought. While conservative trends within contemporary Muslim communities dispute the validity of such reasoning, others argue that progressive *ijtihad* is exactly what is needed in order to "account for and challenge the great impoverishment of thought and spirit brought forth by Muslim literalist-exclusivists" (Safi 2005, 8).

20. According to the *Arab Reform and Foreign Aid: Lessons from Morocco* report, Morocco represents a medium- to high-priority development target for the United States and Europe. See Malka and Alterman's (2006) report for a more in-depth analysis of foreign aid to Morocco and considerations of Western countries attached to providing financial assistance. WB press release of May 2011 informs that WB has supported the INDH since 2005 and has financed over 22,000 projects at an average of 70,000 dollars a project. Moreover, WB provides about 700 million dollars a year in support to Morocco to fund various development projects, such as health and general poverty-alleviation campaigns, to combat climate change and install solar energy, to combat overpopulation, and to fund Morocco's agricultural plan, called Plan Maroc Vert. See: ⟨http://web.worldbank .org/WBSITE/EXTERNAL/NEWS/0,,contentMDK:22907288~pagePK:642 57043~piPK:437376~theSitePK:4607,00.html, accessed May 2011⟩.

21. Alfred Hackensberger did in fact interview both Jbabdi and Yassine, and their interviews were published in the same online edition of *Heise Online/Telepolis*.

22. Outaleb was also referring to the support of CEDAW expressed by Hakkaoui at the 54th UN session, whereas in Morocco her party was fighting against the removal of Morocco's reservations to articles 9 (2) and 16.

23. I was talking about the *hijab* rather than the *niqab*. There is a sort of obsession among the secular feminists with the *niqab* and the prospect of the state imposing one of the most conservative "Islamic" sartorial and other rules if they, the secularists, do not fight against such "dark" forces. This further indicates the extent of the fear of secularists toward the Islamists as well as a lack of understanding and interaction with them. Jbabdi, for example, in an interview for the German online newspaper said with confidence that the Yassine family wants to establish a system similar to the Iranian Islamic Republic. In fact, she goes on to say, "[Nadia Yassine] wouldn't shy away from going even further than the leader of the revolution Khomeini. The father of Nadia Yassine is closer to the Taliban than to the Iranian Ayatollahs. They want to bring back the golden period, which existed in Medina fourteen centuries ago, when the Prophet was still alive" (Hackensberger 2006).

24. Calling someone *hmar* is a serious insult, especially if said by a woman to a man. I would like to thank the anonymous reviewer for pointing this out.

25. Outaleb probably meant an octopus.

26. Although these listening centers were primarily established for women victims of violence, I was told at El Hajeb's *Association Amal pour la Femme et le Développement* (Association Amal for Women and Development) that children, both boys and girls, also come to their listening center in cases of rape or any other type of sexual assault.

27. The sample used in the survey included 2,000 women and 500 men from across the country.

28. Sadiqi and Ennaji argue that "the most spectacular impact of the Moroccan feminist movement resides in its [*sic*!] gradual feminization and, hence, democratization of the public sphere" (2006, 87).

Chapter 3: The State, the Public, and Women's Rights

1. Parts of this chapter are based on a previously published article (Žvan Elliott 2014). The material appears in this book courtesy of University of Indiana Press.

2. Interestingly, marrying off girls without their consent was practiced in many communities but was not sanctioned by law. The original PSC already required consent of both parties for marriage, and the new Family Code only reinforced what had already been contained within the law but not respected in practice. Articles 4 and 14 of the new Family Code, for example, require (mutual) consent of both the woman and man for marriage; and articles 12, 63, and 66 address duress and its legal repercussions.

3. As with the previous footnote, this was the practice of custom rather than an act permitted by law. The 1993 reform of the PSC required informing both wives of the existence of the other wife. Again, the new Family Code only made additional procedural reforms to reinforce what had already been required by the law.

4. See the Preamble and article 400 of the Family Code for the principles of Islam as recognized by the law, as well as the following two king's speeches: "Al-khitab al-maliki as-sami bimunasaba tansib al-lajna al-istišariyya al-khassa bimuraja'a Mudawwanat al-Ahwal al-Šakhsiyya" ("The Speech of His Royal Highness Regarding the Appointment of the Consultative Commission Pertaining to the Revision of the Personal Status Code") delivered on 27 April 2001. I obtained the speech at the UNESCO Chair for Women and Her Rights at the Faculty of Law, Economics, and Social Sciences in Rabat, Morocco. For the "Speech Delivered by His Majesty King Muhammad VI at the Opening of the Parliament's Fall Session" on 10 October 2003 obtained online, see Ministry of Communication 2003.

5. The *fqi* was trying to excuse violent male behavior toward women who transgress religious prescriptions. Islam, according to him, defines honor as pertaining only to women who behave in a modest way. Such behavior protects women from violence. However, when women act in a dishonorable manner—for example, when they actively seek to seduce men outside their homes—they will get punished for not following the rules. Men therefore need to protect their family's honor and can, as claimed by the interviewee, resort to violence.

6. Historically, both Arabs and Berbers inhabiting this pre-Saharan region considered darker or black people to be inferior. Due to their slave origins they were denied rights to own land and were thus working as sharecroppers for the ("light-skinned") Arabs and Berbers. Today, their status has changed; many own land or have males in their family working abroad to help financially. Despite this, racism persists and the issue occasionally cropped up in my interviews with people as well as in conversations with my friends and field-site family. For an analysis of the slave origins of the Heratin, see El Hamel 2002; Ilahiane 2004.

7. For a historical analysis of the origins of Ismkhan living in Tafilalet, an oasis close to Tamazirt, as well as how they differentiate themselves from the Heratin, see Becker 2002.

8. Interestingly, many of my interviewees accorded many more rights to women employed in the public sector than to housewives; yet in Oued al-Ouliya, the vast majority of married women were indeed housewives and have never worked outside the home.

9. I put *Islamic* in parentheses because it is my understanding that it is diverse local interpretations of and local additions to Islamic laws, rather than Islamic law in and of itself, which suggest that the two systems are inherently in conflict.

10. Morocco reaffirmed its commitment to universal human rights in various documents and reports, such as its combined third and fourth periodic report submitted to the Committee on the Elimination of Discrimination against Women on 18 August 2008 (CEDAW/C/MAR/4).

11. The excerpt is translated from its original in French as it appeared in the *Bulletin Officiel* on 30 July 2011.

12. The article offers a compelling discussion on and an argument about the distinction between the notions of equity and equality as a response to continuing "confusion" among some countries, which use both notions interchangeably or, more alarmingly, they replace the term equality with equity for ideological reasons. The authors of the article clarify the distinction and contend that CEDAW requires equality and not equity between women and men.

13. Although CEDAW allows parties to make reservations, it also declares in article 28, paragraph 2 that "[a] reservation incompatible with the object and purpose of the present Convention shall not be permitted." However, many countries, such as Malaysia, Singapore, and United Arab Emirates have deposited so-called impermissible reservations, which may function as evidence for the weakness of the international legal system and, more specifically, of the UN's lack of enforcement mechanism. The UN has issued many reports and declarations attempting to address this failure. See for example 1993 Vienna Declaration and Program of Action (⟨http://www.unhchr.ch/huridocda/huridoca.nsf/(symbol)/a.conf.157.23.en⟩, accessed March 2013), or Part Two (Matters brought to the attention of State parties) of the Eighteenth and Nineteenth UN Report of the Committee on the Elimination of Discrimination Against Women—A/53/38/Rev.1 (⟨http://www.un.org/womenwatch/daw/cedaw/reports/18report.pdf⟩, accessed March 2013).

14. At the meeting of the Committee on the Elimination of Discrimination Against Women in February 2008, Nouzha Skalli in her role as the Minister of Solidarity, Women, Family, and Social Development confidently announced that

only a few more administrative procedures were needed before Morocco would officially withdraw the reservations, giving it a time frame ranging from a few weeks to a few months at the most (Committee on the Elimination of Discrimination Against Women 2008, 4; ADFM 2007).

15. The UN Human Rights Committee publishes its interpretation of the content of human rights conventions in a series of so-called General Comments.

16. The Moroccan government made a minuscule effort to inform the public, justice professionals, and other stakeholders about the ratification of CEDAW, in addition to only having published it in the *Bulletin Officiel* in 2001, eight years after the ratification (ADFM 2007).

17. "Bassima Hakkaoui hawla raf⁺ al-Maghreb al-tahaffudat." The video can be found at: ⟨http://www.youtube.com/watch?feature=player_embedded&v=iZT zgWhw32s#!⟩, accessed April 2012.

18. Article 1 of the PSC was repealed and replaced by the new article 4. According to the former the family was "under the supervision of the husband," whereas the reformed article places the family "under the supervision of both spouses."

19. Global Rights in its 2008 report *Conditions, Not Conflict: Promoting Women's Human Rights in the Maghreb through Strategic Use of the Marriage Contract* makes an important observation as regards this clause. Recognizing the mother as a possible contributor to family maintenance and its well-being has a significant symbolic value for enhancing women's role within the family. But "in so doing, the law opens the door for the husband to evade his responsibilities towards his wife and children by declaring his total or partial incapacity to provide for his family, while such failure to support remains one of six grounds on which the wife may seek divorce" (32). Therefore, by overhauling some discriminating clauses against women, while reinforcing other, less conspicuous, forms of inequality in marital relations, the law opened up additional avenues for avoiding responsibilities, which may aggravate women's lives and deny them their legal rights.

20. In fact, it is not only some men but also certain national laws as well that apply this "rule." Moroccan judge Malika Mezdali, for example, explained at the CEDAW report hearing in 2008 that the existence of marital rape is not recognized in the Penal Code because marriage is a legal relationship and as such creates conjugal duties (CEDAW/C/SR.824: 8). For a discussion on obedience in Muslim Family Laws, see Nasir 2002; Welchman 2011.

21. Nouzha Skalli is Morocco's former Minister of Solidarity, Women, Family, and Social Development and a member of the PPS. At the meeting of the Committee on the Elimination of Discrimination against Women on 24 January 2008 she reported that the new Family Code "clearly established" gender equality (CEDAW/C/SR.824: 2). She also stated that the reformed Family Code abolished divorce by repudiation (*talaq*) and that it no longer allowed men to take a third or fourth wife (CEDAW/C/SR.825: 7). However, none of these statements are true. There are numerous articles dealing with repudiation, notably 39 (3), 61, 70, 71, 72 (2), in addition to Title Three, which specifically regulates repudiation. As regards polygamy, it is true that the Mudawwana makes specific reference to the second wife or "another wife" (for example, Preamble [point 4] and article 43), but merely omitting the mentioning of a third or fourth wife does not ipso

facto mean that the law specifically forbids taking three or four wives. This leads me to conclude that Skalli was either misleading the Committee or that perhaps she was not very familiar with the reformed law. Moreover, Rahma Bourqia was one of the three female members of Muhammad VI's Consultative Commission for the reform of the PSC. In my interview with her she asserted that the reform introduced "the principle of equality in the definition of marriage. . . . This is a very progressive law in the sense, as I have said, that it has introduced the principle of democracy within the family."

22. Perhaps not insignificant is the detail that during the interview, which was conducted in a café in the Rabat's Kasbah des Oudaias at the time of the Arab Spring, Outaleb mentioned that the man sitting at the adjoining table was eavesdropping on our conversation and suggested that he must have been following me.

23. The choice of the word *wadifa* to denote the function of motherhood is significant because people normally use this word to refer to a job in the public service or to a duty.

Chapter 4: Twenty-First-Century Marriage

1. The idea that people have the "right" to have a job in the public sector will be discussed in the following chapter.

2. When I discussed the issue of gender equality (*musawah bayna al-nisa' wa-l-rijal*) with locals I had to explain the term *equality* to them, saying that women and men are the same (*l-'ayalat ou l-rijal kif kif*).

3. The interviewee said "*šita l-mara ou sayf l-rajl*," literally meaning that winter is a woman and summer is a man, which also corresponds to the grammatical gender of winter (female) and summer (male).

4. An example of such "tricking" the law is registering a second marriage in a different region where no record of a first marriage exists. There is still no central computerized system, which would gather marriage-related data from all of Morocco. This is why it is possible to go to a different township to register a second marriage without the "inconvenience" of needing the first wife's approval or the need for the judge to survey the man's ability to take care of the second wife, as is required by the law. There were 0.31 percent of marriages in 2009, 0.32 percent in 2010, and 0.34 percent in 2011 registered as polygamous marriages (Ministry of Justice 2010, 2011, 2012). Although the percentage is relatively low, the number may in fact be higher owing to unreported second (or third and fourth) marriages. Moreover, that the law still sanctions polygamy is perceived as a continuous threat to the stability of the relationship by most of the women I interviewed or talked to. "There's no woman who would accept the second wife," said Mama, the oldest daughter-in-law in my host family. Many women also used a proverb to explain the reason: A woman doesn't accept another woman, even if she is her daughter (*l-mara ma tqabl l-mara, wakha tkun bintha*). "If I saw you with my husband I wouldn't like that," concluded Zoulikha. "I'd explode or even die because women are more jealous than men."

5. Such an opinion harks back to the so-called Nasserist social contract,

briefly discussed in the introduction. Many people continue to expect, and indeed demand, public sector jobs for the educated upon completing their university degrees, despite the government's having long ago reneged on the promise.

6. Katie Zoglin (2009) in a similar manner (to what the judge is saying) found that judges in Morocco have failed to exercise discretion in a way that is consistent with the spirit of the law, notably justice and equality, and that judges make decisions based on their own subjective evaluation of a case.

7. It was women's organizations that pushed for an additional five years at first, but they soon changed their minds. Fouzia Yassine from ADFM explained why: "Because people trick the law in order to get married again or to take advantage of polygamy." Also see Ait Mousa's (2011) article published in one of Morocco's women's magazine called *Nesma*. In it she reported about a government initiative to bring family judges to rural areas—in this case to the province of Taroudant—to further facilitate retroactive registration of marriages.

8. This practice, however, was oftentimes condemned by the other married men disinclined to cheat on their wives. In John's conversations with men, they sometimes referred to "their" prostitutes as girlfriends, so, he joked, he had to ask them whether they paid them or not in order to clarify the nature of the relationship.

9. I put "engaged" in quotation marks because in order for an engagement to be official the suitor has to bring his parents to meet the parents of the girl and bring gifts for the bride-to-be. These men only promised Aziza that they will marry her but avoided having to meet her parents.

10. The March 2012 suicide by sixteen-year-old Amina Filali, after she had been forced by the judge and, according to some news reports, also her mother, to marry her rapist, shows that judges can, in their capacity as social arbiters and keepers of the established moral order, force parents to marry their daughters. Article 21 of the Mudawwana stipulates as follows: "The marriage of a minor is contingent on the consent of his/her legal tutor" and continues in paragraph three that "if the minor's legal tutor refuses to consent, the Family Affairs Judge rules on the matter." It is the judge's ruling rather than that of the legal tutor (or parents) which can, and it seems in the case of Amina did, prevail at the end.

11. Interestingly however, in all the houses I visited in Tamazirt, I never once saw a ventilator, which may be because electricity bills normally represented a significant expense for many a family budget.

12. M. Laetitia Cairoli (2011) in her book on Moroccan girls working in the garment industry also observes that these girls did not identify themselves as workers, which was a consequence of low respectability that such work generated, coupled with low wages and insecurity of employment. Working in the public sector, as will be demonstrated, however, has all the opposite characteristics of a job in the informal sector: respectability, higher salaries, and security of employment, in addition to benefits such as maternity and sick leave, paid holidays, health insurance, and so forth.

13. *Tbaraka llah* is used by people when they want to emphasize a positive idiosyncrasy of a person about whom they are speaking. It is a sign of admiration and approval; though its meaning is "may s/he be preserved from [the] evil [eye]."

14. An acquaintance of mine defied the tradition and moved in with her hus-

band and in-laws immediately after signing the contract and four months before the 'ars [wedding]. To the community, this was a sign that she had lost her virginity before they were officially married in the public eye, which prompted many girls and women to gossip about her and question her modesty. I met her a few months after the wedding, when she told me that she was getting a divorce because of an ongoing conflict with the female in-laws and despite her husband being "a good man."

15. I say "to protect their rights" because one of the possibilities, although a redundant one, is also to stipulate that the husband will allow his wife to continue with education and work outside the home after marriage. Both of these options, however, are rights already granted to women and men by the constitution.

16. For an interesting comparative discussion of the different ways of girls' consent, including the meaning of silence, see Messick 2008 and Welchman 2012.

17. Divorces in Oued al-Ouliya, in fact, are frequent. Again, I do not have statistical data to corroborate my observation; however, during my stay in the community, it became clear to me that particularly for the older generation of women it had not been unusual to get married and divorced a few times before settling down. Younger women, and particularly those of my age (early thirties), on the other hand, found it hard to get remarried. They told me that there were too many young virgin girls sitting around for men to marry an experienced woman. Often women I talked to blamed the wife for the failed marriage because she was either not sufficiently patient with the husband, or she showed some other moral flaw in her character after the wedding. Patience in general was one of the most often invoked positive traits my interviewees associated with an ideal wife.

18. Interestingly, Lisa Wynn (2008) shows in a case study of urban Saudi families that the girl's family uses this option to include conditions into the marital contract in order to protect their daughter and her rights in marriage.

19. Abu-Lughod has written about the state-sponsored socialization of the public in Egypt in the form of soap operas. The aim of such TV series is to promote marriage based on love and mutual understanding. For a more historical account of the calls for a companionate marriage in Egypt, see Kholoussy 2010. In Morocco, too, some local associations directed public-theater shows in which they tackled issues of marriage, laws, domestic violence, and so on.

20. The belief that women get the house in case of divorce and men have to rent a house is a consequence of, what seems to be, a misunderstanding of the new Family Code, if not a rumor spread among people after its reform. I have heard this rumor from a number of people across Morocco who complained that because of this clause and the Mudawwana in general men were reluctant to get married because women only wanted to get married for material reasons—to get the house and other assets once they divorced their husbands. Moreover, two female JSO activists reported in an interview that when men had been told about this purported clause pre-2004 reform, many of them immediately filed for divorce in order not to be evicted from their houses. Such statements, whether true or not, manifest deeper clefts within Moroccan society, one of which is undoubtedly the JSO's vilification of the Family Code as being out of touch with Moroccan reality and enabling easy-to-get divorces and promiscuity.

21. "Going to your husband" means getting married because it is customary

that upon the wedding night (*laylat al-dukhla*) the bride leaves the home of her father and moves to her husband's or, more often, his father's house.

22. Going to the *suq* is something that women have to avoid if possible. The women in my host family were quite shocked when I told them that I was going to the *suq* to browse and experience it. After much bickering because they forbade me to go, it transpired that the *suq* was not only a male (public) space but also, more significantly, situated next to the prostitutes' quarters. The *suq*, therefore, was to be avoided if possible. I succumbed at that particular time, but later "persuaded" Habiba to accompany me. Her father was ill and both of her brothers were away, so there was no one else to go purchase the weekly groceries. We were allowed by our families to go because we accompanied each other.

23. For a comparative view, see Hoodfar 1996; Jansen 1987; Kadioglu 1994; and Latreille 2008.

Chapter 5: Rural, Educated, and Single

1. The article appears to be part of the spinsterhood debate in the region. For similar examples from Egypt, Syria, and Saudi Arabia, see Singerman 2007. That this is not a new debate is shown in Kholoussy 2010.

2. Much of the data contained in this section are based on participant observation as well as on an anonymous written questionnaire I gave to forty-one girls in the informal education program, and it is for this reason that I do not name them when I use their answers.

3. I obtained the document at the Oued al-Ouliya community headquarters situated in Taddert.

4. Unpublished document in the form of a PowerPoint presentation.

5. ⟨http://www.hcp.ma/Analphabetisme_a413.html⟩, accessed March 2012.

6. *Monoghrafia Jama'at [Oued] Al-Ouliya.*

7. Grades seven through nine.

8. Interview by author with Mudir Rachidi in Oued al-Ouliya, 8 June 2010. Name changed upon request. Basic primary school comprises grades one through six.

9. First year of junior secondary school/junior high school.

10. Informal education, as will be discussed, is not compulsory, but teachers nonetheless expect girls to take it seriously, not least because they put in a lot of time and effort, and the government provided books, notepads, and pencils for free. Girls agreed among themselves that for every class they missed they have to pay one dirham into their class fund, which was entrusted to the teacher as a punishment for being absent. But accumulating enough money in the fund was also an incentive for organizing parties and therefore missing a day of school was in the end rewarded.

11. Morocco initiated a family-planning program in 1966. Usage of particularly contraceptives appeared to me to be widespread. Many girls in the month before the wedding went to see a doctor with their mother or another female relative to get a prescription for contraceptives. Some married women I spoke with had been using contraceptives for ten or more years. For a more comprehensive

account of family-planning policies and their social repercussions, see Donna Lee Bowen 1998.

12. Official statistics show that at the beginning of the 1960s 170 children per 1,000 births died in rural areas; in 1982 the number dropped to 102 infants; while in 2010 the number was lower, but still high at 35.3 children (HCP). I do not have official statistics for infant mortality rates in the Tamazirt area, but according to my conversations with women, many children died either at birth or within a few months from birth. A case of a woman who gave birth to seventeen children, of whom ten survived, was not atypical for the community.

13. Singerman (2007) reported that in Egypt at the beginning of the 2000s marriage costs—which among other things involve dowry, gold, the wedding party, and rent—averaged eleven times the annual household expenditure per capita, while for the poorest strata living in rural areas marriage costs were fifteen times per capita household expenditures. Karima told me that when her two brothers got married in 2006 they had spent over 6,000 dollars each on the wedding party, dowry, and other related costs.

14. Both John and I in discussing, what seemed to us, a high dropout rate expressed surprise at how acceptable the decision to do so was to children's parents.

15. According to Mudir Rachidi, this appeared to be a problem only in primary schools.

16. The director of one of the local primary schools, for example, finished *septième année*, or level one, of high school (seventh grade in the United States).

17. Abdelwahid Abdalla Yousif in his 2009 UNESCO Arab report on the state of literacy concludes that the concept of literacy used in the region is limited to the acquisition of the 3Rs—reading, writing, and arithmetic. It is a passive acquisition of basic literacy skills without actively involving learners into the process or lifelong learning.

18. Although there are other types of functional literacy, for the purposes of this chapter I equate functional literacy with household (or everyday) literacy because it is this type of literacy (rather than, for example, for the workplace) which is useful for and utilized most by literate women in Oued al-Ouliya. I understand household literacy to mean the ability to fill out forms and the ability to read and understand utility and other bills, newspapers, food labels, and medicine instruction leaflets.

19. Local private school is particularly ambitious in language training. Children there are taught four, essentially, foreign languages—literary Arabic as the main language of instruction, in addition to Tamazight, French, and English—from grade one onward.

20. School in Morocco is compulsory for children between the ages of six and fourteen. This particular junior secondary school developed four steps to bring the child back to school if she drops out. First, the school sends a letter to parents. Second, if parents do not respond to it, they will receive an official letter from the authorities. Third, if the child still does not return to school, the director arranges a meeting with the father of the child, after which, as their final step, the school will send a well-performing student to talk to the child in the attempt to convince her to return to the classroom. Unfortunately, neither local administration nor the school can do much more beyond these four steps. The director, however, was

pleased with the fact that 80 percent of those enrolled in the third year of junior secondary school (equivalent to eighth grade in the United States) continue to senior secondary school (*lycée*, which is equivalent to one's freshman year of high school, or ninth grade, in the United States).

21. The *stage* period is compulsory for all graduates who wish to become teachers and doctors. In order to complete it, many individuals are sent to remote places away from their families, which is a serious obstacle to pursuing a career particularly for women from more conservative milieus. One of the educated married women in Oued al-Ouliya revealed to me that she had hoped to become a public school teacher of Islamic studies. However, her husband, who was also a teacher, and her family forbade her to apply for the *stage* because she would have to move away for the period of two years. She concluded that in Islam men always have authority over women and therefore she had to comply with his wishes.

22. This despite the fact that some of them earned over 10,000 dirhams a month, in addition to receiving support from their families to subsidize their lifestyles.

23. People oftentimes summed up the reasons for a certain personal issue, such as why she dropped out of school, as *duruf*, or difficult personal circumstances, which forced her to do so.

24. *TelQuel* (Mrabet, Hamdani, and El Hadef 2008), for example, reported about high school and university students who were working as "paraprostitutes," offering their services for gifts rather than money. Though these girls claimed to be virgins, some did admit to having oral and anal sex with their "victims," as they referred to their clients, perhaps as a way to demonstrate that they in fact were exploiting men rather than the other way around.

25. I was surprised when Habiba tried to defend the rule that women cannot perform the duties of an *ʿadul* because they succumb to emotions rather than being driven by reason. "Look at what happens when a girl and a man break up," she explained, "she cries and cries and he just lets it go."

26. Leila Abouzeid explained to me that during the colonial times the French opposed the building of schools for Moroccan children. The few schools that did exist were available only to children of wealthy and urban families "collaborating with the French," she concluded. Even in the postindependent era, conservative attitudes prevailed and many parents were opposed to sending their daughters to school, where they could mix with boys. Nonexistence of infrastructure, Hassan II's division of the country into useful and useless parts, paucity of well-qualified teachers at least in the past, as well as poor educational policies have further contributed to the fact that Morocco to this day performs worse than most MENA countries as concerns literacy.

27. Jennifer Spratt, for example, addressed the issue of accuracy of literacy statistics in Morocco and questioned the method of gathering statistics contained in the national census as well as in other reports dealing with literacy in her 1992 article.

28. Yasmina Baddou, the State Secretary at the Ministry of Solidarity, Women, Family, and Social Development at the beginning of the 2000s and later Health Minister in Abbas al-Fassi's government, asserted in 2003 at the Global Summit of Women held in Marrakech that the empowerment of women is essential for the

country's economic development (quoted in: Willman Bordat and Schaefer Davis 2011).

29. Document obtained in March 2011 at the HCP in Rabat.

30. In Morocco in 2006–2007, 46.5 percent of students enrolled in higher education were female, which is slightly higher than in 1996 and 1997 at 41.4 percent (HCP 2008).

Conclusion

1. "Al-Ramid wa al-intihar Amina." The video can be found at ⟨http://www .youtube.com/watch?v=qXeWPDQlv3I⟩, accessed April 2012.

2. Corruption of judges was substantiated in my conversations with people with anecdotal "evidence" that goes beyond accepting money and rather entails the proverbial *wasta*, or connections. Nadia, for example, reported that her husband was able to marry a second wife because his uncle was an 'adul. She was not asked to sign an agreement, stating that she was aware of her husband marrying a second wife and, in fact, only found out about it after the couple was already registered as married and her husband moved out of the apartment. They lived in a rented apartment because Nadia's family-in-law never accepted the marriage. They had been seeing each other for six years before they finally got married, which is why her in-laws thought of Nadia as an unchaste woman. It was his mother that pressured Nadia's husband to take a second wife.

3. It should be noted, however, that such protection is not always guaranteed even when girls and women fulfill their part of the deal.

4. I am painfully aware of the fact that considering these rural families as living a "comfortable middle-class life" could be misleading and interpreted as superficial. However, within this particular rural context, class divisions were definitely noticeable, and families and their members measured their material well-being against the others within their community rather than on that of *brranis* (outsiders).

5. It is important to note here that living expenses in this community were much less than in urban areas, and hence even a 1,000 dirhams could cover many expenses. A divorced woman once told me that her ex-husband paid 250 dirhams (about thirty dollars) for monthly child support. A rented unfurnished "single-family" apartment costs 300 to 400 dirhams (35 to 48 dollars), monthly utility bills approximately 80 to 400 dirhams (9 to 48 dollars), depending on the amount of electrical appliances, a kilogram of tomatoes 3 to 9 dirhams (0.3 to one dollar—due to severe floods in the northern region in 2010 much of the produce was destroyed, causing prices to escalate for a couple of months), potatoes 3 dirhams (0.3 dollars), a cone of sugar 13 dirhams (1.5 dollars).

6. Both Western-style toilets and tiled bathrooms were quite rare, and I only noticed them in houses that were newly renovated.

7. Both of these descriptions are designations used in the official statistics, such as the national census. A "Moroccan modern house" denotes a house made of modern materials, whereas a "rural-type residence" in this semiarid environment indicates an adobe house.

8. These are households, which according to official statistics are not categorized as either poor or vulnerable but are, also on the basis of my personal observation, living a comfortable middle-class life within this particular rural context. Some of these families have family members living in Rabat and Casablanca where they, according to the information given to me by them, own furniture or other lucrative shops, while others have brothers, uncles, or fathers living abroad.

Appendix

1. People treated the period between signing the contract and the wedding as an engagement of sorts.

Glossary

asel   One's origin, genealogy, identity.

aya   A Quranic verse.

baladiya   Rural commune.

Chrifa   A female descendent from the Prophet.

Darija   Moroccan Arabic dialect.

duruf   (Difficult) personal circumstances.

fqi   Faith healer; though in Moroccan Arabic it can also denote a teacher.

galsa f-dar   Used to denote a housewife; its literal meaning being that of "sitting, staying at home."

Imazighen   Berber.

Khalti   (My) aunt; however, it is used to address older ladies.

ksar (pl. *ksour*)   A fortified village.

Makhzen   Moroccan regime or the Royal palace and its entourage.

Medina   Denotes the old part of a town, distinct from the French-built *ville nouvelle* (New City).

mskina   "Poor thing."

Mudawwanat al-Usra   Family Code.

qanun   Positive law, as differentiated by the people from Islamic law.

sura   A Quranic chapter.

suq   Weekly market.

Tašilhit   Berber dialect, distinct from Arabic.

wali   Legal guardian.

ʿadul (sing. and pl.)   Religious notaries in charge of drafting marital and other contracts.

ʿalim (pl. *ʿulema'*)   Religious scholar.

Bibliography

Abou El Fadl, Khaled
2003 "Islam and the Challenge of Democracy: Can Individual Rights and Popular Sovereignty Take Root in Faith." *Boston Review* (April/May). Print.

Abouzeid, Leila
1989 *Year of the Elephant: A Moroccan Woman's Journey Toward Independence, and Other Stories.* Trans. B. Parmenter. Austin: The Center for Middle Eastern Studies, University of Texas at Austin. Print.

Abu-Lughod, Lila
1998a "The Marriage of Feminism and Islamism in Egypt: Selective Repudiation as a Dynamic of Postcolonial Cultural Politics." *Remaking Women: Feminism and Modernity in the Middle East.* Ed. L. Abu-Lughod. Princeton, N.J.: Princeton University Press. 243–269. Print.

Abu-Lughod, Lila, ed.
1998b *Remaking Women: Feminism and Modernity in the Middle East.* Princeton, N.J.: Princeton University Press. Print.

Abu-Lughod, Lila
1999 *Veiled Sentiments: Honor and Poetry in a Bedouin Society.* Oakland: University of California Press. Print.

Abu-Lughod, Lila
2005 *Dramas of Nationhood: The Politics of Television in Egypt.* Chicago: University of Chicago Press. Print.

Abu-Lughod, Lila
2008 *Writing Women's World: Bedouin Stories.* Oakland: University of California Press. Print.

Abu-Lughod, Lila
2010 "The Active Social Life of 'Muslim Women's Rights': A Plea for Ethnography, Not Polemic, with Cases from Egypt and Palestine." *Journal of Middle East Women's Studies* 6(1): 1–45. Print.

AbuKhalil, As'ad
1997 "Gender Boundaries and Sexual Categories in the Arab World." *Feminist Issues* 15(1–2): 91–104. Print.

Achehbar, Samir, and Nadia Lamlili
2006 "Célibataires ou bikheeer!" *TelQuel* (241): 36–44. Print.

Achy, Lahcen
2010 "Morocco's Experience with Poverty Reduction: Lessons for the Arab World." Web. ⟨http://carnegieendowment.org/files/morocco_poverty1.pdf⟩.

Adely, Fida J.
2012 *Gendered Paradoxes: Educating Jordanian Women in Nation, Faith, and Progress.* Chicago: University of Chicago Press. Print.

ADFM
2007 *Implementation of the CEDAW Convention: Non-Governmental Organization's Shadow Report to the Third and Fourth Periodic Report of the Moroccan Government: Summary.* Obtained at the office of Global Rights, Rabat. Print.

ADFM
2011 "Memorandum Presented to the Advisory Committee for the Revision of the Constitution: For a Constitution that Guarantees Effective Equality of Women and Men as an Indicator of Democracy." Web. ⟨http://www.adfm.ma/IMG/pdf_Memorandum_ADFM_Ang.pdf⟩.

Agnaou, Fatima
2004 *Gender, Literacy, and Empowerment in Morocco.* London: Routledge. Print.

Agueniou, Salah
2010 "70% des actifs n'ont pas de contrat de travail!" *La Vie Éco.* Web. ⟨http://www.lavieeco.com/news/economie/70-des-actifs-occupes-n-ont-pas-de-contrat-de-travail—16436.html⟩.

Ait Mousa, Aziza
2011 "Al-Qur'an bi-l-Fatiha: Zawjat ta'ihat wa ibna' dunna hawiyya." *Nesma* (March): 40–42. Print.

Al Oumliki, Abderrafii
2002 "Société: Des chiffres révélateurs." *Aujourd'hui le Maroc.* N. pag. Print.

Al-Ali, Nadje
2000 *Secularism, Gender and the State in the Middle East: The Egyptian Women's Movement.* Cambridge: Cambridge University Press. Print.

Al-Basri, Abdelrahman
2011 "Al-Maghraoui yakšaf awraqhu fi awl hiwar ba'da 'awdathu min Su'udiyya." *Akhbar Al-Yawm* April 14: 1, 3. Print.

Al-Saaidi, Mouniya
2010 Turafiq talibat bil-ahya' al-jami'iya. *Nesma* (March): 32–38. Print.

Ali, Siham
2010 "Moroccan Bachelors Seek Wives Who Work." Web. ⟨http://www
.magharebia.com/cocoon/awi/xhtml1/en_GB/features/awi/features
/2010/08/09/feature-01⟩.

Allali, Réda, and Hassan Hamdani
2006 "Société. Blad schizo." *TelQuel* (243): 42–49. Print.

An-Na'im, Abdullahi Ahmed
1996 "Toward an Islamic Reformation: Civil Liberties, Human Rights, and
International Law." Syracuse: Syracuse University Press. Print.

Arshad, Amna
2006–2007 "*Ijtihad* as a Tool for Islamic Legal Reform: Advancing Women's
Rights in Morocco." *Kansas Journal of Law & Public Policy* XVI (2): 129–
156. Print.

Ashcroft, Bill, Gareth Griffiths, and Helen Tiffin, eds.
2006 *Post-Colonial Studies Reader*. London: Routledge.

Assaad, Ragui, and Mohamed Ramadan
2008 "Did Housing Policy Reforms Curb the Delay in Marriage among Young
Men in Egypt?" Web. ⟨http://www.shababinclusion.org/files/1226_file
_MEYI_Policy_Outlook_1_English_final.pdf⟩.

B., C.
2002 "Plan d'intégration de la femme: Les raisons d'un échec." *Le Journal* 27
July–2 August: 12–13. Print.

Baker, Alison
1998 *Voices of Resistance: Oral Histories of Moroccan Women*. Albany, N.Y.: State
University of New York Press. Print.

Banerjee, Abhijit V., and Esther Duflo
2011 *Poor Economics: A Radical Rethinking of the Way to Fight Global Poverty*.
New York: Public Affairs. Print.

Bargach, Jamila
2002 *Orphans of Islam: Family, Abandonment, and Secret Adoption in Morocco*.
Oxford: Rowman & Littlefield Publishers, Inc. Print.

Batliwala, Srilatha, and Deepa Dhanraj
2007 "Gender Myths that Instrumentalize Women: A View From the Indian
Front Line." *Feminisms in Development: Contradictions, Contestations and
Challenges*. Eds. A. Cornwall, E. Harrison, and A. Whitehead. New
York: Zed Books. 21–34. Print.

Bauman, Zygmunt
2007 *Liquid Times: Living in an Age of Uncertainty*. Cambridge, UK: Polity
Press. Print.

Beaugé, Florence
2002 "La réforme du statut de la femme au point mort." *Le Monde* (24 January): 4. Print.

Becker, Cynthia J.

2002 "'We are Real Slaves, Real Ismkhan': Memories of the Trans-Saharan Slave Trade in the Tafilalet of South-Eastern Morocco." *Journal of North African Studies* 7(4): 97–121. Print.

Becker, Cynthia J.

2006 *Amazigh Arts in Morocco: Women Shaping Berber Identity.* Austin: University of Texas Press. Print.

Belabd, Houda

2012 "Bassima Hakkaoui: L'abrogation de l'article 475 ne se fera pas sous la pression." Web. ⟨http://www.yabiladi.com/articles/details/9537/bassima -hakkaoui-l-abrogation-l-article-fera.html⟩.

Bell, Diane, Pat Caplan, and Wazir-Jahan Karim

1993 *Gendered Fields: Women, Men & Ethnography.* London: Routledge. Print.

Bennani, Driss

2007 "Reportage: Ces Marocaines qui meurent de froid." *TelQuel* (256): 35–41. Print.

Bennani-Chraïbi, Mounia

2000 "Youth in Morocco: An Indicator of a Changing Society." *Alienation or Integration of Arab Youth: Between Family, State and the Street.* Ed. R. Meijer. Surrey: Curzon Press. 143–160. Print.

Bergman, Elizabeth M.

1994 "Keeping It in the Family: Gender and Conflict in Moroccan Arabic Proverbs." *Reconstructing Gender in the Middle East: Tradition, Identity and Power.* Eds. F. M. Göçek and S. Balaghi. New York: Columbia University Press. 201–218. Print.

Berkou, Lahcen

2010 "Maroc. Bienvenue en Absurdistan." *TelQuel* (407): 38–47. Print.

Bhabha, Homi

2006 "Cultural Diversity and Cultural Differences." *Post-Colonial Studies Reader.* 2nd ed. Eds. B. Ashcroft, G. Griffiths, and H. Tiffin. London: Routledge. 157–159. Print.

Birdsall, Nancy, Ruth Levine, and Amina Ibrahim

2005 *Toward Universal Primary Education: Investments, Incentives, and Institutions—Achieving Millennium Development Goals.* London: United Nations Development Programme—UN Millennium Project, Task Force on Education and Gender Equality.

Boudarbat, Brahim

2005 "Job-Search Strategies and the Unemployment of University Graduates in Morocco." Web. ⟨http://www.iza.org/conference_files/iza_ebrd _2005/boudarbat_b1612.pdf⟩.

Boudarbat, Brahim, and Aziz Ajbilou

2007 "Youth Exclusion in Morocco: Context, "Consequences, and Policies." Web. ⟨http://www.shababinclusion.org/files/542_file_Morocco_Paper _final.pdf⟩.

Bowen, Donna Lee
1998 "Changing Contraceptive Mores in Morocco: Population Data, Trends, Gossip and Rumours." *Journal of North African Studies* 3(4): 69–90. Print.

Brand, Laurie A.
1998 *Women, The State and Political Liberalization.* New York: Columbia University Press. Print.

Buskens, Leon
2003 "Recent Debates on Family Law Reform in Morocco: Islamic Law as Politics in an Emerging Public Sphere." *Islamic Law and Society* 10(1): 70–131. Print.

Butler, Judith
1986 "Sex and Gender in Simone de Beauvoir's *Second Sex.*" *Yale French Studies* (72): 35–49. Print.

Butler, Judith
2006 *Gender Trouble: Feminism and the Subversion of Identity.* London: Routledge. Print.

Cairoli, Laetitia M.
2007 "Girl But Not Woman: Garment Factory Workers in Fez, Morocco." *From Patriarchy to Empowerment: Women's Participation, Movements, and Rights in the Middle East, North Africa, and South Asia.* Ed. V. M. Moghadam. Syracuse: Syracuse University Press. 160–179. Print.

Cairoli, Laetitia M.
2011 *Girls of the Factory: A Year with the Garment Workers of Morocco.* Gainesville: University of Florida Press. Print.

Caplan, Pat
1993 "Learning Gender: Fieldwork in a Tanzanian Coastal Village, 1965–85." *Gendered Fields: Women, Men & Ethnography.* Eds. D. Bell, P. Caplan, and W.-J. Karim. London: Routledge. 168–181. Print.

Chant, Sylvia
1997 "Women-Headed Households: Poorest of the Poor? Perspectives from Mexico, Costa Rica and the Philippines." *IDS Bulletin* 28(3): 26–48. Print.

Chant, Sylvia
2006 "Rethinking the 'Feminization of Poverty' in Relation to Aggregate Gender Indices." *Journal of Human Development* 7(2): 201–220. Print.

Chant, Sylvia
2007a "Dangerous Equations? How Female-Headed Households Became the Poorest of the Poor: Causes, Consequences and Cautions." *Feminisms in Development: Contradictions, Contestations and Challenges.* Eds. A. Cornwall, E. Harrison, and A. Whitehead. London: Zed Books Ltd. 35–47. Print.

Chant, Sylvia

    2007b   *Gender, Generation and Poverty: Exploring the "Feminisation of Poverty" in Africa, Asia and Latin America.* Cheltenham: Edward Elgar Publishing Ltd. Print.

Charrad, Mounira M.

    2001   *States and Women's Rights: The Making of Postcolonial Tunisia, Algeria and Morocco.* London: University of California Press. Print.

Charrad, Wadii

    2014   "Benkirane: 'Il faut reconnaître le rôle sacré de la femme au foyer.'" Web. ⟨http://telquel.ma/2014/06/17/benkirane-reconnaitre-role-sacre-femme-foyer_139344⟩.

Cohen, Shana

    2004   "Searching for a Different Future: The Rise of a Global Middle Class." *Morocco.* Durham, N.C.: Duke University Press. Print.

Colombo, Silvia

    2011   "Morocco at the Crossroads: Seizing the Window of Opportunity for Sustainable Development." Web. ⟨http://ssrn.com/abstract=2000674⟩.

CEDAW

    2006   "Consideration of Reports Submitted by States Parties under Article 18 of the Convention on the Elimination of All Forms of Discrimination against Women: Combined Third and Fourth Periodic Report of States Parties: Morocco (CEDAW/C/MAR/4)." Web. ⟨http://daccess-dds-ny.un.org/doc/UNDOC/GEN/N06/563/69/PDF/N0656369.pdf?OpenElement⟩.

CEDAW

    2008a   "Summary Record of the 824th Meeting (CEDAW/C/SR.824)." Web. ⟨http://www2.ohchr.org/english/bodies/cedaw/docs/CEDAWSR824.pdf⟩.

CEDAW

    2008b   "Summary record of the 825th meeting (CEDAW/C/SR.825)." Web. ⟨http://www2.ohchr.org/english/bodies/cedaw/docs/CEDAWSR825.pdf⟩.

Cornwall, Andrea, Elizabeth Harrison, and Ann Whitehead, eds.

    2007   *Feminisms in Development: Contradictions, Contestations and Challenges.* London: Zed Books. Print.

Crapanzano, Vincent

    1981   *The Hamdasha: A Study in Moroccan Ethnopsychiatry.* Oakland: University of California Press. Print.

Crawford, David

    2002   "Morocco's Invisible Imazighen." *Journal of North African Studies* 7(1): 53–70. Print.

Daoud, Zakya

    1994   *Féminisme et politique au Maghreb (1930–1992).* Paris: Maisonneuve et Larose. Print.

Davids, Tine, and Francien van Driel
2001 "Globalization and Gender: Beyond Dichotomies." *Globalization and Development Studies: Challenges for the 21st Century*. Ed. F. J. Schuurman. London: Sage. 153–175. Print.

de Foucald, Charles
1888 *Reconnaissance au Maroc: 1883-1884*. Paris: Challamel. Print.

de Haas, Hein, and Aleida van Rooij
2010 "Migration as Emancipation? The Impact of Internal and International Migration on the Position of Women Left Behind in Rural Morocco." *Oxford Development Studies* 38(1): 43–62. Print.

Dimitrovova, Bohdana
2009 *Reshaping Civil Society in Morocco: Boundary Setting, Integration and Consolidation*. Centre for European Policy Studies (CEPS). Print.

Dwyer, Daisy Hilse
1978 *Images and Self-Images: Male and Female in Morocco*. New York: Columbia University Press. Print.

Eisenstein, Hester
2005 "A Dangerous Liaison? Feminism and Corporate Globalization." *Science & Society* 69(3): 487–518. Print.

El Azizi, Abdellatif
2007 "Enquête. Tabit: La vraie histoire." *TelQuel* (281): 52–58. Print.

El Feki, Shereen
2013 *Sex and the Citadel: Intimate Life in a Changing Arab World*. New York: Pantheon Books. Print.

El Hamel, Chouki
2002 "'Race,' Slavery and Islam in Maghribi Mediterranean Thought: The Question of the *Haratin* in Morocco." *Journal of North African Studies* 7(3): 29–52. Print.

Elder, Sara, and et al.
2010 "Global Employment Trends for Youth." Web. ⟨http://www.ilo.org /wcmsp5/groups/public/—ed_emp/—emp_elm/—trends/documents /publication/wcms_143349.pdf⟩.

Ennaji, Moha
2007 "Education, Gender and (Un)employment." *Femmes et éducation dans la région Méditerranéenne*. Eds. F. Sadiqi and M. Ennaji. Fez: Sipama. 77–90. Print.

Ennaji, Moha
2008 "Steps to the Integration of Moroccan Women in Development." *British Journal of Middle Eastern Studies* 35(3): 339–348. Print.

Ennaji, Moha
2011 "Women's NGOs and Social Change in Morocco." *Women in the Middle East and North Africa: Agents of Change*. Eds. F. Sadiqi and M. Ennaji. London: Routledge. 79–88. Print.

Esposito, John L.

   2001 "Women in Muslim Family Law." New York: Syracuse University Press. Print.

Euromed Gender Equality

   2010 "National Situation Analysis Report: Women's Human Rights and Gender Equality: Morocco." Web. ⟨http://www.euromedgenderequality.org /image.php?id=291%20%20target=⟩.

Facio, Alda, and Martha I. Morgan

   2009 "Equity or Equality For Women? Understanding CEDAW's Equality Principles." Web. ⟨http://www.iwraw-ap.org/publications/doc/OPS14 _Web.pdf⟩.

Freeman, Amy

   2004 "Re-locating Moroccan Women's Identities in a Transnational World: The 'Woman Question' in Question." *Gender, Place and Culture* 11(1): 17–41. Print.

Friedan, Betty

   2010 *The Feminine Mystique.* London: Penguin Books. Print.

Galal, Ahmed, et al.

   2008 "The Road Not Travelled: Education Reform in the Middle East and North Africa." *World Bank MENA Development Report.* Web. ⟨http://site resources.worldbank.org/INTMENA/Resources/EDU_Flagship_Full _ENG.pdf⟩.

Galal, Salma

   1995 "Women and Development in the Maghreb Countries." *Gender and Development in the Arab World: Women's Economic Participation: Patterns and Policies.* Eds. N. F. Khoury and V. M. Moghadam. London: Zed Books Ltd. 49–70. Print.

Ghazzala, Iman

   2001 "Sculpting the Rock of Women's Rights: The Role of Women's Organizations in Promoting the National Plan of Action to Integrate Women in Development in Morocco." Web. ⟨http://www.hhh.umn.edu/centers /wpp/pdf/case_studies/sculpting_the_rock/sculpting_rock_women _rights.pdf⟩.

Ghoussoub, Mai, and Emma Sinclair-Webb, eds.

   2006 *Imagined Masculinities: Male Identity and Culture in the Modern Middle East.* London: Saqi. Print.

Global Rights

   2006 *The Moroccan Family Code (Moudawana) of February 5, 2004: An unofficial English translation of the original Arabic text.* Rabat: Global Rights. Print.

Global Rights

   2008 *Conditions, Not Conflict: Promoting Women's Human Rights in the Maghreb through Strategic Use of the Marriage Contract.* Rabat: Global Rights. Print.

Global Rights
2011 *Promoting Women's Human Rights in Morocco, Algeria and Tunisia through Strategic Use of the Marriage Contract: Researching and Documenting the Use of Marriage Contracts among Local Authorities.* Rabat: Global Rights. Print.

Global Rights, and Advocates for Human Rights
2012 "Morocco: Challenges with Addressing Domestic Violence in Compliance with the Convention Against Torture." Web. ⟨http://www.global rights.org/site/DocServer/2011-10-14_Final_Shadow_Report_to _CAT.pdf?docID=12983⟩.

Göçek, Fatma Müge, and Shiva Balaghi, eds.
1994 *Reconstructing Gender in the Middle East: Tradition, Identity and Power.* New York: Columbia University Press. Print.

Gray, Doris H.
2008 *Muslim Women on the Move: Moroccan Women and French Women of Moroccan Origin Speak Out.* Plymouth: Lexington Books. Print.

Guessous, Nadia
2011 "Genealogies of Feminism: Leftist Feminist Subjectivity in the Wake of the Islamic Revival in Contemporary Morocco." Diss. Graduate School of Arts and Sciences, Columbia University.

Hachimi Alaoui, Nadia
2002 "Portrait Saîd Saadi: L'homme qui aimait les femmes . . ." *Le Journal* 6–12 July: 39. Print.

Hackensberger, Alfred
2006 "Der Koran und der muslimische Feminismus." Web. ⟨http://www .heise.de/tp/artikel/22/22833/1.html⟩.

Halaq, Aziza
2010 "Mohammed Saïd Saadi: Al-musawat qadiya al-rajul awalan." *Nesma* (March): 28–30. Print.

Hallaq, Wael B.
2009 *Sharī'a: Theory, Practice, Transformations.* Cambridge: Cambridge University Press. Print.

Harris, Walter B.
1895 *Tafilet: The Narrative of a Journey of Exploration in the Atlas Mountains and the Oases of the North-West Sahara.* London: William Blackwood and Sons. Print.

HCP
2011 "Activité, emploi et chômage: Résultats détaillés. Direction de la statistique." Web. ⟨http://www.hcp.ma/downloads/Activite-emploi-et -chomage-resultats-detailles_t13039.html⟩.

HCP
2008 "La femme Marocaine en chiffres: Tendances d'évolution des caractéristiques démographiques et socioprofessionnelles." Obtained at HCP, Rabat. Print.

Herz, Barbara, and Gene B. Sperling
    2007 *What Works in Girls' Education: Evidence and Politics from the Developing World*. New York: U.S. Council on Foreign Relations. Print.

Hobsbawm, Eric
    2009 "Introduction: Inventing Traditions." *The Invention of Tradition*. Eds. E. Hobsbawm and T. Ranger. New York: Cambridge University Press. 1–14. Print.

Hobsbawm, Eric, and Terence Ranger, eds.
    2009 *The Invention of Tradition*. New York: Cambridge University Press. Print.

Hoffman, Katherine E.
    2008 *We Share Walls: Language, Land, and Gender in Berber Morocco*. Oxford: Blackwell Publishing. Print.

Hoodfar, Homa
    1996 "Egyptian Male Migration and Urban Families Left Behind: 'Feminization of the Egyptian Family' or Reaffirmation of Traditional Gender Roles?" *Development, Change, and Gender in Cairo: A View from the Household*. Eds. D. Singerman and H. Hoodfar. Bloomington: Indiana University Press. 51–79. Print.

IFES
    2010a "Focus on Morocco: Educational Attainment and Career Aspirations." Web. ⟨http://www.ifes.org/Content/Publications/Papers/2010/Focus-on-Morocco-Educational-Attainment-and-Career-Aspirations-Topic-Brief.aspx⟩.

IFES
    2010b "Focus on Morocco: Social Attitudes Towards Women." Web. ⟨http://www.ifes.org/Content/Publications/Papers/2010/Focus-on-Morocco-Social-Attitudes-Toward-Women.aspx⟩.

Ilahiane, Hsain
    2004 *Ethnicities, Community Making, and Agrarian Change: The Political Ecology of a Moroccan Oasis*. Oxford: University Press of America. Print.

Jansen, Willy
    1987 *Women without Men: Gender Marginality in an Algerian Town*. Leiden: Brill. Print.

Jay, Cleo
    2013 "Acting Up: Performance and the Politics of Womanhood in Contemporary Morocco." *Journal of African Cultural Studies* 25(3): 305–318. Print.

Joffé, George
    2009 "Morocco's Reform Process: Wider Implications." *Mediterranean Politics* 14(2): 151–164. Print.

Joseph, Suad
    1994 "Brother/Sister Relationships: Connectivity, Love, and Power in the Reproduction of Patriarchy in Lebanon." *American Ethnologist* 21(1): 50–73. Print.

Joseph, Suad
1993 "Connectivity and Patriarchy among Urban Working-Class Arab Families in Lebanon." *Ethos* 21(4): 452–484. Print.

Joseph, Suad
1996 "Patriarchy and Development in the Arab World." *Gender and Development* 4(2): 14–19. Print.

Kabeer, Naila
2003 *Gender Mainstreaming in Poverty Eradication and the MDGs: A Handbook for Policy-Makers and Other Stakeholders.* Ottawa: Canadian International Development Agency. Print.

Kadioglu, Ayse
1994 "The Impact of Migration on Gender Roles: Findings of Field Research in Turkey." *International Migration* 32(4): 533–560. Print.

Kamphoefner, K. R.
1996 "What's the Use? The Household, Low-Income Women, and Literacy." *Development, Change, and Gender in Cairo: A View from the Household.* Eds. D. Singerman and H. Hoodfar. Bloomington: Indiana University Press. 80–109. Print.

Kandiyoti, Deniz
1988 "Bargaining with Patriarchy." *Gender and Society* 2(3): 274–290. Print.

Keddie, Nikki R.
2007 *Women in the Middle East: Past and Present.* Oxford: Princeton University Press. Print.

Kenny, Charles
2010 "Learning about Schools in Development." Web. ⟨http://www.cgdev .org/files/1424678_file_Learning_About_Schools_in_Development _FINAL.pdf⟩.

Kholoussy, Hanan
2010 *For Better, For Worse: The Marriage Crisis that Made Modern Egypt.* Stanford: Stanford University Press. Print.

Khoury, Nabil F., and Valentine M. Moghadam, eds.
1995 *Gender and Development in the Arab World: Women's Economic Participation, Patterns and Policies.* London: Zed Books Ltd. and United Nations University Press. Print.

Kingdom of Morocco
2005a "Morocco: National Report Beijing +10." Web. ⟨http://www.un.org /womenwatch/daw/Review/responses/MOROCCO-English.pdf⟩.

Kingdom of Morocco
2005b "Objectifs du millénaire pour le développement: Rapport national 2005." Web. ⟨http://www.pnud.org.ma/rapports/Rapport_OMDa2005 -.pdf⟩.

Kingdom of Morocco
2010 "Objectifs du millénaire pour le développement: Rapport national 2009." Web. ⟨http://www.pnud.org.ma/pdf/rapports/omd2009Fr.pdf⟩.

Kirsch, Gesa E.

2005 "Friendship, Friendliness, and Feminist Fieldwork." *Signs: Journal of Women in Culture and Society* 30(4): 2163–2172. Print.

Kouaouci, Ali

2004 "Population Transitions, Youth Unemployment, Postponement of Marriage and Violence in Algeria." *Journal of North African Studies* 9(2): 28–45. Print.

Kozma, Liat

2003 "Moroccan Women's Narratives of Liberation: A Passive Revolution?" *Journal of North African Studies* 8(1): 112–130. Print.

Kristof, Nicholas D., and Sheryl WuDunn

2009 *Half the Sky: Turning Oppression into Opportunity for Women Worldwide.* New York: Alfred A. Knopf (Random House Inc.). Print.

Lahlimi Alami, Ahmed

2010 *La présentation des résultats de l'enquête national démographique à passages répétés 2009–2010.* Speech presented in Rabat, Morocco.

Latreille, Martin

2008 "Honor, the Gender Division of Labor, and the Status of Women in Rural Tunisia: A Social Organizational Reading." *International Journal of Middle East Studies* 40(4): 599–621. Print.

Layachi, Azzedine

1998 or 1999 *State, Society and Democracy in Morocco: The Limits of Associative Life.* Washington D.C.: Center for Contemporary Arab Studies, Georgetown University. Print.

Lazreg, Marnia

1994 *The Eloquence of Silence: Algerian Women in Question.* London: Routledge. Print.

Maddy-Weitzman, Bruce

2005 "Women, Islam and the Moroccan State: The Struggle Over the Personal Status Law." *Middle East Journal* 59(3): 393–410. Print.

Makhlouf Obermeyer, Carla

2000 "Sexuality in Morocco: Changing Context and Contested Domain." *Culture, Health & Sexuality* 2(3): 239–254. Print.

Malka, Haim, and Jon B. Alterman

2006 "Arab Reform and Foreign Aid: Lessons from Morocco." Web. ⟨http://www.mafhoum.com/press10/290S21.pdf⟩.

Martin-Muñoz, Gema

2000 "Arab Youth Today: The Generation Gap, Identity Crisis and Democratic Deficit." *Alienation or Integration of Arab Youth: Between Family, State and Street.* Ed. R. Meijer. ed. Surrey: Curzon Press. 17–26. Print.

Masquelier, Adeline

2005 "The Scorpion's Sting: Youth, Marriage and the Struggle for Social Maturity in Niger." *Journal of the Royal Anthropological Institute* 11(1): 59–83. Print.

Mayer, Ann Elizabeth
   2007 *Islam and Human Rights: Tradition and Politics.* Oxford: Westview Press.
   Print.

Mdidech, Jaouad
   2003 "Islamistes et modernistes . . . pas si opposés que ça." *La Vie Éco,* 17
   October: 46. Print.

Meeker, Michael
   1976 "Meaning and Society in the Near East: Examples from the Levantine
   Arabs and the Black Sea Turks (1)." *International Journal of Middle East
   Studies* 7 (2) (April): 243–270. Print.

Meeker, Michael
   1976 "Meaning and Society in the Near East: Examples from the Black Sea
   Turks and the Levantine Arabs (2)." *International Journal of Middle East
   Studies* 7 (3) (July): 383–422. Print.

Meijer, Roel, ed.
   2000 *Alienation or Integration of Arab Youth: Between Family, State and Street.*
   Surrey: Curzon Press. Print.

Mernissi, Fatima
   1993 *Islam and Democracy: Fear of the Modern World.* London: Virago Press
   Limited. Print.

Messick, Brinkley
   2008 "Interpreting Tears: A Marriage Case from Imamic Yemen." *The Islamic
   Marriage Contract: Case Studies in Islamic Family Law.* Eds. A. Quraishi,
   and F. E. Vogel. Cambridge, Mass.: Harvard University Press. 156–179.
   Print.

Miller, Carol, and Shahra Razavi, eds.
   1998 *Missionaries and Mandarins: Feminist Engagement with Developing Institutions.* London: Practical Action. Print.

Ministry of Communication
   2003 "Opening of the Parliament Fall Session—10 October 2003." Rabat:
   Ministry of Communication. Print.

Ministry of Economy and Finances, and UNIFEM
   2008 "Examen exhaustif des statistiques sensibles au genre au Maroc." Rabat:
   Ministry of Communication. Print.

Ministry of Justice
   2008a Les actes de mariage et les actes de divorce: Année 2007. Web. ⟨http://
   adala.justice.gov.ma/production/statistiques/famille/FR/Actes%20
   de%20marriage%20et%20actes%20de%20divorce.pdf⟩.

Ministry of Justice
   2008b "Tableau n3: Comparaison des actes de mariages entre les années 2006
   et 2007." Web. ⟨http://adala.justice.gov.ma/production/statistiques
   /famille/FR/Comparaison%20des%20actes%20de%20mariages%20
   entre%20les%20annees%20%202006%20et%202007.pdf⟩.

Ministry of Justice
  2010 "Ihsa'iyat hawla našat qada' al-usra 2009." Rabat: Ministry of Justice. Print.

Ministry of Justice
  2011 "Ihsa'iyat hawla našat qada' al-usra 2010. Rabat: Ministry of Justice. Print.

Ministry of Justice
  2012 Statistique des sections de la justice de la famille: Année 2011. Web. ⟨http://adala.justice.gov.ma/production/statistiques/SJF/FR/30–10–12 %20VR%20Finale%20Statistique%20Francais.pdf⟩.

Mir-Hosseini, Ziba
  1997 *Marriage on Trial: A Study of Islamic Family Law.* London: I. B. Taurus. Print.

Moghadam, Valentine M.
  1998a "Feminisms and Development." *Gender & History* 10(3): 590–597. Print.

Moghadam, Valentine M.
  1998b *Women, Work and Economic Reform in the Middle East and North Africa.* London: Lynne Rienner Publishers. Print.

Moghadam, Valentine M.
  2003a "Engendering Citizenship, Feminizing Civil Society." *Women & Politics* 25(1): 63–87. Print.

Moghadam, Valentine M.
  2003b *Modernizing Women: Gender and Social Change in the Middle East.* London: Lynne Rienner Publishers. Print.

Moghadam, Valentine M., ed.
  2007 *From Patriarchy to Empowerment: Women's Participation, Movements, and Rights in the Middle East, North Africa, and South Asia.* Syracuse: Syracuse University Press. Print.

Moghadam, Valentine M.
  2011 "Feminism and Family Law in Iran: The Struggle For Women's Economic Citizenship in the Islamic Republic." *Women in the Middle East and North Africa: Agents of Change.* Eds. F. Sadiqi and M. Ennaji. London: Routledge. 114–128. Print.

Moghissi, Haideh
  1999 *Feminism and Islamic Fundamentalism: The Limits of Postmodern Analysis.* London: Zed Books Ltd. Print.

Molyneux, Maxine
  1985 "Mobilization Without Emancipation? Women's Interests, the State and the Revolution in Nicaragua." *Feminist Studies* 11(2): 227–254. Print.

Mrabet, Ayla
  2009 "Nostalgie: Les poids des mots." *TelQuel* (361): 60–62. Print.

Mrabet, Ayla, Hassan Hamdani, and El Hadef Azzeddine
2008 "Tabou: Étudiantes et prostituées." *TelQuel* (347): 54–59. Print.

Naciri, Mohamed
1986 "Les ksouriens sur la route: Émigration et mutation spatiale de l'habitat dans l'oasis de Tinjdad." *Annuaire de l'Afrique du Nord*. Eds. A. Raymond and H. Michel. Paris: Editions du Centre national de la recherche scientifique. 347–364. Print.

Naciri, Rabea
1998 "Engaging the State: The Women's Movement and Political Discourse in Morocco." *Missionaries and Mandarins: Feminist Engagement with Developing Institutions*. Eds. C. Miller and S. Razavi. London: Practical Action. Print.

Nasir, Jamal J. Ahmed
2002 *The Islamic Law of Personal Status*. Third Revised and Updated Version. London: Kluwer Law International. Print.

Newcomb, Rachel
2009 *Women of Fes: Ambiguities of Urban Life in Morocco*. Philadelphia: University of Pennsylvania Press. Print.

Noelle-Neumann, Elisabeth
1984 *The Spiral of Silence: Public Opinion, Our Social Skin*. Chicago: Chicago University Press. Print.

Office of the High Commissioner for Human Rights
1994 "General Comment No. 24: Issues Relating to Reservations Made upon Ratification or Accession to the Covenant or the Optional Protocols Thereto, or in Relation to Declarations under Article 41 of the Covenant (CCPR/C/21/Rev.1/Add.6, General Comment No. 24 (d))." Web. ⟨http://www1.umn.edu/humanrts/gencomm/hrcom24.htm⟩.

Ossman, Susan
2002 *Three Faces of Beauty: Casablanca, Paris, Cairo*. London: Duke University Press. Print.

Oyewumi, Oyeronke
2000 "Family Bonds/Conceptual Binds: African Notes on Feminist Epistemologies." *Signs* 25(4): 1093–1098. Print.

Peristiany, John George, ed.
1974 *Honour and Shame: The Values of Mediterranean Society*. Chicago: Chicago University Press. Print.

Quraishi, Asifa, and Frank E. Vogel, eds.
2008 *The Islamic Marriage Contract: Case Studies in Islamic Family Law*. Cambridge, Mass.: Harvard University Press. Print.

Rhiwi, Leila
2004 "Trois femmes et une Moudawana: Une philosophie de l'égalité." *Le Journal* 6–12 March: 16. Print.

Richards, Alan, and John Waterbury
  2008 *A Political Economy of the Middle East.* Boulder, Colo.: Westview Press. Print.

Rosen, Lawrence
  1980–1981 "Equity and Discretion in a Modern Islamic Legal System." *Law and Society Review* 15(2): 217–246. Print.

Rosen, Lawrence
  1995 "Law and Custom in the Popular Legal Culture of North Africa." *Islamic Law and Society* 2(2): 194–208. Print.

Rosen, Lawrence
  1998 *The Anthropology of Justice: Law as Culture in Islamic Society.* Cambridge: Cambridge University Press. Print.

S., J.
  2003 "Entretien: Saïd Saadi: 'Notre société demeure misogyne.'" *Le Journal* 25–31 January: 18–19. Print.

Saadouni, Mohamed
  2012 "Rabat Salafists Assault Woman Over Dress." Web. ⟨http://www.magha rebia.com/cocoon/awi/xhtml1/en_GB/features/awi/features/2012/05 /11/feature-02⟩.

Sadiqi, Fatima
  2008 "The Central Role of the Family Law in the Moroccan Feminist Movement." *British Journal of Middle East Studies* 35(3): 325–337. Print.

Sadiqi, Fatima, and Moha Ennaji
  2006 "The Feminization of Public Space: Women's Activism, the Family Law and Social Change in Morocco." *Journal of Middle East Women's Studies* 2(2): 86–114. Print.

Sadiqi, Fatima, and Moha Ennaji, eds.
  2007 *Femmes et éducation dans la région Méditerranéenne.* Fez: Sipama. Print.

Safi, Omid
  2005a "Introduction." *Progressive Muslims: On Justice, Gender, and Pluralism.* Ed. O. Safi. Oxford: Oneworld. 1–29. Print.

Safi, Omid, ed.
  2005b *Progressive Muslims: On Justice, Gender, and Pluralism.* Oxford: Oneworld. Print.

Salime, Zakia
  2011 *Between Feminism and Islam: Human Rights and Sharia Law in Morocco.* London: University of Minnesota Press.

Schaefer Davis, Susan, and Douglas A. Davis
  1989 Adolescence in a Moroccan Town: Making Social Sense. New Brunswick, N.J.: Rutgers University Press. Print.

Schuurman, Frans, ed.
  2001 *Globalization and Development Studies: Challenges for the 21st Century.* London: Sage. Print.

Seftaoui Jamila (responsible editor)
   2006 *La Moudawana, autrement.* Rabat: Royaume du Maroc: Secrétariat d'État chargé de la Famille, de l'Enfance et des Personnes Handicapées avec l'appui de la coopération Allemande au développement GTZ. Print.

Sen, Amartya
   1999 *Development as Freedom.* New York: Anchor Books (Random House Inc.). Print.

Sharabi, Hisham
   1988 *Neopatriarchy: A Theory of Distorted Change in Arab Society.* Oxford: Oxford University Press. Print.

Silver, Hilary, and S. M. Miller
   2003 "Social Exclusion: The European Approach to Social Disadvantage." *Indicators* 2(2): 1–17.Print.

Singerman, Diane
   2007 "The Economic Imperatives of Marriage: Emerging Practices and Identities among Youth in the Middle East." Web. ⟨http://www.shabab inclusion.org/content/document/detail/559/⟩.

Singerman, Diane, and Homa Hoodfar, eds.
   1996 *Development, Change, and Gender in Cairo.* Bloomington: Indiana University Press. Print.

Skalli, Loubna H.
   2006 *Through a Local Prism: Gender, Globalization, and Identity in Moroccan Women's Magazines.* Oxford: Lexington Books. Print.

Spratt, Jennifer E.
   1992 "Women and Literacy in Morocco." *Annals of the American Academy of Political and Social Science* 520(March): 121–132. Print.

Spratt, Jennifer E., Beverly Seckinger, and Daniel A. Wagner
   1991 Functional Literacy in Moroccan School Children. *Reading Research Quarterly* 26(2): 178–195. Print.

Terrab, Sonia
   2009 "SOS: Femmes en détresse." *TelQuel* (374): 62–63. Print.

Tibi, Bassam
   1994 "Islamic Law/Shari'a, Human Rights, Universal Morality and International Relations." *Human Rights Quarterly* 16(2): 277–299. Print.

Tucker, Judith E.
   2008 *Women, Family, and Gender in Islamic Law (Themes in Islamic Law).* Cambridge: Cambridge University Press. Print.

UN Division for the Advancement of Women
   Ongoing   "Declarations, Reservations and Objections to CEDAW." Web. ⟨http://www.un.org/womenwatch/daw/cedaw/reservations-country .htm⟩.

UN: The Fourth World Conference on Women
   1995 "Beijing Declaration and Platform for Action." Web. ⟨http://www.un .org/womenwatch/daw/beijing/platform/⟩.

UNDP

  1995 *Human Development Report.* Oxford: Oxford University Press. Print.

UNDP Bureau of Development Policy

  2005 "En Route to Equality: A Gender Review of National MDG Reports." Web. ⟨http://www.undp.org/content/undp/en/home/librarypage /womens-empowerment/en-route-to-equality-a-gender-review-of -national-mdg-reports-2005.html⟩.

UNIFEM

  2002 *Progress of the World's Women 2002: Gender Equality and the Millennium Development Goals. Vol. 2.* Web. ⟨http://hdrnet.org/562/⟩.

United Nations Treaty Collection

  2012 CEDAW Status as at: 17–01–2012. Web.

Wadud, Amina

  1999 *Qur'an and Woman: Rereading the Sacred Text from a Woman's Perspective.* Oxford: Oxford University Press. Print.

Wagner, Daniel A.

  1993 *Literacy, Culture and Development: Becoming Literate in Morocco.* Cambridge: Cambridge University Press. Print.

Wagner, Daniel A.

  2009 "Youth and Adult Literacy Policies and Programs in Morocco: A Brief Synopsis (Draft)." Web. ⟨www.balid.org.uk/GMR/Wagner_GMR _Morocco_Apr22_9.doc⟩.

Welchman, Lynn

  2000 *Beyond the Code: Muslim Family Law and the Shari'a Judiciary in the Palestinian West Bank.* London: Kluwer Law International. Print.

Welchman, Lynn

  2004 *Women's Rights and Islamic Family Law: Perspectives on Reform.* London: Zed Books. Print.

Welchman, Lynn

  2011 "A Husband's Authority: Emerging Formulations in Muslim Family Laws." *International Journal of Law, Policy and the Family* 25(1): 1–23. Print.

Welchman, Lynn

  2012 "Muslim Family Laws and Women's Consent to Marriage: Does the Law Mean What it Says?" Web. ⟨http://www.socialdifference.org/files /SocDifOnline-Vol12012.pdf⟩.

Welchman, Lynn, and Sara Hossain, eds.

  2007 *Honour: Crimes, Paradigms, and Violence against Women.* London: Zed Books. Print.

Willman Bordat, Stephanie, and Saida Kouzzi

  2009 "Legal Empowerment of Unwed Mothers: Experiences of Moroccan NGOs." Web. ⟨http://www.wluml.org/sites/wluml.org/files/LEWP _BordatKouzzi.pdf⟩.

Willman Bordat, Stephanie, and Susan Schaefer Davis
  2011 "Women as Agents of Grassroots Change: Illustrating Micro-Empowerment in Morocco." *Journal of Middle East Women's Studies* 7(1): 90–119. Print.

World Bank
  2000 *World Development Report: Attacking Poverty.* Oxford: Oxford University Press. Web and print. ⟨http://www.ssc.wisc.edu/~walker/wp/wp-content/uploads/2012/10/wdr2001.pdf⟩.

World Bank
  2004 *Kingdom of Morocco: Poverty Report—Strengthening Policy by Identifying geographic Dimension of poverty.* Web. ⟨http://siteresources.worldbank.org/INTMOROCCOINFRENCH/Resources/MR-poverty-report-GB.pdf⟩.

Wynn, Lisa
  2008 Marriage Contracts and Women's Rights in Saudi Arabia: *Mahr, Shurut,* and Knowledge Distribution. *The Islamic Marriage Contract: Case Studies in Islamic Family Law.* Eds. A. Quraishi and F. E. Vogel. Cambridge Mass.: Harvard University Press. 200–214. Print.

Yousif, Abdelwahid Abdalla
  2009 *The State and Development of Adult Learning and Education in the Arab States: Regional Synthesis Report.* Hamburg: UNESCO Institute for Lifelong Learning. Print.

Zoglin, Katie
  2009 "Morocco's Family Code: Improving Equality for Women." *Human Rights Quarterly* 31(4): 964–984. Print.

Žvan Elliott, Katja
  2009 "Reforming the Moroccan Personal Status Code: A Revolution for Whom?" *Mediterranean Politics* 14(2): 213–227. Print.

Žvan Elliott, Katja
  2014 "Morocco and Its Women's Rights Struggle: A Failure to Live Up to Its Progressive Image." *Journal of Middle East Women's Studies* 10(2): 1–30. Print.

Consulted webpages

http://www.adfm.ma/index.php?lang=fr
http://www.uaf.ma/fr/file.php (defunct)
http://www.worldbank.org
http://www.un.org/en/
http://www.globalrights.org/site/PageServer?pagename=www_africa_morocco
http://www.hcp.ma/
http://www.mincom.gov.ma
http://adala.justice.gov.ma/AR/home.aspx
http://www.ifes.org

http://www.youtube.com
http://www.magharebia.com/
http://telquel.ma

Interviews with activists and public officials

Abouzeid, Leila. Personal interview in Rabat. 18 April 2011.
'Adul. Personal interview in Oued al-Ouliya. 18 April 2010.
Aicha and Khadija (JSO). Personal interview in Fez. 27 March 2008.
Arsalane, Fathallah (JSO). Personal interview in Rabat. 8 April 2011.
Bargach, Jamila. Personal interview in Casablanca. 16 April 2011.
Bourqia, Rahma. Personal interview in Rabat. 14 April 2011.
Dkkali, Souad, and Merieme Yafout (JSO). Personal interview in Sale. 16 April 2011.
Farchadou, Muhammad. Personal interview in Rabat, 7 April 2011.
Mudir Rachidi. Personal interview in Oued al-Ouliya. 8 June 2010.
Outaleb, Fatima (UAF). Personal interview in Rabat. 15 April 2008 and 19 April 2011.
Sadiqi, Fatima. Personal interview in Rabat. 4 January 2007.
Willman Bordat, Stephanie (Global Rights). Personal interview in Rabat. 4 April 2011.
Yafout, Merieme (JSO). Personal interview in Rabat. 31 March 2011.
Yassine, Fawzia, and Fatiha (ADFM). Personal interview in Rabat. 12 April 2011.
Yassine, Nadia (JSO). Personal interview in Rabat. 10 April 2011.

Index